HERBIE HANCOCK

HERBIE HANCOCK

POSSIBILITIES

WITH LISA DICKEY

VIKING

VIKING
Published by the Penguin Group
Penguin Group (USA) LLC
375 Hudson Street
New York, New York 10014

USA | Canada | UK | Ireland | Australia | New Zealand | India | South Africa | China
penguin.com
A Penguin Random House Company

First published by Viking Penguin, a member of Penguin Group (USA) LLC, 2014

Photograph credits
Insert page 3 (top and bottom): Photographs by Francis Wolff © Mosaic Images | 4: © Raymond Ross Archives / CSTIMAGES | 5 (bottom): © Lisl Steiner | 6 (top): Tom Copi / Michael Ochs Archive / Getty Images | 6 (bottom), 10 (bottom): Roberto Rabanne | 7 (top): Photo by Kurt Wahlner, originally appeared in *Softalk Magazine* | 7 (bottom), 8 (top): © Kaz Tsuruta | 8 (bottom): © Roger Ressmeyer / Corbis | 9 (top): © Bettmann / Corbis | 9 (bottom): © Lynn Goldsmith / Corbis | 10 (top): Herb Greene | 11 (top and bottom): Sam Emerson | 12 (top): © Etienne George / Sygma / Corbis | 13 (top): © Corbis | 13 (bottom): © Newport Jazz Festival / Ayano Hisa | 14 (top), 15 (bottom): © Elisa K. Morris / Thelonious Monk Institute of Jazz | 14 (middle): Photo: Keystone / Laurent Gillieron | 14 (bottom): © Mike Blake / Reuters / Corbis | 16 (top and middle): Courtesy of Jessica Hancock | 16 (bottom): Photo by Nathan East | Other photographs courtesy of Herbie Hancock

Library of Congress Cataloging-in-Publication Data
Hancock, Herbie, 1940– author.
Herbie Hancock : possibilities / Herbie Hancock with Lisa Dickey.
pages cm
Includes index.
ISBN 978-0-670-01471-2 (hardback)
1. Hancock, Herbie, 1940- 2. Jazz musicians—United States—Biography.
I. Dickey, Lisa, author. II. Title.
ML417.H23A3 2014
781.65092—dc23
[B] 2014013964

Printed in the United States of America
1 3 5 7 9 10 8 6 4 2

Set in Adobe Garamond Pro with EngraversGothic BT
Designed by Daniel Lagin

*For my priceless jewel, my beautiful eternal wife, Gigi,
and our precious treasure, our lovely daughter, Jessica*

HERBIE HANCOCK

CHAPTER ONE

'm onstage at a concert hall in Stockholm, Sweden, in the mid-1960s playing piano with the Miles Davis Quintet. We're on tour, and this show is really heating up. The band is tight—we're all in sync, all on the same wavelength. The music is flowing, we're connecting with the audience, and everything feels magical, like we're weaving a spell.

Tony Williams, the drumming prodigy who joined Miles as a teenager, is on fire. Ron Carter's fingers are flying up and down the neck of his bass, and Wayne Shorter's saxophone is just screaming. The five of us have become one entity, shifting and flowing with the music. We're playing one of Miles's classics, "So What," and as we hurtle toward Miles's solo, it's the peak of the evening; the whole audience is on the edge of their seats.

Miles starts playing, building up to his solo, and just as he's about to really let loose, he takes a breath. And right then I play a chord that is just *so* wrong. I don't even know where it came from—it's the wrong chord, in the wrong place, and now it's hanging out there like a piece of rotten fruit. I think, *Oh, shit*. It's as if we've all been building this gorgeous house of sound, and I just accidentally put a match to it.

Miles pauses for a fraction of a second, and then he plays some notes that somehow, miraculously, make my chord sound right. In that moment I believe my mouth actually fell open. What kind of alchemy was this? And then Miles just took off from there, unleashing a solo that took the song in a new direction. The crowd went absolutely crazy.

I was in my early twenties and had already been with Miles for a couple of years by this time. But he always was capable of surprising me, and that night, when he somehow turned my chord from a wrong to a right, he definitely did. In the dressing room after the show I asked Miles about it. I felt a little sheepish, but Miles just winked at me, a hint of a smile on his chiseled face. He didn't say anything. He didn't have to. Miles wasn't one to talk a whole lot about things when he could show us something instead.

It took me years to fully understand what happened in that moment onstage. As soon as I played that chord I judged it. In my mind it was the "wrong" chord. But Miles never judged it—he just heard it as a sound that had happened, and he instantly took it on as a challenge, a question of *How can I integrate that chord into everything else we're doing?* And because he didn't judge it, he was able to run with it, to turn it into something amazing. Miles trusted the band, and he trusted himself, and he always encouraged us to do the same. This was just one of many lessons I learned from Miles.

We all have a natural human tendency to take the safe route—to do the thing we know will work—rather than taking a chance. But that's the antithesis of jazz, which is all about being in the present. Jazz is about being in the moment, at every moment. It's about trusting yourself to respond on the fly. If you can allow yourself to do that, you never stop exploring, you never stop learning, in music or in life.

I was lucky enough to learn this not only from playing with Miles but over the decades of playing that have followed. And I'm still learning it, every single day. It's a gift that I never could have imagined back when I first started plunking around on my friend Levester Corley's piano at the age of six.

||||||||||

Levester Corley lived in the same building as my family, on the corner of Forty-Fifth Street and King Drive on the South Side of Chicago. We lived in a poor neighborhood, but it wasn't the worst one in 1940s Chicago. It was probably a step up from the worst, meaning that we didn't live in the projects but they were close by.

I never thought of our neighborhood as being a "bad" one, though parts of it were rough. There were gangs, and there was a run-down house down the block we called the Big House—slang for prison. Most days there were young men hanging out in front of the Big House, and when you saw that, you knew to walk on the other side of the street. But for the most part I never felt unsafe or threatened. I just assumed that my neighborhood was pretty much like everyone else's.

I was born in 1940, and when I was really little, I thought we were rich, because we always had everything we wanted. We had clothes to wear and food to eat, and a Christmas tree and toys every year, so what did I know? I had never met anyone from outside our neighborhood, and compared to some of the other families on our block, we seemed to be doing great. In the basement of our own building, there was one family living with about ten people crammed into a single room. In comparison, we had a two-bedroom for five people—my parents, my brother, Wayman, my sister, Jean, and me—which felt like a luxury.

Levester lived on another floor in our building, and when he turned six, his parents bought him a piano. I'd always liked just hanging around with Levester, but once he got that piano, all I wanted to do was go to his apartment and play it. I loved the feel of the keys under my fingers, even though I didn't really know what I was doing. We'd plunk around on it, and I'd try to play songs, and when I went back to our apartment, I'd tell my mom about it. After a while she said to my father, "We need to get this boy a piano." And so when I was seven, they gave me a used piano they'd bought for about $5 in a church basement.

It's not surprising that my mother, Winnie Griffin Hancock, was eager for me to have a piano. She was always anxious to instill an appreciation of culture in her children, even naming me—Herbert Jeffrey Hancock—after an African American singer and actor, Herb Jeffries. To my mother, culture meant music, so she made sure we grew up listening to Tchaikovsky, Beethoven, Mozart, and Handel. She also loved the music that came out of the black community—jazz and blues—and felt we should be connected to it as part of our heritage. But "good music" to her was classical music, so when I got my piano, she sent my brother and me to take classical lessons.

My mother's feelings on class and culture were rooted in her unusual childhood in the South. Her mother—my grandmother Winnie Daniels—grew up poor in Americus, Georgia, in a family of sharecroppers working the property of a wealthy family called the Griffins. But when my grandmother came of age, she married one of the Griffin sons, and just like that, she went from being a sharecropper to being a landowner's wife. So my mom and her brother, Peter, were born into a wealthier environment than most southern black kids at the time.

Growing up, I was always told that my grandfather Griffin was black, but in the few pictures I saw, he didn't look it. Years later, my mother told me he was actually white, so to this day I couldn't tell you which is the truth. What I do know is that sometime during the 1920s, my grandfather lost his entire fortune. He died soon after, and my grandmother picked up and moved the family to Chicago to start over.

It was a rough transition. After enjoying a life of relative privilege in Georgia, my grandmother and my mother were forced to take work as maids in Chicago. My mom cleaned houses for white families throughout high school, and understandably she hated it. She spent two years in college, which enabled her to get a job as a secretary, and eventually she became a guidance counselor for the Illinois State Department of Employment. She worked hard, carried herself with dignity, and raised all three of her children to believe we could achieve great things.

That was my mother's good side. But there was another side, too. She was bipolar, though we didn't know what that was—in those days people just used words like "headstrong" and "high-strung." She'd get into fights with family members, big screaming arguments where she'd shout and cry and argue until her neck veins popped out. In our house, it was my mother's way or the highway, but my dad tried to dismiss her rages as "just Winnie being Winnie." He loved her, and he tended to put her on a pedestal, because she carried herself in that dignified manner. But he also knew better than to get in her way. Whenever we asked him for something, he was quick to say, "Go ask your mother."

My father was a sweet, easygoing man, the guy cracking jokes in any group. He was raised by my grandmother and grandfather Hancock, but what very few people know is that at birth he wasn't actually a Hancock at all. He was born during my grandmother's first marriage, to a man with the last name of Pace. I don't know anything about my grandfather Pace, except that my grandmother always said he was a bad guy. She left him and married Louis Hancock, who adopted my father and gave him his—and now my—name.

Growing up, my dad wanted to be a doctor. But for a poor black family from Georgia in the 1930s, that was completely out of the question. In fact, he didn't even get to finish high school, dropping out after his sophomore year following a family discussion about finances. By then the family had moved to Chicago, and my dad knew that if he worked hard enough, his two younger brothers could go to college, so he sacrificed his own education to make that happen. From the time he was a teenager, my dad worked in the grocery business, and although he never went back to school, he eventually managed to buy his own store.

Unfortunately, he was too giving to be a good businessman. He was always extending people credit, and then he had a hard time pressing them for money. Or he'd buy cuts of meat from the stockyards for other mom-and-pop stores, acting as the middleman, and then it was the same story: He let them pay on credit, and then he could never ask them for the money. Dad's generosity threatened to bankrupt his business, and he ultimately sold his store. He worked a lot of different jobs while I was growing up, unskilled positions like cabdriver and bus driver, since he had just two years of high school. Eventually he became a government meat inspector at the Chicago stockyards.

My uncles thought of my dad as a hero for having sacrificed his own education for them. But my mother, sharp-tongued and opinionated, would sometimes tease him cruelly about his lack of education, calling him dumb or worse. She didn't do it often, and it was most likely because of her illness, but she knew how to use words to wound him.

I knew that my parents loved each other, and I watched as my dad tried to be patient with my mom, even when she got into a "headstrong" state. But every once in a while, her rages got physical. One afternoon I happened to see my dad in his undershirt, and I could see scratch marks all down his back. He never talked about it, and in fact I never heard him say a single bad word about my mother. No matter how mercurial she might be, he was always steady, which is probably a big reason why I remember my childhood as a stable, happy time.

But there's another reason for that, too: From the time I was very young, I've always tended to see the good in situations rather than the bad. Not because I was trying to be a Goody Two-Shoes or make a point to anyone else—I just somehow never really noticed or paid attention to the bad things. I'm an optimist at heart, always have been.

Years after my sister, Jean, grew up and moved away from Chicago, she wrote a short autobiography for a class. This was how she described the neighborhood where we grew up:

> Girls became pregnant upon puberty, boys worshipped and eventually copied the habits of heroin dealers, and kitchen gossip chronicled the purchase of stolen goods, weekend knife fights, and the "turning out" of a young lady with a nice body. Our area of commerce was heavily weighted with liquor stores, smelly groceries, well-fortressed currency exchanges, and tawdry five-and-dimes.

Was this all true? I suppose it was. But whenever I think of our neighborhood, I think of shooting marbles with my brother, or getting Goldenrod ice cream down at my dad's store, or standing on a corner with friends and singing R&B songs by groups like the Five Thrills and the Ravens. Ever since I can remember, I've tended to focus on the good rather than the bad. It's a trait I feel lucky to have.

||||||||||

Some older brothers don't want anything to do with their younger siblings, but my brother, Wayman, wasn't like that. Even though he was three years older, he took me everywhere with him.

He loved playing games and sports, so he'd bring me along to shoot marbles or play softball even though I was terrible at it. I was small for my age and had no interest in sports, but he still seemed to like having me there.

He remembers one softball game in which his team was up by about twenty runs and they encouraged me to take a turn pitching. I was probably about six years old, and they put me right up close to the plate, but I just couldn't pitch strikes. I walked the first five batters, and when I finally got one over the plate, the whole team erupted into cheers.

My relationship with my sister wasn't as easy. Jean was the only girl, and she was the youngest, so she sometimes felt left out. She'd get so frustrated because she just wanted to be one of the boys. One time we even caught her in the bathroom trying to pee standing up, which we never let her forget.

Jean was three years younger than me, but she could be smart and sharp-tongued like my mother. Because she was so smart, she could talk her way through anything, and once she had an opinion, she held tight to it like a bulldog. She could have been a debate champion, because she knew exactly how to manipulate an argument. She and I got along really well, but when we did argue, she'd somehow get me backed into a corner. Once I got so frustrated I just wanted to hit her. But for the most part, during our early childhood anyway, we got along.

Even though Jean was younger than me, she could be intimidating. She could be fierce, and both she and my mother knew how to hurt someone verbally. Maybe because they were so similar in that way, my mom and sister used to have confrontations. My mother's bipolar illness escalated during my sister's childhood, so as Jean got older, she bore the brunt of it in ways that my brother and I hadn't.

In many ways, that was the story of my sister's life—that through no fault of her own, she often got the short end of the stick. She was absolutely brilliant, skipping grades in school, teaching herself to play the guitar, playing sports. She could do just about anything better than most people. But as a young black woman growing up in the '50s and '60s, there were few expectations, and even fewer opportunities, for her. She had to scratch and claw for everything she got, which was something I never really thought about until years later, after her too-short life had ended.

The other thing I didn't realize until much later was how badly my sister wanted my approval. Jean was a deeply passionate human being, much more passionate than I am. She was emotional, whereas I've always been a more rational, reasoning kind of person. She would sometimes try to provoke responses out of me, but I never saw that for what it was: a need on her part, rather than just a provocation. As with so many things that didn't directly affect me, I just never really thought about it. I've always tended to focus on whatever is right in front of me, which causes me to miss the nuances of what's happening to others.

From the time I was very young, I had the ability—the compulsion, really—to get completely absorbed in whatever I was doing. I was obsessed with mechanical things, and I'd spend hours taking apart clocks and watches, poking around inside. I just had a driving need to understand how a thing worked, and if I couldn't figure it out, I'd block out everything else and focus obsessively until I got it. At first I was just messing around with whatever gadgets I could find in the house. But when my parents bought me the piano, I turned the same kind of obsessive focus to learning how to play it.

Once we got that piano, all I wanted to do was play music. My brother and I both took lessons from the same teacher, Mrs. Jordan, who taught about a dozen primarily black students. We all studied classical, which is what any black person who took piano at the time would study—there weren't lessons in blues or R&B or anything like that. Studying piano meant studying classical music, which suited my mother just fine.

Mrs. Jordan put on recitals and competitions, and it wasn't long before I decided I wanted to be a concert pianist. From that point on, music was my life. I spent every spare moment at the piano, picking out chords and melodies, learning to read music, training my hands. No matter how much I learned, there was always more to learn, and I loved that. I still do.

I also loved playing piano because, unlike sports, I was good at it. I always felt inferior at sports, because I was small and uncoordinated, but here was an activity where I could be as good as my brother and his friends. Wayman was a pretty good piano player, but he didn't have the same single-minded focus on it that I did, so before long I could actually play better than he could. Once we got that piano, I never went back to playing sports with my brother and his friends.

Also, playing piano was considered cool in our neighborhood. Because I was small, other kids would occasionally mess with me—including one time, in front of the Big House, when a couple of kids jumped me. But once word got out that I could play piano, I found myself in a different category. Playing music changed everything about my life. It gave me purpose, it changed others' perceptions of me, but most important, it changed the way I felt about myself.

‖‖‖‖‖‖‖

When I was eleven years old, Mrs. Jordan entered me in an annual competition held by the Chicago Symphony Orchestra. As part of its young people's series, the CSO invited students to play a movement of a concerto, and the winner of the competition would get to play it live, onstage, with the CSO.

By that point I'd been taking lessons for four years, and playing piano was pretty much all I did. I practiced Mozart's Piano Concerto no. 18 in B-flat Major, K. 456, every day for nearly a year, and when my audition came, I was ready. The audition was held at Orchestra Hall (now called Symphony Center), and each student was required to play alone, onstage, in front of the assistant conductor, George Schick.

I walked onto the stage, sat down at the piano, and looked out into the seats. Mrs. Jordan was there, and I saw two other ladies come in and sit in the back, near her. Then I turned my attention to the piano, and from the moment I played the first notes, the rest of the world might as well have not existed. I played the first movement, and only when the final notes had faded did I look up again.

Well, that was pretty good, I thought. When I came offstage and saw Mrs. Jordan, she gave me a hug and told me that, yes, I had done well. In fact, she told me that the two women I'd seen coming in were also piano teachers, and that after I'd finished playing, the two of them were crying. That was pretty heady stuff for an eleven-year-old.

A few months later, I got a postcard in the mail saying, "Congratulations!" I had won the competition and was invited to play with the Chicago Symphony Orchestra on February 5, 1952. Unfortunately, the postcard also said that the CSO had been unable to locate the orchestral parts to that particular concerto, so I would have to either learn a new piece or forfeit my chance to play.

I stared at the postcard in shock. How could this be? Over the past year, I had learned that concerto cold, and now I'd only have a couple of months to learn a brand-new one. And this wasn't for just any recital—it was my debut onstage with the Chicago Symphony Orchestra! But there was no way I was letting my big opportunity slip away. We chose another Mozart concerto—no. 26 in D Major—and I began feverishly practicing. I played that piece for hours upon hours, and as the date of the concert approached, I knew it, though not as well as I knew no. 18.

Finally the big night arrived. I wasn't at the top of the program, so I waited nervously in the wings while the orchestra played its first piece. There was an elevator platform near the conductor's podium, and just before I was to play, a big grand piano came up through the floor into position. I took a deep breath and walked onto the stage to take my seat at that massive piano.

I must have looked pretty funny walking out there, because at age eleven I was a short, spindly little kid who could barely reach the piano pedals. I don't remember exactly what I was wearing, but I think it was a jacket, short pants, and knee socks. I was small for my age, so I can't imagine what was going through the minds of people in the audience. But just as at the audition, the moment I started playing, everything else faded away—it was just me and the music.

When I finished, the audience exploded into applause, and after the concert a few people even asked me for my autograph. I signed one for a girl my age, writing out "Herbert Hancock" in my most careful cursive. I felt proud of myself, and relieved that I'd been able to learn the new concerto in so little time.

A week or two later, as a congratulatory gift, Mrs. Jordan invited me to see the British pianist Dame Myra Hess perform with the Chicago Symphony. We were both stunned when we saw what was on the program: Mozart's Piano Concerto no. 18! Somehow they'd managed to find all the orchestra music. Or perhaps it was never really lost? It would have been easy to feel suspicious, to wonder whether someone at the CSO just wanted to discourage the young African American kid who'd surprised everyone and won their prestigious competition. For a black person growing up in '40s and '50s America, small acts of racism were simply a fact of life. But even at age eleven, I tended to ignore possible racial slights rather than give them any weight. It was just my nature.

CHAPTER TWO

The first time I ever met a white kid was in high school. At my elementary school, Forestville, all the students were black (though some of our teachers were white). No white families lived in my neighborhood, and I never really went anywhere else, so I just never met any. In our part of Chicago, the only white people we saw were the ones coming to collect money—the insurance man, or the landlord.

The only thing I knew about white kids came from the stories my dad told me from his childhood. He'd spent his first years in the segregated South, then went to a mixed elementary school after he moved to Chicago, and often had gotten into fights. So when I was about to start my freshman year at Hyde Park High School, where three-quarters of the students were white, I was definitely wary.

I had skipped a grade in elementary school, so I was young for a freshman—just twelve when I first set foot in the halls of Hyde Park. We weren't really supposed to go to school there, since we didn't live in Hyde Park's district, but it was better academically than the high school in our district, so my mother was determined to send us there.

We had an aunt and uncle who lived in the right district, so my parents used their address when they enrolled us.

My head was full of the stories my dad had told me, so when I went to school on the first day of freshman year, I fully expected something to go down. I was primed for a fight, but to my surprise, the white kids turned out to be . . . just kids. I went running home after that first day of school, and as I burst through the door to our apartment, I yelled, "Mama! Mama! They're just like us!" It sounds funny now, but that really was a big surprise to me.

Hyde Park was a liberal school, so we students thought of ourselves as progressive, racially and otherwise. But as progressive as we thought we were, it was the 1950s, so a lot of people frowned on blacks and whites dating each other. Still, I probably experienced more overt racism from members of my own extended family than I did from my high school friends. I had darker skin than most of my relatives, and in black families, that's an easy target. Sometimes, when I was bad, I'd get called "a black, evil rascal." But to the best of my recollection, nobody in high school ever called me names based on my color.

Even if they had, I'd have done my best to ignore it, because I made a conscious decision in high school not to focus on race at all if I could help it. Racism existed, of course; in the 1950s casual racism was woven into the fabric of American life. You didn't have to go searching for it, because it was omnipresent, everything from whites getting preferential treatment for loans, employment, and housing to white people addressing a black man as "boy." But early on, I realized I had a choice: The easy road was to sit back and expect racist acts to happen—to see injustice and ill intent at every turn, to essentially say, *I'm black and will never get a fair shake,* and to live life accordingly. I made a choice to do the opposite.

Some black people look for racism, but I made a point of *not* looking for it, because looking for it feeds a victim mentality, which doesn't help anyone. That victim mentality was rampant in our neighborhood, but somehow I managed to find my way out of it. This was partly thanks to my parents, who raised all three of us to believe we could achieve anything we put our minds to. But it also had a lot to do with my own curiosity. When I started high school, for the first time in my life I found myself surrounded by many different kinds of people. And rather than feeling like I was an outsider or being judged by them, I wanted to know everything about them.

After growing up exclusively around black people, I suddenly had friends who were Jewish, Italian, Asian—and I didn't know anything about their cultures. I wanted to hear how they talked, see how they lived, learn about their beliefs. Most ethnic groups stuck together at Hyde Park, but I knew I didn't want to stay in the black-kids group.

One of my first girlfriends was white, a girl named Barbara Laves, who played violin with the orchestra. She was a petite brunette with amazing light blue eyes, and I used to walk her home after school each day. Barbara and I didn't stay together all that long, and I dated black girls, too, including my prom date, Peggy Milton. But I never really worried about anybody's race. If I liked a girl, I asked her out. And if other people had a problem with that, I either didn't know about it or, more likely, didn't pay attention to it.

||||||||||

My parents tried for a while to turn us into churchgoers, but it didn't stick. The first church they took us to was Ebenezer Baptist, one of dozens of Baptist churches sprinkled throughout our South Side neighborhood. The music was fantastic. There was a young people's gospel choir and an adult gospel choir, and I liked the part of the service when they sang. But the sermons were all fire and brimstone, which didn't really speak to me, or to my mother. There just didn't seem to be much to learn from listening to someone talk about hell and damnation all the time.

Next, my parents took us to an African Methodist Episcopal

church a few blocks away. Their choirs were good, too, but I didn't love the hymns, and I still didn't love the message—I just never responded to the notion of heaven and hell and retribution and punishment. Apparently my parents didn't, either, because the next church we went to was Unitarian, which didn't preach any kind of fire and brimstone at all. My mother liked this church, as it was more open and seemed to have an intellectual, rather than emotional, basis. But even so, we didn't go to this one for very long, either.

None of the churches really spoke to me, yet from the time I was very small, I was always curious about the big questions of existence. At night, after my brother went to sleep, I'd sit on the windowsill of our bedroom looking up at the stars, wondering about life and death and the universe. At some point, I figured out for myself that life never ends, and I came early to the belief that even when we die, we reemerge later as another being. Years later, I would learn that these were core beliefs of Buddhism.

The notion of heaven and hell just never made sense to me. I couldn't imagine that, when you die, you just pop out and disappear to some unknown place. I didn't see anything else in the world just disappearing like that; matter and energy transform, but they don't disappear. A seed becomes a tree, a tree becomes a chair, a chair becomes ash, and the cycle continues. It just wasn't logical to me that the way we live and die could be so different from that.

This was how my brain worked, by seeking out the logical sequence of things. As a kid, I loved mechanics and science, and I spent hours taking apart clocks and toasters because I had a driving need to know how things worked. I was drawn to the rational order of these systems, enraptured by the way that taking apart an object could lead to a complete understanding of that object.

One day in high school, I decided to apply that same kind of logic to other parts of my life. I'd done something that got me in trouble with my parents, and they decided to punish me by not letting me go to a party I was looking forward to. The punishment didn't seem fair, and I was really angry. I didn't get mad often, but this seemed so undeserved that I was furious. It was a barrier I couldn't get around—I felt helpless, almost victimized, by the injustice of it all. I stewed about it for days.

Sulking in my room on the afternoon of the party, I finally thought, *Okay, let me examine rationally what's going on here.* I decided to take apart the situation just as I'd take apart a mechanical object. The party started at ten, and because of my curfew, I would have had to leave at midnight. That was two hours of my life; once those two hours were done, I'd be on to the next thing, whether I went to the party or not. Suddenly everything became clear: *All I have to do is get through those two hours, and then life will go on as usual.*

So that's what I did. From ten until midnight, I read books and hung out in my room, and once midnight had passed, that was the end of it. I didn't feel like a victim anymore; in fact, I was proud of myself. I had taken control of my emotions and figured out a way to get past my anger. From that point on, there was no way I could be punished, because I knew I could choose how to respond to any given situation. I had learned how to keep my emotions under control.

This felt like a great development: I would never again feel victimized by external factors, because I could control how they affected me emotionally. In many ways this was a useful trait, but over time, I carried it to an extreme, desensitizing myself. I had never been a particularly emotional kid, but from high school onward I really kept my emotions in check; I almost never cried, no matter how sad or upset I felt. If something started to upset me, I'd shut myself down rather than feel those negative emotions.

There was one glaring exception, and it happened just as I was starting my senior year in high school: the murder of Emmett Till.

Emmett Till was fourteen, just one year younger than me, and he was also from the South Side of Chicago. In August of 1955, he went to

Mississippi to visit relatives. His mother warned him before going that the South was different from the North and he needed to behave accordingly. But when Till and some friends went into a convenience store to buy some candy, one of the other boys dared him to talk to the twenty-one-year-old white woman working at the store, Carolyn Bryant. He apparently wolf-whistled at her, showing off for his friends, and when Bryant told her husband, Roy, about it, he decided to take action.

Several days later Roy Bryant and a number of other men kidnapped Till and pistol-whipped him. They put the bleeding boy in the back of a pickup truck, covered him with a tarp, and drove him to a cotton gin, where they picked up a seventy-pound fan. Then they drove Till to the banks of the Tallahatchie River, shot him in the head, and tied the fan around his neck to weigh down his body before throwing it into the river.

Three days after that, kids fishing in the river found Till's corpse. His grieving mother insisted that his body be put into a pine coffin and sent by train back to Chicago, rather than being buried in Mississippi. The coffin arrived at the A. A. Rayner funeral home in early September, and when Till's mother looked in and saw her son's horribly mutilated face, she decided to have an open casket at his funeral, so the whole world could see what those men in Mississippi had done to him.

The day Till's body arrived back in Chicago, we happened to drive past the Rayner funeral home, which wasn't far from our apartment on the South Side. I could see people stumbling out the door, weeping, and I watched in shock as one man came out sobbing, uttering gibberish as he waved his hands in the air. I had never seen people unhinged like that, and it scared me.

Jet magazine published a full-page close-up photo of Emmett Till's swollen, destroyed face, and although my parents tried to shield us from seeing it, curiosity got the better of me. When I picked up the magazine and flipped to the photo, fear and horror shot right through me. No matter how much control I thought I had over my emotions, nothing could have prepared me for seeing the cruelly disfigured face of a boy my age, from my own neighborhood, who'd been brutally murdered for nothing at all. I had nightmares for weeks afterward.

||||||||||

My earliest exposure to jazz was on WGES deejay Al Benson's radio show. Known as the Godfather of Chicago Black Radio, Benson spun records all day, mostly blues or R&B but with the occasional jazz cut thrown in. The first jazz performance I took notice of was "Moonlight in Vermont," played by the guitarist Johnny Smith, with Stan Getz on tenor sax. It was a ballad, just a pretty song that I liked, rather than some kind of big epiphany about jazz. At the time it came out, in 1952, I mostly listened to R&B music, like the rest of the kids in my neighborhood.

We used to stand around on street corners and sing, imitating our favorite groups—the Orioles, the Midnighters, the Five Thrills, the Ravens. Later I heard the Four Freshmen, a vocal quartet that gained fame in the mid-'50s with songs like "Mood Indigo" and "Day by Day."

The Four Freshmen sang harmonies that were beyond the four-part barbershop harmonies that had been popular in the '30s. They sang more jazzlike harmonies, with major sevenths and even a few ninth chords, which mesmerized me and made me want to learn how to sing them myself. I also loved the Hi-Lo's, another vocal group, whose piano player, Clare Fischer, arranged many of their songs. Fischer's arrangements had a tremendous influence on my understanding of harmony.

I loved this type of singing so much that I even put together my own vocal group at Hyde Park. But even though I was interested in R&B and other musical genres, it never really occurred to me that I could play anything other than classical music on the piano.

I used to play for the high school orchestra's rehearsals, to help guide the violinists and others who were struggling to learn parts. But the orchestra never performed with a piano, so in concerts I played cymbals and percussion instead. Hyde Park did have a dance band, but their piano player was a guy named Don Goldberg, who was in my class, though I hadn't yet met him. Don was also in a student jazz trio, and when I finally saw them play one afternoon during my sophomore year, he did something that changed my life.

Every semester the senior class at Hyde Park put on a variety show for all grades. Don's trio—piano, upright bass, and drums—took the stage, and as they started playing, I was of course watching Don. His performance absolutely floored me: He was improvising! I had no idea people our age could do that; I thought it was something only older players did. Mind you, "older" to me at age fourteen meant nineteen or twenty.

I had been playing classical music since I was seven, so I was pretty good at reading music, but Don could do something on my instrument that I couldn't. He was creating the music himself, in the moment, rather than reading it off a page. My heart started beating like crazy, and as soon as the trio finished their three songs, I hurried backstage and found him. I quickly introduced myself, and then I couldn't hold back.

"Man, how did you learn to play like that?" I asked him. "I don't really understand what you did, but I liked it. I want to learn how to do it, too—how to play jazz."

Don laughed and said, "Well, if you like what I did, the first thing you need to do is get yourself some George Shearing records." He told me to listen to how Shearing played and then try to imitate the parts I liked. That was how he'd learned, and at age fifteen he was already pretty good at improvising.

As soon as the school bus dropped me off that afternoon, I ran home, burst through the front door, and said, "Mama! We've got to get some George Shearing records!" She looked at me like I had three heads. "Herbie," she said, "you already have some."

"No, Mama," I said. "You don't understand. We need *George Shearing* records. Not just any records."

"Herbie," she said, "do you remember last year when I brought you home some records, and you got mad at me because you wanted some other ones and said I'd gotten the wrong things? Those were George Shearing records. Go look in the cabinet."

I crossed the living room to the cabinet, which was filled with 78s, and sure enough, there they were: a few albums by George Shearing and his quintet. I had never even listened to them. I'd always thought of jazz as older people's music, something that had no relevance to me. But now that I'd seen someone my age improvising, making that kind of music exciting, I just wanted to do it myself.

I slid a record out of its sleeve and put it on the turntable. Don's trio had performed three songs that the George Shearing Quintet played: "Lullaby of Birdland," "I'll Remember April," and "A Nightingale Sang in Berkeley Square." I laid the needle down on "I Remember April," and as I listened to Shearing play, it sounded like Don! That was it for me—if Don could do it, why couldn't I? That afternoon I started trying to learn how.

My first attempts were terrible. I sounded exactly like what I was, a classical musician learning how to improvise. But then my love of science and mechanics kicked in, and I decided to approach improvising the same way I approached taking a clock apart: analytically. I'd find a phrase I liked, and then try to pick out the notes by listening to it over and over—even just to find a single-note improvisation on the right hand. I tried to listen past the melody to the improvised parts to figure out the individual notes I needed to play.

Once I found the right notes, I'd try to play along with the record, but in the beginning I couldn't seem to make it sound the same. So I'd go past that phrase to get to the next one, learning longer and longer phrases until I could play them the way they sounded on the record.

I kept working to find the phrases I liked, and then I'd transcribe them onto music paper. I didn't know it at the time, but I was also doing ear training—I was sharpening my relative pitch at the same time I was learning the phrases. I did this for hours each day, branching beyond George Shearing into other piano players, like Erroll Garner and Oscar Peterson. The more I learned, the more I wanted to learn.

Because of the way my mind works, I noticed patterns. I'd play a phrase, write it down, and think, *Wait a minute—he just used those same notes in another phrase earlier in the song.* I didn't know how jazz was constructed, so I had to figure it out as I went along. To me, improvisation sounded like stream of consciousness. But at the same time I knew it couldn't be, because it was so organized.

Despite the fact that I could play classical music well, my knowledge of other musical forms was pretty limited. I knew major chords and minor chords, but everything else I had to teach myself. I began to spend a lot of time talking to the few other kids at school who were into jazz, including Don Goldberg and a French horn player named Ted Harley. They were both good musicians; Don went on to become a professional composer and arranger, changing his name to Don James and working on big shows, such as the Ice Capades and *Baryshnikov on Broadway.* Talking with Don and Ted helped me to figure out more of the theory and structure behind improvisation.

Whenever people ask me how to learn to improvise, I tell them the same thing Don told me: Find a player you like, and then copy what he or she is doing. That analytical, mechanical approach will enable you to learn the basics, but then the trick will be to figure out how not to get stuck in copying. You have to start creating your own lines, to find your own voice.

If you're playing a particular form—say, on a thirty-two-bar song—you're playing the melody, the head of the tune, and then you improvise off that form's particular chord structure. There's a lot of freedom within that structure—space, rhythm, chords, shadings. Whatever you decide to play, whatever comes out moment to moment, is an expression that's shaped by a combination of elements, which includes, if you're in a group, what the other musicians are playing. You have to be fully present, because there's a lot going on, and it's happening so rapidly that you can't get slowed down by thinking about it.

Improvisation—truly being in the moment—means exploring what you don't know. It means going into that dark room where you don't recognize things. It means operating on the recall part of your brain, a sort of muscle memory, and allowing your gut to take precedence over your brain. This is something I still work on every day: learning to get out of my own way. It's not easy, but the times when you can do that are truly magical. Improvising is like opening a wonderful box where everything you take out is always new. You'll never get bored, because what that box contains is different every single time.

Jazz is not something you can ever completely master, because it is in the moment, and every moment is unique, demanding that you reach inside yourself. Classical music seemed more cerebral, but jazz was both cerebral and intuitive. It pulled me like a magnet, and I couldn't wait to learn more about it.

CHAPTER THREE

n the fall of 1956, I headed off to Grinnell College. Grinnell was a small liberal-arts school in Iowa, of all places, so it wasn't the most obvious choice for me. But one of my parents' closest friends, our South Side neighbor Mrs. Smith, had gone there, so I decided to apply. I won a Pullman scholarship and set out for Iowa at age sixteen, and what I found when I got there was a warm, welcoming campus with students from all over the world. Going to Hyde Park High School had opened my eyes to people from different walks of life, and my time at Grinnell would broaden my horizons even more.

Even before I set foot on campus, I started examining my options analytically. Should I major in music? Or in science? I loved them both, but I wanted to make the smart choice. So I asked myself: *What are the chances you can make a living from jazz? Questionable. Now, what are the chances you can make a living from science? Probably really good.* As much as I loved jazz, I decided to take the pragmatic path and major in engineering. I even promised my mother, who wanted me to get a degree in something useful, that I wouldn't major in music.

I didn't sign up for any music courses my freshman year, but I did take piano lessons and spent hours on my own studying jazz. My grades were just average, because I never buckled down that much to study my engineering classwork. Although there weren't many other jazz musicians at the school, I did find a couple of guys who were pretty good, so I spent time playing and talking about music with them. There was a drummer from Denmark named Bjarne Nielsen, a bass player named Dave Kelsen, and two trumpet players who could play pretty well—John Scott and Bob Preston. John became a close friend; we even wrote a song together that I would later record for my second album, *My Point of View*.

Some professional classical musicians practice for eight or so hours a day, but not me. I never actually practiced at the piano for more than about an hour a day—but I spent untold hours studying, learning, and analyzing music. I'd talk endlessly with the other guys about structure, theory, and improvisation, and we'd swap notes until late into the night. I never got tired of it, and the more I learned, the more excited I got.

I continued to be fascinated by improvisation. When I'd listen to Oscar Peterson records, I'd think, *How'd he do that?* I loved playing and jamming, because it was a blank slate for expressing yourself. You didn't have to just read the music someone else wrote; you could express yourself by creating your own music in the moment.

In my sophomore year I decided to put together Grinnell's first jazz concert. How hard could it be, right? I'd just listen to a few big-band recordings, figure out what the other instruments were playing, and transcribe all the arrangements myself. Then I'd just have to find enough musicians who could play the various parts, show them how to phrase and use dynamics, and get them concert-ready. Somehow, in my seventeen-year-old head, this seemed an achievable goal.

Grinnell had only about twelve hundred students total, and it was smack in the middle of Iowa. Where was I going to find enough jazz musicians for a whole concert? I put up notices on bulletin boards all over school, seeking out anyone who had experience playing and especially anyone who'd been in a high school dance band. I knew that the University of Iowa, about sixty miles east of Grinnell, actually had a jazz band, so I borrowed some arrangements from them and from Iowa State. Somehow I managed to cobble together five saxes, three trombones, four trumpets, bass, drums, and a small vocal group.

Then I started figuring out the arrangements from a few Count Basie records, just as I'd worked out those George Shearing songs: by listening to the record, then writing down the various instrumental parts on blank music paper. This was complicated and time consuming, but I learned a lot doing it.

Once the parts were ready, I started section rehearsals for each instrument of the band. What I discovered was that while everybody could play the notes, only two people knew anything about jazz phrasing. I didn't want to go through all this trouble to put on a mediocre concert, so I personally conducted every section rehearsal—the saxophone players, the trombone players, the trumpet players. And because nobody knew how to solo, I had to write those parts out, too. For the whole semester I spent all my time teaching these players, trying to get them ready for the show. I was so consumed by preparing for the concert that there was no room for anything else in my mind, and I began flunking all my courses.

This was the second semester of my sophomore year, and the concert was scheduled just before finals. As the date drew near I stopped going to classes altogether—there was too much to do! I was working with the musicians day and night, hardly sleeping at all. But when the big day arrived, we were ready. Or as ready as we'd ever be, anyway.

The concert was held in May of 1958 in the Alumni Recitation Hall auditorium. People had never thought they'd get to hear a jazz concert in Grinnell, Iowa, so, given everyone's low expectations, we sounded fantastic. With every song, the audience was clapping and cheering like crazy. I loved being onstage improvising with a group of jazz musicians, just letting loose in whatever direction I felt like playing. The whole night felt magical.

But then came the nasty wake-up call: I had ignored my classes so completely that, unless I aced my finals, I was in danger of flunking out of school. For the next week, all I did was study. I crammed everything I could into my brain, and when I showed up for the finals, some of my professors—who hadn't seen me in weeks—seemed surprised. I knew how crushed my parents would be if I failed, so I was desperate to do at least well enough to stay in school.

And somehow I did. I aced all my finals, which enabled me to pass the semester with three Cs and a D. One professor was so shocked that he even thought I had cheated. He called me into his office and demanded to know how I could have been failing all semester, only to come in and do so well on the final exam. He began firing questions at me, trying to see if I really knew the material or not. When I was able to answer all his questions, he had to back down.

After that I went back to my dorm room, completely exhausted, and stared at myself in the mirror. My eyes were bloodshot, and I looked like hell. "Who are you trying to kid?" I asked the face in the mirror. I'd tried very hard to fit myself into the engineering box, but it was obvious where my passion was. At that point it was no longer even a choice. That day I decided to switch my major to music.

|||||||||||

When I started taking music classes my junior year, I was happy to find that I already knew a lot of the material we were covering. I'd spent so much time studying theory and harmony and structure that I was able to skip most of my classes and just show up for tests.

To bring in extra money, I had a job at the restaurant in the student union, taking orders and serving food. But one weekend I got a gig playing piano in Des Moines, and to my shock I got paid more for that one night than I did for a week of working at the union. That realization just turned me upside down: The idea of logging all those hours slinging food in a restaurant when I could make so much more doing something I loved made it impossible for me to keep doing that job. So I quit.

The funny thing was, the Des Moines trip wasn't actually all that pleasant. The gig was okay—but a strange thing happened afterward.

I was only eighteen or so at the time, but somehow these guys who were playing at a nightclub had heard about me. I had agreed to go to Des Moines to play with them, and then, to save money, I was planning to go right back to Grinnell in the early-morning hours instead of paying for a hotel room. But one of the musicians told me I could just stay at his house with him and his wife. I thought, *Cool! An adventure!* This guy was a real working musician, and I was going to get to hang with him.

The gig wrapped up at about two in the morning, and as the guy and I walked to his car, he said, "I gotta make a couple of stops before we get to my place." I said, "I don't mind!" I didn't care where we went—I was just happy to be along for the ride.

Another couple of people were waiting at the car, and we all piled in. The guy pulled out of the parking lot, and after driving for a while we ended up outside a house. As soon as we pulled up, all the lights in the house went off. I thought that was a little weird—were they not expecting us?—but someone hopped out and went up to the front door, and then came back to the car with a little paper bag. We then drove to another house and picked up the guy's wife, and I noticed with bewilderment that even though it was pretty warm out, she was shivering.

We made a few more stops to drop off the other people in the car, and then it was just the musician, his wife, and me. He drove us to their building, and we climbed some back steps to get into their apartment. When he opened the door, my mouth fell open: It was one tiny room, with one bed in it. The guy and his wife lay down on the bed and gestured for me to join them.

"Do you want to get high?" he asked me, and then emptied the contents of the paper bag onto the bed. I looked at the hypodermic needle that had tumbled out, and the baggie of powder, and said, "No, thank you." I had never gotten high before, on anything, and I had no intention of getting into that stuff. But I was curious, so I said, "Can I watch?" As long as I was there, I wanted to see how it was done.

I observed him as he put the powder in a spoon with a little water, lit the lighter, and heated the bottom. The powder turned into a black liquid, which he then poured into the syringe. He wrapped his arm with a piece of rubber and tapped his vein, just like in the movies, and then he shot up. His wife was shivering because she was coming down from a high, but when he offered her the syringe, she took it, too. I could hardly believe I was sitting here watching them shoot up; watching their faces to see if anything changed, I started feeling nervous. Were they about to get weird? There was only one bed, after all. But evidently they didn't think much of the heroin, so after complaining for a little bit, the guy said, "We're just gonna go to sleep." And I thought, *Okay, but where the hell am I supposed to sleep?*

I ended up lying on one side of the bed, with the guy in the middle and his wife on the other side, and I was so nervous I don't think I closed my eyes the entire night. They didn't seem all that high to me, but I'd never been with people shooting up heroin, so what did I know? I was a complete novice when it came to any kind of drug use, though I had recently started drinking. But this was a completely foreign world to me. I hadn't been tempted by drugs at all, though that would change.

||||||||||

In 1960 I left Grinnell and returned to Chicago, one credit shy of graduating because I had flunked a course in my junior year. I wanted to get my degree, but I wanted even more to start playing jazz seriously, and Grinnell wasn't the place to do that.

So I moved back in with my parents and took a job with the post office while I sought out work as a pianist. I delivered mail five days a week, and whenever I had gigs, I'd play music from nine p.m. until four or five in the morning. The hours were just brutal—I had almost no time left over to sleep. And I often had to take the train to and from the gigs, so I'd be slumped over in exhaustion on the "L" as it shuddered down to the South Side in the early-morning hours.

But until I could make enough money playing piano, I needed that post office job, so I was still delivering mail in the fall of 1960 when I got a call to play with Coleman Hawkins. Hawkins was a legendary saxophonist, the man who brought the tenor sax to prominence in jazz. He'd been playing since the early 1920s, when he started with Mamie Smith's Jazz Hounds, and in the four decades since then he'd played with all the big names: Louis Armstrong, Django Reinhardt, Miles Davis, Benny Goodman, Thelonious Monk, and Oscar Peterson. I mean, I would have been excited just to be in the same room with a player like Coleman Hawkins, much less actually get to play with him.

To keep his costs down, Hawkins usually worked with pickup bands, which meant he hired local musicians—a pianist, drummer, and bass player—in each city he played. For this gig in Chicago, the first-choice pianist, a guy named Jodie Christian, wasn't available, so Hawkins's drummer, Louis Taylor, suggested he give me a try. I was pretty green at that point, but I'd played with Taylor a few times, and he thought I deserved a chance.

Coleman hired me to play with him at the Cloisters nightclub for a fourteen-day stand. He was the first internationally known musician I had ever worked with, and his recording of "Body and Soul" was considered the ultimate saxophone solo of that classic song. I felt honored to share the stage with him and excited at the thought of what I might learn, but I was also nervous, hoping I could hold up my end of the bargain. He encouraged me and tried to make me feel comfortable onstage, and I think he was pleased with how I played.

I never got much of a chance to talk to Coleman, because I always had to hurry home after the last set. The hours were crazy—four sets a night, and five on Saturdays, with no days off—so I was playing music into the wee hours every night and then trying to deliver mail all day. By the third day I was a complete wreck. That morning I was standing in front of somebody's apartment, thumbing through the mail, and I actually fell asleep standing up—which wasn't good, because the apartment was at the top of a concrete staircase. I was really dragging, and not surprisingly, I got sick, too.

Louis Taylor, the drummer who had gotten me the gig, said, "Herbie, that post office job is interfering with the music. You've got to quit." I knew there was no way for me to keep doing both, but I was scared to quit the post office, since it offered me stability and a steady income.

But on the fourth day, dragging myself home at four a.m. from that night's gig, I knew I had no choice. That morning I told some of the guys at the post office that I was going to quit. A lot of them were musicians themselves, and they urged me not to do it. More than one guy said, "Man, you're going to lose your health insurance!" I knew that if I did leave, I'd never get hired back there if music didn't work out, but that was a chance I had to take. So I walked into my supervisor's office and told him I was done.

After I finished that two-week gig with Coleman Hawkins, I just waited by the phone, hoping someone would call with another one. It was strange not to have a steady job, and I wasn't sure I'd be able to make enough money playing piano. But my parents took care of me, letting me live at home rent-free and feeding me dinner every night. I felt very lucky to have their support as I kept trying to make my dream of being a professional jazz musician come true.

||||||||||

In December of 1960, a couple of months after the Coleman Hawkins gig, I got a call from John Cort, the owner of the Birdhouse, a small club in a second-floor walkup on Dearborn Street, on the North Side. "Donald Byrd and Pepper Adams are playing in Milwaukee this weekend," he told me. "You want to play with them?"

"Are you kidding?" I said. "Yeah, I want to play with them!" I couldn't believe it—I'd just been invited to gig with one of the best jazz trumpeters around. Donald Byrd was a veteran of Art Blakey's Jazz Messengers, and he'd earned a master's degree at the Manhattan School of Music. He'd performed with many of the jazz greats over the years, including John Coltrane and Thelonious Monk, and in 1958 he'd started a quintet with the baritone saxophonist Pepper Adams. That was the group I was being invited to play with.

"Well," John said, "put on your maroon jacket and get on down here!" I'd played several times before at his club, so he knew my maroon jacket—the only jacket I had for playing gigs. I hurried down to the Birdhouse as quickly as I could get there.

As it turned out, Donald had hired another piano player, but a blizzard was blowing through the Midwest and the pianist had gotten stranded. So they just needed me to fill in for the weekend gig at Curro's in Milwaukee, and then on Monday they'd have their regular guy back. I met Donald and Pepper and the other guys at the Birdhouse, and we all went downstairs to pile into a car for the drive. But by now the blizzard was howling, and we didn't get very far before realizing there was no way we could make it to Milwaukee in time for the gig.

I was disappointed, but then Donald said, "Well, are there any jam sessions happening in Chicago tonight? Maybe we could at least hear you play." I knew of one, a loose gathering led by the trumpet and sax player Ira Sullivan, so I gave Donald directions, and we made our way there. As we walked into the club all I could think was *Herbie, don't screw this up!* This was my big chance, an audition of sorts for Donald Byrd. He was sharply dressed, highly educated, and a really charming guy, and I wanted so badly to impress him that my hands were shaking when I went up onstage to take my turn with the other musicians.

And I guess they never really stopped shaking, because I sounded terrible. I was so nervous that I couldn't play anything right. After struggling through one tune, I knew I was done. I slumped off the stage and back to the table where the guys were sitting, my head hanging down in embarrassment.

I turned to Donald and said, "Well, I want to thank you for this opportunity. I'm sure after that you're not going to want me now, but I appreciate the fact that you gave me a chance." Donald just started laughing and clapped me on the back. "Come on, Herbie!" he said. "We're taking you to Milwaukee tomorrow. I figured you'd be nervous—don't worry about it!" Relief flooded through me. I hadn't blown it after all, and I'd have a chance to show Donald what I really could do.

We drove to Milwaukee the next day, and that evening I played a lot better than at the jam session. But I did have trouble with one song, a jazz standard from the '30s called "Cherokee." I knew the chord structure, but Donald's quintet played it really fast, and although I usually did pretty well with ballads and medium-tempo songs, I always struggled with soloing on faster songs.

After the gig I decided to bring it up with Donald. "I know I didn't do so well on 'Cherokee,'" I told him. "I always have a hard time with fast tempos. Do you have any tips that might help me out?"

"Barry Harris gave me a tip a long time ago," Donald said, referring to a piano player from his hometown of Detroit. "He told me, 'The reason you can't play fast is 'cause you never heard yourself play fast.'" And then he explained to me how Barry suggested overcoming that problem.

Barry's tip was to start with a particular form—either a twelve-bar blues or a rhythm form (based on the chord structure of Gershwin's "I Got Rhythm"), which are the only two true traditional forms in jazz—and then work out choruses. If it's a blues form, you write out the twelve-bar structure and then an improvised solo on that structure for several choruses. Then, once you've written out the whole structure, you just practice what you've written on the page, playing it over and over again, and then doing it faster.

The next day I did exactly what Donald had told me. I didn't worry about playing the piece exactly as it was written; the important thing was just getting used to playing and hearing myself do it quickly. That night at the second gig in Milwaukee, when Donald called "Cherokee," I played it fast! This was the first time I'd been able to solo really well on a fast song, and it was amazing to feel my fingers flying over the keys like that.

After the gig Donald and I talked again. He knew I had a lot to learn, but he'd obviously taken notice of the fact that I'd paid attention to his advice and worked so hard, because he said, "Herbie, I've been talking it over with the band, and we like the way you play. We want you to join the band."

"But you already have a piano player," I said, confused.

"We'll fire him," Donald told me. "We want *you*. But you'll have to move to New York. What do you think?"

I wanted to go, of course, because New York was the center of jazz, the big time. Chicago was a great jazz town, and there were amazing pianists there, guys like Ahmad Jamal and Ramsey Lewis. But I'd felt all along that Chicago was just the stepping-stone to get to New York, where the real action was happening. I just hadn't imagined I'd be taking that step so soon.

"I would love to," I told Donald. "But you'll have to ask my mother." Even though I was twenty, my mother was still the one in the family who did all the decision making. My whole life, I'd heard my father say, "Go ask your mother." And now that there was such a big decision on the table, it would have felt wrong to make it myself without talking to her.

Donald just smiled and said, "Of course." The next day he called my mother from the club and asked permission to take her younger son to New York City to play in his band.

My parents had always said they'd support all of us kids in whatever we wanted to do, but my mom wasn't too sure about this particular move. She expressed concern to Donald about my age and my safety in New York, and Donald, who was all of twenty-eight, said in his inimitable style, "Have no fear! I will take care of Herbie and make sure he's fine."

So it was that, less than a month later, in January of 1961, I took my very first airplane trip, from Chicago's Midway Airport to New York's Idlewild. I arrived with three bags and a couple hundred dollars in my pocket, and I took a bus into Manhattan to start my new life.

CHAPTER FOUR

Riding the bus into Manhattan, I couldn't stop staring out the window at all the skyscrapers. Even though I had grown up in Chicago I hadn't spent any time downtown, and there were no skyscrapers on the South Side and in Hyde Park, so I was as green as any tourist. I just couldn't believe I was really in New York City, right here in the Mecca of jazz and on my own for the first time in my life.

I got off the bus in Midtown Manhattan, not far from Times Square, and lugged my three overstuffed bags to the curb. Bags didn't have those little wheels back then, so I had to somehow drag or carry them to the place where I was staying: the Alvin Hotel, on Fifty-Second Street between Broadway and Eighth Avenue. The Alvin was cheap, and I'd heard that a lot of musicians stayed there. It was also just around the corner from Birdland, and that was a place I knew I wanted to be.

Birdland was a legendary jazz club, where all the greats had been coming to play since 1949. There was a sign out front calling it THE JAZZ CORNER OF THE WORLD, and it really did feel like that, with musicians like Count Basie, Charlie Parker, John Coltrane, Stan Getz, and Art

Blakey making regular appearances. Miles Davis was a regular, too, although just five months earlier he'd been beaten up by police outside the club for the crime of walking a white woman to her car. Birdland was where everything was happening, and "Lullaby of Birdland," the George Shearing song that was one of the first jazz tunes I ever tried to copy, was actually named for the club. So it felt only right that my first few nights in New York should be in the shadow of this great jazz venue.

I couldn't afford to stay in a hotel—even a cheap one—for long, so when Donald's bass player, Laymon Jackson, asked if I wanted to get an apartment with him, I jumped at the chance. We found a dirt-cheap place in a sketchy West Side neighborhood, a tiny walkup on West Eighty-Fourth with no furniture but plenty of cockroaches. There was only one bed, a mattress on the floor, so Laymon and I shared it. We didn't have enough money to buy another one, even if there had been room for it. But we did manage to find a couple of chairs on the street, so at least we each had a place to sit.

Those first weeks in New York were rough. Before I moved there, I had no idea what life was actually like for New York musicians. I knew Donald had a successful jazz career and that his records sold all over the world, so I figured that as regulars in his quintet we'd make plenty of money. But I soon discovered that the reality was very different. We played fewer gigs than I thought and got paid less than I expected. Laymon and I were sharing the cheapest apartment we could find, in a neighborhood of poor black people and Hispanics, and we still could barely afford it.

We got to know the handful of other musicians who lived in the neighborhood, including a vibes player named Jinx Jingles and his wife, who was a singer, and they were usually broke, too. The worst it got for me was a month or so after I arrived in the city, when I emptied my pockets to find just twelve cents to my name. But we all looked out for each other, so that afternoon we pooled our money together and for a little more than a dollar we bought a loaf of Wonder bread, a soup bone, a potato, and some flour. Jinx's wife made soup, which we sopped up with the bread, and I was so hungry that it seemed absolutely delicious. We had to ration the bread, because it had to last us until someone could scrape together a little bit more money.

I called my parents every few weeks, and though I never told them how bad things were, they still seemed to know. "Do you want to come home now?" my mother would say, and of course I always told her no. I'm sure they would have sent money if I had asked, but I was determined to make it on my own. I had my pride to consider.

My first New York gig with Donald Byrd's group was at the Five Spot, a cabaret-style club on Cooper Square in the Bowery. Since opening in 1956, the club had become a magnet for artists and writers like Allen Ginsberg, Jack Kerouac, and Willem de Kooning, as well as famous musicians like Thelonious Monk and later Joni Mitchell. Before the gig, Donald gave me a little pep talk. "Listen, Herbie," he said. "When we play at the Five Spot, there's going to be some other piano players there, people whose music you love." He told me Horace Silver might show up, or Bill Evans, and that if I saw them there in the audience, lined up like a jury to check out the new kid, I should try not to let it worry me. "Don't get nervous, okay?" he said. Yeah, no pressure.

Well, of course I was nervous. But I must have managed to do okay, because soon after that I started getting calls from other musicians about gigs. Everyone knew I was Donald's pianist, but the quintet wasn't always working, so I had plenty of time to play on other dates and work on recording sessions with guys like Jackie McLean, Kenny Dorham, and Lou Donaldson. Once that started happening, I began making a more reasonable income, to my great relief.

||||||||||

One afternoon shortly after the Five Spot gig, Donald drove down from the Bronx to my place on Eighty-Fourth Street for a visit. He pulled up in a Jaguar, with his girlfriend in the passenger seat, and I thought, *All right, Donald must be doing really well!* He parked the car and came up to the apartment, and after having a look around, he said, "Herbie, you've got to get out of here. I'm going to take you up to the Bronx. You can share my apartment with me."

I could only imagine what kind of luxury Donald must be living in, so I eagerly accepted his offer. But when I moved into his apartment a few days later, after lugging my stuff up five floors, I was surprised to see that his place was a one-bedroom. There was a hideaway bed in the living room, so that's where I would stay. Oh, and it turned out the Jaguar wasn't Donald's, either—it belonged to his girlfriend, but he would never let her drive it.

Donald had three rules for the apartment: First, everything had to be really clean, to cut down on the ever-present cockroaches. Second, I had to make up my bed every morning. And, third, if anybody rang the doorbell before nine a.m., I had to wake Donald up first before answering the door.

I had no idea what that third rule was about, but one morning I found out. The doorbell rang just before nine a.m., and I went into Donald's bedroom to let him know. He was groggy, but he jumped right out of bed, opened the window, and hustled out onto the fire escape. He told me to shut the window behind him and then go and see who was there. When I opened the door, it was an investigator with the Internal Revenue Service, coming to talk with Donald—just as he'd known it would be. I guess Donald hadn't paid any taxes in a while, but as long as he could avoid the IRS agents, he could stay a step ahead.

Donald had promised my parents he'd take care of me, and he did. But he was a free spirit, and it's fair to say that his kind of care wasn't quite the same as theirs. Not long after I moved in with him, he introduced me to weed. We were on the road for a gig, somewhere in the Midwest, maybe Detroit, and I just remember laughing through the whole night. That first time I tried it was great, but ultimately I didn't really enjoy smoking weed all that much. I didn't like being away from reality, or the way it often brought my mood down and made me feel paranoid. I'm more of a high-energy kind of person, so marijuana wasn't really the drug for me. I did like drinking, and I got to where I could do a lot of it. But for the most part, I kept on the straight and narrow that first year in New York.

By the end of 1961, I had played on my first two records: Donald Byrd's *Royal Flush* and Donald and Pepper's quintet's *Out of This World*. Donald even chose one of my own compositions to record on *Royal Flush*, a song called "Requiem." At that point I didn't have much experience writing songs. When we were kids, Wayman, Jean, and I made up one called "A Summer in the Country," and I had written a couple when I was at Grinnell. As a local musician in Chicago I had worked on other people's compositions, helping guys who didn't have as much of a harmonic background, so that gave me a little more experience. I knew I wanted to compose more, and when Donald told me he was making a new record, I wrote "Requiem" in hopes that he'd like it enough to use it.

Playing on those records and getting my song recorded felt like a pretty good start. But a year after I'd arrived in New York, I still wasn't working nearly as much as I'd expected, so in January of 1962 I decided to enroll at the Manhattan School of Music. I figured I might as well further my education rather than sitting around, so I signed up for music courses in classical composition and orchestration.

Donald had gotten his master's from the school, and every once in a while he'd come down and meet me there for lunch. One day he walked in and saw a young pianist he knew, a guy named Larry Willis. He introduced us, and Larry looked at me and said, "You're *the* Herbie Hancock?" I laughed, not sure if he was joking. But Larry didn't have any recordings yet, and I had two, so at twenty-one I guess I was already getting some kind of reputation in New York.

The irony was, as soon as I signed up and paid for my courses, so much work started rolling in that I couldn't even finish the semester. I played numerous gigs that winter, including one in January at Birdland with trombonist Al Grey that was recorded for his *Snap Your Fingers* record. Donald decided it was now time for me to take the next step.

"Herbie, it's time for you to make your own record," he said.

"No," I told him. "I'm not ready."

"Yes, you are," he insisted. "And I'm going to tell you how to make it happen."

Donald had a contract with Blue Note, the top jazz label, which prided itself on putting out records by the young lions of jazz—hot new players who were just starting out. Freddie Hubbard, Wayne Shorter, and Horace Silver were all with Blue Note, and their careers were on the upswing. But there was one hitch: The executives didn't want to take on a young artist unless they already knew he could sell records. It was the old chicken-and-egg problem, where no one will let you make a record until you've proved that you can make money by making a record.

But Donald had a plan. "Here's what you do," he said. "Go down to Alfred Lion"—one of the co-founders of Blue Note—"and tell him you've been drafted." This was the brief period between the Korean War and the Vietnam War, so we weren't fighting anywhere, but the draft was still happening. "Tell him you want to make a record before you go off to the army," Donald said. "That's the first thing.

"The second thing is, you have to make half the record for yourself and the other half for Blue Note," he went on. I didn't know what that meant, so he explained it. Half the songs on the record could be my original compositions, but for the other half I should be prepared to do covers of standards. "You've got to do something people know," Donald said, "'cause that's what's going to sell the record. It's a business, Herbie."

I thought about Donald's advice for a couple of days, especially what he'd said about original songs. I liked playing standards as much as the next guy, but I wanted to write songs that would capture people, and I found myself wondering, *Why can't record sales be driven by original compositions?* I knew that composers like Horace Silver had written songs that could sell, and that his funkier tunes sold the best. Could I write a funky original song that would help me sell a record?

I wanted to write something that was authentically from the African American experience—but not about being in prison or in a chain gang or picking cotton in the South. I'm black, but I'm a northerner and a city guy—I didn't know anything about cotton fields and chain gangs. I had lofty ideals about my integrity as a musician, and I wanted my songs to be true to my own life, so I thought, *Okay, why not try to write something that speaks to my own experience as a black person from Chicago?* And that's when the figure of the watermelon man, the most ethnic character from my childhood, popped into my head.

In my South Side neighborhood in the 1940s, the watermelon man used to come through with his wagon, rolling down the alleyways to sell his wares. The alleys were paved with cobblestones, so I grew up hearing the *clackety-clack, clackety-clack* of his horse-drawn wagon. I'd heard that rhythmic clacking so many times, it was easy to turn it into a song pattern. But what would the melody be?

I remembered that the watermelon man used to call out in a sing-song cry, "Watey-mee-low! Red, ripe watey-mee-low!" He'd shout up to people's windows, telling them he'd "plug" the watermelon, which meant cutting them out a little triangular piece to test it. Yet even though the watermelon man was calling out rhythmically, his wail wasn't really melodic. Then I thought about the women who would sit out on their porches, facing the alley. Whenever they'd hear him coming, they'd call out, "Hey-eyyy, watermelon man!" And there it was— the melody for my song. I wrote out a funky arrangement, with the melody lilting over a rhythmic pattern that represented the wagon wheels going over the cobblestones in the alley, and I named it "Watermelon Man."

I really liked the song, and I was happy to have created it from a true childhood memory—a piece of my heritage. But I knew that not everybody would be thrilled with a song by a black musician called "Watermelon Man." At that time the dominant image of black people and watermelons was a caricature of a pickaninny with braided hair, big white eyes, and shiny teeth. It was a negative caricature, and writing a song called "Watermelon Man" felt a little embarrassing. I couldn't quite convince myself that this wasn't a mistake.

So, just as I did with everything, I took the situation apart analytically. I asked myself two questions: *Is there anything wrong with watermelons? No. Is there anything inherently wrong with the watermelon man? No.* I didn't like the fact that something as innocent and inoffensive as a watermelon had been so completely co-opted by racism, and I didn't want to give in to it, because giving in to it felt like giving in to that victim mentality, the tendency to accept, subconsciously or otherwise, the negativity that racism directs at us.

By naming my song "Watermelon Man," I wanted to reclaim the image. Truthfully, I was relieved, because I really did like the song and wanted to record it—and I never could come up with any alternative title that sounded right. There was a vegetable man who came clacking through those South Side alleyways, too, but that just didn't have the same ring to it.

|||||||||

In the spring of 1962, at Donald's urging, I went to meet with Alfred Lion and Frank Wolff, whom I'd already met through my work on Donald's record *Royal Flush*. Alfred and Frank were German immigrants, childhood friends who immigrated to the United States and then founded Blue Note records in 1939. They both had thick accents, and some of the jazz musicians had fun doing impersonations of them. You'd have thought people were mocking them, but the truth is, everybody could see how much heart Frank and Alfred had and how much they cared about jazz. Musicians loved them for that.

Just as Donald had advised me, the first thing I told Frank and Alfred was that I was about to be drafted. Then I told them I'd written three songs and that I could do those plus covers of two standards and a blues, for a six-song record, which was typical for a jazz LP. They asked me to play my three original compositions, and when I was finished, Alfred said, "Can you write three more original songs, Herbie?" This was surprising, because it was very unusual for Blue Note to record all original songs from a new young artist.

Maybe they heard something in "Watermelon Man" that made them believe it could sell records, so they were willing to take a chance on a whole album of originals. I was stunned—I'd walked in that day just hoping to get a record deal, and now they were offering me a better situation than I'd imagined was possible.

But we weren't done yet. Donald had given me one other piece of advice before my meeting. "I'll help you set up your own publishing company, because they're gonna tell you that you have to put your compositions into their publishing company," he'd told me. "And you have to say no." I told Donald I was afraid to do that—afraid that Blue Note would pull out of any record deal if I did. "No, they won't," Donald assured me. "They're going to record you."

I didn't know anything about the record business at the time, but I trusted Donald. So at the meeting, when Alfred said to me, "Of course, you'll publish your songs through our publishing company," I did what Donald had said.

"I'm sorry, I can't do that," I told him. When he asked why not, I lied and said, "Because I've already put them in my own publishing company." I couldn't believe I actually said it, and I started sweating. I just hoped these men in their suits wouldn't crush my dream before it even got started.

"Well," Alfred said, glancing at Frank, "I guess we can't record you, then." And all the air went out of me at once. I was so disappointed, I couldn't speak. But I couldn't go back on what I'd said. I stood up to leave, and it was just like in the movies: I was halfway out the door when Alfred suddenly said, "Herbie, wait a minute." The two men conferred, and then Alfred said, "Okay, you can keep the publishing on your tunes."

At the time I was just happy to have my record deal back on. Later I would see the full wisdom—and reap the full financial rewards—of Donald's advice. The very next day I created Hancock Music, and I put all the songs from that first record, called *Takin' Off*, into my publishing company. And when "Watermelon Man" became a hit, I made a lot of money from it—money that would have otherwise gone straight to Blue Note. Once again I'd managed to take a big leap in my jazz career, thanks to Donald Byrd.

We recorded *Takin' Off* at Rudy van Gelder's studio in Englewood Cliffs, New Jersey. For years Rudy was an optometrist by day and a sound engineer on the side, but in the late 1950s he built a fantastic new recording studio and started doing music full-time. Most studios had flat ceilings, but Rudy's had a cathedral-like spiral ceiling. Not only were the acoustics amazing, but the space was designed so that the musicians could play in a semicircle, without having to be in separate rooms or having high baffles between them. That unique design made it possible for the musicians to hear each other and for Rudy to control each musician's recording in the mix even though we were all in one room.

Rudy was famous for being super meticulous about his equipment. He wore white gloves whenever he touched anything in the studio, and the musicians knew they'd better not touch anything themselves. If you needed anything moved, even a microphone stand, you asked him to move it—because if you did it yourself, he'd stop the session and come out of the booth muttering. Even though Rudy wasn't a big guy, he could scare the shit out of you, because he looked like he wanted to kill you if you'd touched anything.

I ended up doing a lot of records with Rudy, and he became like family to me. Years after that first recording session, I was in the studio and needed to plug my headphones into a different jack. "Rudy," I said, "I need these headphones moved. There's a jack right near me." When he answered, "Go ahead, move 'em," all the other musicians in the room looked at me in shock. I thought I'd died and gone to heaven—Rudy said I could move the headphones myself! I looked over at him, and he had a little smile on his face. That was the moment I knew I had arrived.

As we were recording the tracks for *Takin' Off* I learned something new about Frank Wolff, too. When you're laying down a track, you're not watching anyone in the booth, because you're just doing your thing. But when you go into the booth afterward to hear the playback, that's when you can get an idea of what everybody else thought about the take. With Blue Note, all you had to do was watch Frank. He had this little bouncy shuffle he'd do if he was feeling the music, and if he did that during the playback, you had your take. If not, it was back into the studio to record it again. And his instincts were always right.

Alfred had suggested the personnel for the record: Billy Higgins on drums, Butch Warren on bass, Freddie Hubbard on trumpet, and Dexter Gordon on saxophone. (Dexter had just gotten back from living in Denmark for a number of years, an experience that would serve him well later when he got the lead role in the movie *Round Midnight,* which I wrote the score for and acted in, too.) The sessions went smoothly, and the only moment I remember worrying about was just before we played "Watermelon Man." How would Billy Higgins, who was a bebop and post-bebop drummer, play this funky tune? But Billy had this way of playing that fell somewhere between straight eighth notes and the swinging triplets of jazz, and he gave the song a great funky-jazz flavor. Everything just came together beautifully.

Takin' Off was released in May of 1962, and it climbed to number 84 on the *Billboard* 100. At that time *Billboard* didn't have different charts for different genres, like pop, jazz, and R&B. There was just one chart for all the records released, so for a jazz record to reach the top 100 was considered pretty good. "Watermelon Man" was the single that propelled the record, and when I started hearing it on the radio, it was really cool.

Once *Takin' Off* came out, I started getting even more calls about playing with other musicians. That same year I played with Freddie Hubbard on his record *Hub-Tones* and with Roland Kirk on his record *Domino*. Another musician who had a profound effect on me was the great flute and saxophone player Eric Dolphy.

Eric was a leader in the avant-garde movement, which was a relatively new exploratory underground movement in jazz. I'd heard and admired his music—he put out four records in 1960 and 1961 and played all over New York—but I didn't really understand how it worked. It was just so different from the kind of jazz most of the rest of us were playing—much looser, freer, and less structured. Eric invited me to go on a short tour with him in the fall of 1962, but at first I wasn't sure I understood how to play with him.

"Do you have tunes you play?" I asked him. "Or do you all just start playing?"

Eric laughed. "Yes, we have tunes," he told me. "We have chord changes."

This surprised me, because the music surely didn't sound that way. I realized that if I was going to play with Eric, I'd have to look at chord changes completely differently, because the way I'd been dealing with them wouldn't work. I was nervous, but I thought, *Maybe if I break some of the rules I normally use, that may lead me in the right direction.* I decided to give it a try.

When I played with Eric, I purposefully broke rhythmic rules, harmonic rules, the rules of playing solo improvisatory lines. I just decided to go for it, extending myself into a way of playing that I'd never even considered before. It was scary to go outside the lines of what I'd spent so much time developing, but it was exhilarating, too.

And I learned something really important from doing it: I learned to play from my guts. Playing this way took more fearlessness, more honesty, more digging down deep into my raw emotions, but the payoff was huge.

Eric was a great musician to learn from, because he was such a sweet, mellow guy, always encouraging to other musicians and open to new ideas. He was able to walk a tightrope between the conventions in jazz and the avant-garde, producing music unlike anything else out there. The sad thing is, we could have enjoyed a lot more creative, beautiful music from Eric, but he died tragically in Berlin less than two years after I played with him. He collapsed at a show, but when he was taken to the hospital, the medical staff apparently assumed he was on drugs and left him to detox. Eric didn't do drugs—he was diabetic. If he'd gotten a shot of insulin, he might be alive today, but instead he died in that hospital at just thirty-six years of age.

The weeks I spent with Eric Dolphy in the winter of 1962–63 were a crucial step in my own development, because this was the first time I had to figure out how to fit into that kind of loose musical structure. The things I learned from Eric would influence not only how I later played with Miles Davis but the formation and evolution of the Mwandishi band, too. Playing with Eric pried open my brain as to what was possible in jazz.

And this was the beauty of being in New York's jazz scene in the 1960s. There were so many talented musicians playing, so many different jazz directions being explored all over town, that it was like taking a master class in music. The possibilities for how to play were endless, from cool jazz to hard bop to avant-garde to Latin jazz, and you could go to any number of clubs and hear some of the best musicians in the world. We were all just like kids in a candy shop.

In late 1962 I got my first gig working with a Latin group. The leader was a Cuban conga player named Mongo Santamaria, and his piano player—who I found out many years later was actually Chick

Corea—had just left the band. Mongo needed a pianist for the weekend, so I agreed to fill in. I had never played Latin music before, but Mongo told me he'd just teach me some simple *montunos,* or Latin patterns, and that I'd get through it just fine.

We were playing at a supper club in the Bronx, not far from the apartment where Donald and I were living, and on the third night Donald came by to see how it was going. He was like a big brother to me by now, always checking in on me and making sure I was doing all right. That night the atmosphere in the supper club was pretty dead. People were sitting at their tables, talking and drinking, but the dance floor was empty. We made it through the first set, and Donald strolled over to the bandstand to say hello.

During the intermission Donald and Mongo struck up a conversation. Donald was a real student of music, and he loved to talk about music history and theory with anyone who was interested. He and Mongo got into this deep conversation about Afro-Cuban music and African American jazz. Mongo told Donald he'd been searching for a link between the two, but he'd never quite found what he was looking for, though he was sure it was out there, that link from the African diaspora.

I was only half listening, because this felt like a pretty heavy conversation to be having during the intermission of a supper club show. Then Donald said, "Hey, Herbie—play 'Watermelon Man' for Mongo." I wasn't sure how my funky little jazz tune was relevant to the conversation they were having, but I sat down at the piano and started to play.

Mongo started nodding his head and then said, "Keep playing!" He went up to his congas and joined in with a Latin beat, something he called *guajira*—and it fit perfectly. The bass player stole a look at my left hand to see what I was playing, and he picked up the bass line, and pretty soon the whole band joined in, jamming to this new Latin-flavored version of "Watermelon Man."

Meanwhile, the people who'd been sitting in their chairs all night started getting up, two by two, and heading for the dance floor. Within minutes the whole place was jumping, people dancing and shrieking with joy. Mongo had a huge smile on his face, and all of us in the band were looking at each other like *What just happened here?* We all started laughing, because this song was so much fun to play. When we finished the tune, people were saying, "It's a hit! It's a hit!" and slapping me on the back. Mongo said, "Can I record it?"

"Please do!" I told him. I couldn't even believe what had just taken place. I had never imagined putting a Latin beat on "Watermelon Man," but it brought the whole song to life in a new way.

Mongo Santamaria released his version of "Watermelon Man" in early 1963, and it became a huge hit, eventually reaching number 10 in *Cash Box* and number 11 on the *Billboard* chart. I could walk down the street and hear it blasting out of people's windows, hear it coming out of people's cars as they drove by. I was twenty-two years old, almost twenty-three, and I had a big hit record! And, thanks to Donald's advice about publishing, I would actually make some money from it.

After the success of Mongo's version of "Watermelon Man," I hired the entertainment lawyer Paul Marshall, who told me I needed to register with BMI as a publisher, not just a writer, so they could track down any royalties I should be getting. I'd registered as a writer when I first came to New York, but what I didn't know was that if you register as a publisher or writer with BMI when you have some degree of success, you can get an advance on future sales. So when Marshall called BMI on my behalf, he told them he wanted a $3,000 advance for me. And just like that, a courier delivered the check to me within an hour or so.

In the entire previous year, I had made only about $4,000. When I pulled that BMI payment out of the envelope, it was the biggest check I'd ever seen, let alone held in my hand. What in the world would I do with all this money? I gave it some thought, then made a decision.

I would buy a station wagon.

|||||||||

"A station wagon?" Donald said, puckering. "Man, are you *serious*?"

I'd just told Donald my plan. With the success of "Watermelon Man," I'd started thinking that I might have to get a band together, to get out there and promote the song. If I had my own band, I'd need a car to take gear to and from gigs. The most efficient and sensible vehicle for doing that was a station wagon.

Donald put his hand on my shoulder and peered into my face. "Herbie, have you ever thought about getting a sports car?"

"No," I said. And that was the truth—it had never occurred to me to spend money on a sports car, maybe in part because I'd never had anywhere near enough money to buy one. But Donald knew what it was like to tool around New York in a beautiful, expensive automobile— even if the one he was driving actually belonged to his girlfriend.

"Listen," he told me, "there's this new car called an AC Cobra. It's the street version of a racecar that's been beating Ferraris." He told me all about the Cobra, how it was made by Ford and was the hottest new thing that car enthusiasts were talking about. There was a showroom on Broadway where I could test-drive one. "Go have a look," he told me, "and see if you still want a station wagon after that." I agreed to check it out, even though a little super-fast sports car really didn't make sense for my needs.

I went down to Charles Kreisler Automotive and walked into the showroom. A few salespeople were sitting behind a big desk, but none of them even bothered to look up when I came in. One guy in particular seemed determined not to notice I was there, so I finally leaned over and said, "Excuse me. I understand you have a Cobra here." He still didn't look at me but just jabbed a finger in the direction of the car.

I knew what he was thinking: *This poor black dude, he's in here poking around, but there's no way he can buy anything.* In fairness, I had just turned twenty-three, and I'd walked in wearing jeans and a shirt, with no jacket. I probably didn't look like someone who could afford a slick, expensive convertible, but that was no reason for him to treat me contemptuously. As I walked over to look at the car I felt my blood heating up.

Having never bought a car before, I had no idea what I was supposed to be looking for. So I just walked around the car, kicked a tire, and bent over to inspect the headlights. But instead of cooling down, I just kept getting angrier. I strode back over to the salesman's desk and said, "I'm interested in the Cobra."

Finally, the man looked up. "Do you know how much that car costs?" he asked.

"Yeah," I snapped. "It's six thousand dollars, and I'm buying it. I'll bring you the cash tomorrow." I was so furious, I didn't care what I was buying anymore—I just wanted to show that guy.

The next day Donald drove me to the dealership in his girlfriend's Jaguar, and I walked in wearing a nice sport coat and carrying $3,000 for my initial payment. Everybody at the dealership treated me completely differently now, of course, and as I was signing the paperwork I happened to see the great saxophonist Jimmy Heath walking along Broadway with a couple other musicians I knew. They all broke out into big smiles when they saw what was happening, and they came over to check out my new car. Jimmy actually got the first ride in it—one of the mechanics took him for a spin around the block while I finished signing the paperwork, a big smile on my face.

It was just as well that the mechanic took Jimmy for that ride, though, because the truth was, I was scared to death to drive the Cobra. Earlier that day, when the salesman had taken me for a ride around the block, I couldn't believe how fast the car went. And the clutch was really stiff because of engine torque, so I didn't trust myself to drive it. When

I finished signing the paperwork, Donald flipped me the keys to the Jaguar, and I gave him the keys to the Cobra so he could drive it back to the Bronx for me.

I had rented a space in a garage in the Bronx, and for the next two weeks I'd come see my Cobra every day, sit in it, and pretend I was driving. I'd practice pushing the clutch in, bracing myself against the seat, and eventually I felt brave enough to take it out.

The irony is that, as worried as I was about scratching or denting that car, Donald wound up wrecking it about six weeks after I bought it. The accident wasn't his fault, and I was glad he wasn't hurt, but it cost a lot of money to repair it. But like Donald's other advice to me— to publish my own songs and play "Watermelon Man" for Mongo Santamaria—his suggestion to buy the Cobra turned out to be financially sound. I found out later that I was the first person to buy a Cobra on the East Coast, and my car was just the sixth production model built. Because they're so rare now, it's worth many times the $5,825 I paid for it. And I still have that car.

CHAPTER FIVE

I t was the spring of 1963 when I first heard that Miles Davis was looking for me.

Miles had disbanded his most recent quintet, and a rumor was going around that he was forming a new one. By this time Miles was already a legend. He had been making records since the mid-1940s, recording with and leading some of the greatest jazz musicians of all time—Charlie Parker, Dizzy Gillespie, Thelonious Monk, and the list goes on. In the mid-1950s he formed what is now known as the Great Quintet, which arguably set the bar for post-bebop jazz, with John Coltrane, pianist Red Garland, bassist Paul Chambers, and drummer Philly Joe Jones; and in 1959 he released one of the greatest jazz albums of all time, *Kind of Blue*. His musical artistry and razor-sharp cool had made him legendary even beyond the jazz world.

I had met Miles once, about a year earlier. Because Donald saw me as his protégé, he wanted Miles to know who I was, so he arranged for us to meet one afternoon at his house. As we walked up to the front door all I could think was *Shit! I'm about to meet Miles Davis!* He was unquestionably my favorite musician—I had all his records and was always amazed at the daring and innovation he brought to his solos.

Miles represented everything I wanted to be in jazz, though at age twenty-two I couldn't imagine achieving it.

Meeting Miles was a thrill for me, but he was interested in more than just social niceties. About five minutes into our visit, he looked at me and said, "Play something." So I sat down at the little spinet piano in his living room and played the safest song I could think of, a ballad called "Stella by Starlight." I was definitely nervous, but it must have sounded all right, because when I finished, Miles said, "Nice touch." I was so happy, I thought I might burst. Donald and I were there for about a half hour, but the only thing I remember about that visit were those two words: "Nice touch."

Despite that compliment, when the rumors started going around the next year that he was looking for me, I still found it hard to believe. Everybody wanted to play with Miles, so it seemed unimaginable that of all the jazz pianists in the world, I was the one he wanted. I didn't put any stock in the rumors, but they kept on buzzing.

Donald must have believed them, because one afternoon in early May, as we were sitting in the apartment, he said, "Okay, Herbie. When Miles calls, you've got to tell him you're not working with anybody."

"Come on, Donald," I said. "I don't know if he's going to call, but even if he does, how could I do that to you?" Donald had brought me to New York, and I'd been in his band ever since. He was like a brother to me, and I told him so. "You've helped me so much, with the record contract and the publishing deal—"

"Shut up, man!" he snapped. "If I stood in the way of you getting this job, I couldn't look at myself in the mirror." Donald loved to joke around, but he wasn't joking now. "When Miles asks, you do what I told you."

The next afternoon, the phone rang in our apartment. I picked it up and heard the raspy, unmistakable voice of Miles Davis. "Hello, Herbie," he said. "You workin' with anybody right now?" Miles wasn't one to waste words.

"No, not right now," I said.

"Good," he said. "Come to my house tomorrow at one thirty."

I started to say, "Okay, Miles," but—*click!*—he'd already hung up the phone. He didn't give me the address! In my excitement and nervousness, it didn't occur to me to ask Donald—all I could think was that Miles Davis had invited me to come play, and I didn't remember where he lived. When the phone rang again, I snatched it off the hook, hoping it was Miles, but it was Tony Williams on the line.

Tony had just turned seventeen, but even at that young age he was the hottest jazz drummer around. I had met him in late 1962, when he was living in Boston and I was gigging there with Eric Dolphy, but I didn't get to hear him play at that time. Then, when he moved from Boston to New York in early 1963, he called me to let me know he lived in the city now. Well, what was I supposed to do with a teenage drummer? Hang out? I didn't know what to do with him, so I just kind of put him off. About a week later I got a call from the saxophonist and bandleader Jackie McLean. Jackie was putting together a group for a gig in Brooklyn, at the Blue Coronet, and he asked me to play. "Who's on the gig?" I asked. And he said, "Eddie Kahn on bass, Woody Shaw on trumpet, and Tony Williams on drums."

"Look, Jackie," I asked, "can Tony really play? Or does he just sound good for a seventeen-year-old kid?"

"I'll tell you what, Herbie," Jackie answered. "Just make the gig, and find out for yourself."

So I did. We didn't have any kind of rehearsal, but we were doing standards, stuff we all knew. When Jackie counted off the first tune, I played the opening chord—and then Tony started playing some amazing rhythm I'd never heard before. I took my hands off the piano and turned around to look at him, my mouth just hanging open. I couldn't believe what I was hearing from this little scrawny kid! I had no idea how he was conceiving such rhythms, and it took me a couple of choruses before I could actually collect myself and play anything.

Tony had absolutely mind-blowing talent. He could play drums like no one else I'd ever seen, and even at that young age he had complete confidence in his abilities. Some musicians seem as if they were born playing their instrument, and Tony was one of those guys. He was magical to watch and listen to, because energy and creativity just flowed out of him. Just a week earlier I had put him off, but the day after the gig I called him and said, "Hey, man, what's happening? You doing anything? Can I come over?" And that's how I became friends with Tony Williams.

So when I picked up the phone that day and Tony told me that Miles had invited him to come to play, too, I was really excited. I was also relieved that Tony actually had Miles's address, so I'd know where I was going.

The next afternoon I made my way to Miles's place, on West Seventy-Seventh Street. He answered the door and then led me down a flight of steps to his basement recreation room, where I found Tony, bass player Ron Carter, and saxophonist George Coleman. We all chatted for a little bit until Miles called a tune, counted it off, and we started playing, just kind of feeling each other out. Miles played a few bars, and then he threw his horn down on the couch and disappeared up the staircase. Ron took over calling tunes from there.

Ron, who was a couple of years older than I was, had been on the scene for a while, and he'd played with Eric Dolphy, too. Like me, he'd started out in classical music, studying cello as a boy in Michigan before switching to jazz and the double bass. I had met Ron but didn't know him well. And I didn't really know George Coleman, either, but we started to get to know each other the way jazz musicians do everywhere: by sitting down and running through some tunes together.

We played that whole afternoon and into the evening, and every so often Miles would come downstairs, pick up his horn and play a few notes, and then he'd throw it down on the couch again and run back up. I didn't know it until many years later, but Miles actually had an intercom system in his house, so he was up on the third floor, listening to everything we did. He knew that a bunch of young players like us might feel intimidated by his presence, and he wanted to hear what we could do, so he put Ron in charge, leaving a few pieces on the piano for us to play. Ron played bass with a beautiful tone and impeccable timing, and he was also really organized and responsible, so he kept us focused.

This went on for three days straight. We kept playing, exploring chord progressions and learning each other's styles, while Miles popped in and out as the spirit moved him. Finally, on the third day, Miles came down and played a couple of songs with us all the way through. Then he said, "Okay, that's it. Come to the 30th Street Studio on Tuesday." And he started up the stairs again.

"Miles," I said, confused, "am I in the band?"

Miles turned to look at me, a hint of a smile on his face. "You makin' a record, muthafucka!" he said. And then he was gone.

That Tuesday, May 14, I went down to the CBS 30th Street Studio with the rest of the guys. We still had never really played the tunes for the record together, but Miles wasn't interested in rehearsing. He just wanted us to play, with the tape recorders rolling, to capture whatever was going to happen. I later found out that this was the way Miles always recorded: He wanted to capture the first, most honest version of a song, even if there were mistakes in it. Miles believed that if you rehearse a song too much, you stifle the creative moment. Music was about spontaneity and discovery, and that's what he tried to capture on his records. The first time the horns made it through the entire melody, that was the take that would be on the record.

Miles didn't waste words, and he didn't waste time. In 1956, with his first quintet, he recorded four full records in one day—*Cookin'*, *Relaxin'*, *Workin'*, and *Steamin'*—with just a few tracks added from an earlier session. He just went into the studio and played. When you record like that, it's scary at first, but then it sharpens you up. You're forced to go in with confidence, because you know you just have to do it.

And that day we just did it. We laid down tracks for the record *Seven Steps to Heaven,* and it was an amazing session. Everybody, especially seventeen-year-old Tony Williams, was killing. It was so much fun playing with these amazing musicians, I wanted it to last forever.

At the end of the sessions, I smiled and asked Miles again, "So am I in the band now?"

"You made the record, didn't you?" he asked. I had my answer.

My last gig before going full-time with Miles was at the Village Gate in Greenwich Village, where I was playing sideman for Judy Henske. Judy was a husky-voiced, six-foot-tall brunette who sang bawdy blues and backroom ballads, and she was opening for Woody Allen during his stand at the Village Gate. I was scheduled to play with Judy for a couple of nights, and after one of them Miles showed up at the club.

"You need a lift?" he asked me.

"No, thanks," I said. "I just bought a car, and I drove it down tonight."

Miles eyed me for a moment. "But it ain't a Maserati," he said. Miles was, of course, known for his beautiful cars, clothes, and women.

"No, it's not," I said. "But it's kind of cute."

We walked up the stairs and out onto Bleecker Street, and my Cobra was parked right in front. I pointed it out to Miles, and he said indulgently, "Aw, that *is* cute." He went off down the street, and I got in my car, pulled out, and turned right on Houston, then right onto Sixth Avenue for the straight shot north toward Ninety-Third Street, where I had recently gotten my own apartment.

Miles came gliding up beside me at a stoplight. He looked at me, I looked at him, and we both knew what was going to happen next. As soon as that light turned green, we both floored it.

We flew up Sixth Avenue, where the lights all turned green at once rather than being staggered. My Cobra just dusted his Maserati, and by the time Miles caught up to me at a red light about twenty blocks away, I'd had time to light a cigarette. I looked over at him, feeling just as smug as could be. Miles rolled his window down and said, "Get rid of that car."

"What?" I said. "Why?"

"It's too *daaaan*gerous," he rasped. And right then, as if he'd planned it, the light turned green and he shot off into the night.

|||||||||||

In the beginning, the quintet was Miles, Tony, Ron, George, and me. When George left the following year, Miles brought in Sam Rivers to replace him, but it wasn't until Wayne Shorter replaced Sam toward the end of 1964 that the quintet really became complete. Wayne brought his artistry not only as an amazing saxophonist but as a composer, writing songs that were ideal for what we were trying to accomplish. The addition of Wayne is what ultimately turned the group into the Second Great Quintet.

The beauty of playing with Miles was that he gave us so much freedom. He never told us what to do or how to do it—he just gave us a platform to explore. We would start playing a song, and the deeper we got into it, the more each player would branch out into new improvisatory places. No song ever sounded the same twice, and often they wouldn't even be recognizable by the time they ended. Even the most familiar jazz standards became swirling, unpredictable explorations—"controlled freedom" was what we called it.

Every player took turns soloing, and that was when we really took off in unknown directions. Miles didn't put any limits on us, always encouraging us to be as adventurous as we could. Sometimes we would get so far out in our explorations, we'd almost lose track of the original song, but then Miles had the ability to step in and play a solo that somehow brought everything back together again.

Each night was a high-wire act, and every once in a while even Miles lost track of where we were. My brother, Wayman, tells a story from one of our gigs in Chicago:

The band started playing up onstage, and they sounded great. Miles would play for a while, and then he would leave the stage, pass through the audience, and go outside to smoke a cigarette while the other band members went through their respective solos. They always started off with some song everybody would recognize, but by the time everybody had finished their solos, you knew they were all just jamming and riffing.

One time Miles finished smoking a couple of cigarettes and sauntered back in, and when he got to my table, he said, "I forgot what tune we were playing." I told him what it was, and he went right back up and finished.

We never rehearsed in the traditional sense, though sometimes we'd get together for a kind of brainstorming session. Miles might say, "We're going to record next week. Bring your tunes." And we'd toss around ideas for how to develop them on the stage.

Miles never said much about our playing. He just wasn't the kind of leader who gave notes or made suggestions unless we asked him to. Even then, he usually responded with cryptic comments, almost like little puzzles we had to solve. And Miles never talked about the mechanics of music, the notes and keys and chords of it. He was more likely to talk about a color or a shape he wanted to create. Once, when he saw a woman stumble while walking down the street, he pointed at her and told us, "Play that."

While Miles preferred to talk about music in metaphors and images, after each performance Tony, Ron, and I would stay up late into the night deconstructing what we'd played. We'd spend hours talking about what had gone down that night, and about the "what ifs" of what we might play the next night. I loved discussing music with those guys, and I learned so much in those late-night sessions. I just drank it in, eager to learn everything, because I knew that being in Miles's quintet meant being a part of a legacy, a bloodline that reached back through some of the greatest jazz players in history. And maybe somehow down deep, I didn't want to let them down.

Early on I was trying too hard. In my efforts to show Miles what I could do, I was doing too much. Miles would be playing an intro, and I'd practically concertize behind him, filling up the space with flourishes and thick chords. A couple of times he walked over to the piano and mimicked cutting off my hands, to get me to shut up. I figured this was just Miles being Miles, but later I found out there was more serious intent behind it.

I kept filling up the space, always thinking about how I could enhance the song or push my limits further outward. But there were some moments when I wasn't sure how to do that, or what was expected of me. So after a show one night, I decided to ask Miles about it.

"Miles, sometimes I just don't know what to play," I told him.

"Then don't play nothin'," he replied, not even looking up. Simple as that.

I had never thought of just *not playing* during a song. But as soon as Miles said the words, it made perfect sense. I realized that this was why he'd joked about cutting off my hands: The absence of an instrument changed a song's sound as drastically as—if not more than—simply changing what that instrument was playing. This was classic Miles, teaching me something profound about music in just a couple of words.

The bassist Buster Williams told me about a similar experience when he first played some gigs with the quintet in the late 1960s:

> The first week I'm with him, Miles is making me feel so comfortable. In intermissions, he's spending the time talking with me

about cars, clothes, that kind of thing. And then, when we were onstage, he'd just say, "Play your ass off, muthafucka!" He'd make me feel confident.

I had questions, so I decided to ask him one. I said, "Miles, everybody is so free on the bandstand. Herbie just lays out, and Tony looks like a big ball of smoke. And then you're playing, and every now and then, something comes through heaven, through your head, and down through your horn. What do you want me to do? When everyone is playing so free, and the form is there and the changes are there, but you only know that because you know it. Nobody is locked into anything, so I'm not sure what to do. Should I stay with the changes? Should I be describing the foundation? Or can I be as free as everyone else?"

And Miles just looked at me with that big smile. He said, "Buster, when they play fast, you play slow. And when they play slow, you play fast." And somehow that actually cleared everything up, even though he still didn't really tell me what to do.

This, too, was quintessential Miles: answering a question with a puzzle, and counting on you to figure it out. He would never hand out a pat answer when he could make you think instead. That's the mark of a great teacher.

Once he was in a club listening to a group of young musicians play. They knew he was there, so naturally they wanted to impress him. When they finished, one young man walked over to Miles and said, "Mr. Davis, what did you think about the way I played?" Miles just looked at him and said, "Do you dance with your girlfriend like that? Do you kiss her like that?" The kid hadn't played with any passion, but Miles would never say that directly. Instead, he wanted the kid to think about what passion was and to connect that feeling with what he should be doing with music.

Miles was always trying to stretch himself, too. Once when we were playing at a club in Detroit, he turned to Tony and me and asked, "Why don't you play behind me the way you play behind George?" He had noticed that we tended to mix up the rhythms when George Coleman was soloing, and that our playing sounded freer as a result. We would "break up the time," playing displaced rhythms, which tended to push the soloist into a freer interpretation of the song.

The reason we did that was because George was influenced by John Coltrane at the time, and Trane's band was really out there in terms of rhythm and meter. George liked it when Tony and I played more unconventionally, because it opened him up, too. Then, when Miles came in to solo, Tony and I would revert to a more familiar path for whatever song we were playing. I'd been listening to Miles's records for so many years that I assumed he'd want us to play like what we heard on the records. But it didn't work like that. Miles wanted Tony and me to help him challenge himself.

When Miles asked us why we played differently behind George, Tony and I looked at each other in surprise and then promised him we'd mix it up behind him, too. And that night in Detroit, we did. I started creating different approaches, different atmospheres, than what Miles was used to. At first he struggled. He'd play a short spurt of a phrase—just start and stop—because Tony, Ron, and I were breaking up things underneath him. The palette he was accustomed to hearing wasn't there, and it threw him off—I could tell by the way he was moving his shoulders, contorting his body to try to get on top of the rhythm.

Miles didn't complain, so we just kept laying it down like that all night. His solos sounded kind of erratic, but the next night he told us he wanted more. We played even more unpredictably, but Miles handled it better and was able to play longer phrases. He was starting to get into it now. And by the third night he was tearing it up and I was the one jumping and jerking, trying to keep up with him. That night I realized we'd hit a whole new level, and that my function in playing was going to be different than what it had been before.

This was a step forward but, true to form, Miles wanted to push us even further. Mixing up the rhythm led me to play more open harmonies—but why couldn't I play those anyway? Miles liked it when I played unconventional chords and harmonies, freeing up options for the soloist, regardless of the rhythm.

Playing in the quintet meant we were stretching and learning every day, but sometimes you could get into a rut. The solution was usually just to play through it, but one night as we were playing at the club Lennie's-on-the-Turnpike in Peabody, Massachusetts, I was really struggling, feeling like everything I played just sounded the same. Sensing my frustration, Miles came up behind me onstage and whispered five words into my ear: "Don't play the butter notes."

I had no idea what he meant, but I knew that if he'd bothered to say it, it was important. So I started to mull it over. What is butter? Butter is fat. Fat is excess. Was I playing to excess? Butter also could refer to something easy, or obvious. *Like butter.* Was there something obvious about how I'd been playing? If so, how could I change it?

Harmonically, the most obvious notes in a chord are the third and the seventh. Those are the notes that tell you whether it's major or minor, and whether it's dominant or tonic. So I started to think, *What if I left out the third and the seventh? Just didn't play them at all?* It would certainly open up more possibilities. And because I wasn't used to playing that way, it could lead me somewhere else entirely.

I decided to try it, not only on chords, which would be hard enough, but with improvised lines on my right hand, too. This would be really tricky, because it went against the grain of how I'd always played. But I was determined to do it. And because Miles always gave us free rein to try whatever we wanted, I knew he wouldn't mind. In fact, I figured he'd be glad I was working on something new.

Because the quintet never rehearsed, I just began my experiment right up on the bandstand one night. I had to focus so hard that it was more like an exercise, like doing scales, than playing music. Everything

I played was very erratic, and I had to stop myself frequently, because my fingers inevitably wanted to go to those third and seventh notes. I thought I sounded clumsy, but that night I got bigger applause than I had all week. People could feel that I was stretching, trying something new, and they liked it.

Normally a chord has three basic notes. When I took out the "butter notes," instead of playing a full chord, I'd play one or two notes. Sometimes I'd play two notes right next to each other—seconds. But I never played the third and the seventh, so my chords left a lot open. This gave the soloist more room, giving him a lot more choices of direction. It sounded minimalist and unusual; more important for me, it opened up a whole new way of looking at music and the compositional element of improvisation.

Once I got accustomed to playing without butter notes, I could start playing them again. Because now they were no longer butter notes: I wasn't playing them because I *had* to, like before. I was playing them because I *wanted* to. And that changed everything for me. All because Miles spoke those five little words.

The funny thing is, many years later I heard a rumor that Miles actually had told me, "Don't play the bottom notes," but I misheard it! Whatever the case, the five words I heard—or thought I heard, anyway—changed my life.

||||||||||

Tony Williams was just seventeen when he started playing with the quintet, and that posed a problem: He was too young to be in the clubs where we played. Miles told him to grow a mustache, but even then Tony still looked like the teenager he was.

Club owners tried a few tricks to make it legal. They'd rope off a section of the club for underage patrons, where people could only drink sodas. Or they'd stop selling alcohol altogether when Tony was onstage. We played one gig where Miles brought in another drummer for the first set, so people could get some booze into their systems, and then when Tony came on for the second set, the alcohol sales stopped. Some people at the no-alcohol gigs assumed it was because Miles took the music so seriously and wanted the room quiet, without the tinkling of ice in highball glasses. But it was really only because of Tony.

Miles loved the way Tony played, so he made other concessions for him, too. For the first couple of years we played all our tunes up-tempo, just flying through them, even ballads—everything was just *boom-boom-boom,* sometimes triple the normal tempo. This was exciting but exhausting, and one day we'd finally had enough, so we staged a revolt. Ron went to Miles and said, "It's too much to play so fast every time. We need some slower-tempo numbers, and to play some ballads as ballads." After that Miles started mixing it up a little bit.

At first I couldn't figure out why Miles always wanted us to play so fast. But as I thought about it, I decided it was for Tony. In those early days of the quintet Tony wasn't as comfortable playing medium and slow tempos, and because he was such a major component of the quintet's sound, I think Miles wanted to play to his strengths while the rest of his skills caught up. I never did ask Miles about it, so I could be wrong. But that's the only conclusion I could come up with.

Miles and Tony had an intense relationship, both personally and professionally. Tony actually lived in an apartment Miles owned, a couple of floors above where Miles lived, and they'd sometimes get into confrontations over rent or loans. Tony could be a hothead, and he'd bump up against Miles like a young buck testing out his antlers. Sometimes they even stopped speaking to each other, and each would grumble about what the other had done. During those times Miles would snap, "Don't ask me, ask him," whenever we wanted to discuss something. But I wouldn't have gotten in the middle of those two for all the tea in China.

Tony even dared to get on Miles about his playing, something I didn't hear about until much later. Tony would study obsessively, learning everything he could about different styles, even to the point of memorizing all the parts of particular songs. He'd suddenly launch into a lecture on the "modal period of European harmony, going back to the twelfth century," as if it were a topic we all had on the tips of our tongues. He worked so obsessively that he'd get irritated with Miles, who didn't share his interest in rehearsing and studying.

"Man, why don't you practice?" Tony would ask, as if there was nothing strange about a teenage drummer lecturing the greatest jazz trumpeter of his generation, a man old enough to be his father. Tony's sole criterion for whether a person could critique another person was talent—not age, not experience, just talent. Years later, when Bryan Bell, who created and built much of my electronic music technology, told Tony he was a great drummer, Tony replied, "Bryan, you're not good enough to make that judgment."

Bryan was a little taken aback, but he said, "Well, I enjoyed your performance."

To which Tony replied, "*That*, you can say."

Whenever Tony would get irritated with one of us in the quintet, he'd punish us by refusing to play when we soloed. He'd just drop right out, leaving you hanging, to teach you a lesson. Tony could be very temperamental and moody, but whatever problems his moods created were more than offset by his monstrous skills. And because he was so young, we gave him slack. He was a teenager playing with arguably the hottest band on the scene, and being thrust into that position puts a lot of pressure on a person. I'm not sure what Tony's problem was, but I suspect at least part of it was the insecurity of having so much attention on him at such an early age.

Tony and I became really close during our years with Miles. Before Wayne came along, he was my buddy in the band, the guy I talked most with about life, music, and everything else. He pushed himself relentlessly to become a better player and composer, and I learned as much from him as I did from anyone during that time. And as much as Tony believed in his own skills, I never knew him not to have a teacher. He was always studying, always learning.

When Tony was composing songs for his first album, *Life Time,* he would sit at the piano and plunk out tunes with the index finger of each hand, like a kid learning to play. But he didn't want to become a pianist—he just needed a way to work out melodies. I'd spend hours helping him, transcribing the melody he was playing and then using trial and error to figure out what harmonies he was looking for. Tony's songs were complex, not like pop songs and not particularly singable.

And Tony helped me by opening up my mind about other kinds of music. The age difference between us was only six years, but they were six crucial years, because like everyone born after 1945, Tony had grown up in the age of rock and roll. By the time rock music became really popular, I was already steeped in jazz, and jazz and classical were the only genres of music that I would listen to. I was a terrible music snob, and Tony—and Miles, who listened to everybody from Janis Joplin to James Brown to Cream—helped me get past that.

Tony also taught me a lot about the cutting edges of jazz. He got into the avant-garde scene before I did, and he was more comfortable with the direction that music was heading in. I used to ask him a lot of questions, just to find out what influenced him. He had this ability to come up with new stuff, to draw sounds out of his drums that nobody had ever heard before. He was absolutely fearless when it came to music, and that fearlessness infused the rest of us in the quintet, too.

||||||||||

One evening in Chicago, after we'd played a show at the Lyric Theatre, George Coleman came into the dressing room and said, "Hey, man— Billy Eckstine's in his dressing room with some cats, and he's been drinking. He's saying some shit about Miles." Eckstine was a legendary singer and the leader of the Billy Eckstine Orchestra, a seminal big band. He'd had some of the greatest musicians of all time in his band, including Charlie Parker, Dizzy Gillespie, Art Blakey, and Dexter Gordon—and years before, Miles had played in his band, too. What in the world was he saying about Miles now?

"Come on," George said, and he and I went down to Eckstine's dressing room to see what was happening.

Eckstine was really drunk, and he was going on about Miles—I can't remember exactly what he was saying, but none of it was flattering. I guess someone told Miles, because a couple of minutes later he suddenly walked in the door. And Eckstine looked at him and blurted, "Hey, Inky!"

Oh, my god, I thought, *Miles is gonna go nuts!* Eckstine was a light-skinned black man with light-colored eyes, considered a heartthrob—and of course Miles was famously dark-skinned. Calling out a darker man's color like that was just not done, unless it was meant to provoke. I knew Miles had been a boxer, so I figured he was about to drop Eckstine to the floor. Some poor janitor was going to have to clean up Billy Eckstine's blood tonight.

But Miles didn't say or do anything—he just let the comment go by. I couldn't believe it! Someone insults Miles to his face, and he doesn't even defend himself? I felt disappointed in him.

The more I thought about it, though, the more I realized how much strength Miles had shown in that moment. Billy Eckstine was Miles's elder, and he had given Miles a job back when he was just starting out. Miles was capable of breaking all kinds of rules, but he had a real code of ethics when it came to dealing with people. And the fact that he stood there and took it when Eckstine called him "Inky"—in front of a roomful of people!—was evidence of Miles's strength, not of weakness. On the other hand, it was a good thing Eckstine wasn't white, because Miles would have knocked him out.

This was the thing about Miles: He looked so fierce, and cared so little about what others thought of him, that people didn't see his softer side. I was intimidated by Miles at first—everybody was. But whenever we were in a hotel on the road, he'd call and invite us all up to his room, and we'd find a table loaded with food. He'd order up all kinds of dishes, and then he'd never touch them himself—he just wanted to make sure we were well fed. He cooked for us at his house, too. Once he sautéed dinner for us while wearing a tuxedo—no apron, no nothing. He had two kitchens in his house, and he was a great cook.

There was a real lightness to Miles, especially when he was playing music. He loved to play, and he played like a stone skipping across a pond. It never felt like work to him, and he didn't want it to feel that way for us, either. And it didn't. It was too much fun to feel like work.

CHAPTER SIX

O n Halloween night in 1964 my friend Larry Willis and I headed to the Village Gate, where the trumpeter Hugh Masekela was performing. Hugh was a friend of ours, but seeing him wasn't the only reason we were going. On the way to the club I said to Larry, "Let's pick up some girls."

I was twenty-four years old, playing in Miles Davis's band, and had a hot car and my own apartment now, so picking up girls was the name of the game. Since moving to New York, I'd had a few girl-friends, but mostly I was having fun and sowing my wild oats. I was making up for lost time, really, because in high school and college I wasn't exactly a ladies' man.

Although I'd dated a couple of girls in high school, I was still a virgin when I got to college. At Grinnell I went out with a few women, but the dating pool at a school of twelve hundred students in the middle of Iowa was a whole lot smaller than in New York City, which was filled with beautiful, interesting women. Now I was having way too much fun to settle down with anybody.

So that Halloween night we were looking for some pretty girls to "talk to." But Hughey came over to our table after his last set, and we got into a conversation and lost track of time. When we finally wrapped things up with him, the waiters were sweeping the floor and putting the chairs upside down on the tables, and all the women who'd been in the club were gone.

"Oh, shit," I said. And we started to walk out of the club.

Except . . . there was one group of people left. A guy I knew named Bobby Packer, who was actually a waiter at the club but had taken the night off, was sitting at a table with three women. "Come on, Larry," I said. "Bobby doesn't need all three for himself. Let's get over there."

As we walked up to the table I could see that two of the girls were pretty but one of them was really fine. She had jet-black hair, pale blue eyes, and an amazing figure. And there was something about the way she carried herself, a self-confidence, that was really sexy. Her name was Gigi, and I knew right away she was somebody I'd like to get to know.

Unfortunately, she didn't have the same feeling about me. I thought I was looking pretty sharp that night, in a gray silk suit and a leather jacket, but I also had a brand-new Nikon camera hanging on a strap around my neck. That summer I'd toured Japan with the quintet, and I guess I was still in tourist mode. As Gigi told me later, she looked at me and thought, *That one's kind of cute, but what a square!*

The six of us left the Village Gate and went to a bar called the Red Garter, where we had drinks and played cards. And even though Gigi wasn't all that interested in me, one of the other girls, Effie, said, "Gigi's having a dinner party at her place on Monday, and you're all invited." I said I'd go, mainly because I wanted to see Gigi again.

What was it about Gigi? She was different from other women I'd met, so much more intriguing. She was gorgeous, but it wasn't just her looks. She seemed feisty and strong, like my mother. She was brutally honest, no matter who she was talking to, and so full of energy and life that I couldn't imagine there would ever be a dull moment with her around.

Gigi had grown up in East Germany, and she didn't know anything about jazz, a fact I liked. That first night, when I told her I was a musician, she said, "Ah, that's nice. But what do you do for a living?"

"That," I said.

"You play in a band?"

"Yes, with Miles Davis."

"Who's he?" she asked. She had never heard of Miles—and in fact, that night was the only time she'd ever set foot in a jazz club. She obviously wasn't bowled over by my looks or my job, so I was going to have to find another way to make an impression. But at least I knew that if she did end up liking me, it wasn't just because she was some kind of jazz groupie.

That Monday I went to Gigi's apartment for the dinner party. I got there a little late, and Gigi was tied up in conversation with another guy. I kept looking for a moment to approach her, but she always seemed to be talking with someone else. After a while I just gave up and started paying attention to her roommate, a woman named Kristin.

Kristin was nice, but at a certain point, having failed to get Gigi's attention throughout the party, I'd had enough. "I've got to go," I said. "Thank you for dinner." Kristin got up to walk me out, and just as we got to the door I heard Gigi's voice from inside the apartment: "Kristin! You have a phone call!" Kristin went back inside to take it—and Gigi instantly appeared at my side. She walked me to the elevator, and I knew it was now or never. "I'd like to see you again," I said. "Do you want to go to the movies sometime?"

"Okay," she said. "How about Wednesday?" And we made a date.

When I stepped into the elevator, I was floating on air. *All right!* I said to myself. Thank goodness for the perfect timing of that phone call.

But of course there was no phone call. Gigi had made it up to distract Kristin so she could walk me out herself. Sometime during the evening she had decided I was worth getting to know after all, so she had to act quickly when I started to leave unexpectedly. As I would soon learn, Gigi is not a woman who hesitates when she wants something.

We started dating, and from the very beginning it was unlike any other relationship I'd ever had. Gigi always spoke her mind, and we challenged each other, like sparring partners. On one of our first dates we went to a bar and ended up in a heated disagreement. I don't even recall what it was about, but I do remember the passion we argued with, and the exhilaration I felt just being with her.

On another of our early dates Gigi invited me to dinner at her apartment. She was preparing coq au vin, but because she didn't have the right wine, she ended up making "coq au whiskey." It was delicious, and I thought, *Wow—all this, and she can cook, too!* But by the third or fourth time she made me dinner, it was still coq au vin, and she finally had to admit that it was the only dish she knew how to make.

Gigi could always make me laugh, but she taught me a lot, too. She ran the film department at the American Federation of Arts, and she was well versed in visual arts, such as painting, sculpture, and photography—none of which I knew anything about. I had always been focused exclusively on music. But she introduced me to the work of Roy Lichtenstein, Andy Warhol, and other Pop artists of the sixties, as well as filmmakers like Fellini, Bergman, and Truffaut. In our relationship she was the eyes and I was the ears, and we never got tired of talking about our respective passions.

There was so much I liked about her. We could talk for hours, and I always felt comfortable with her, right from the start. Our budding relationship wasn't built on just sexual attraction, or on our comfort level together, or even on mutual admiration, though it had all those elements. It was the balance of them all that made me want to keep seeing her. And she made me feel special, too, because women loved her, men loved her—everybody loved her. But she was dating *me.*

||||||||||

From the time I started playing with Miles, he had one rule when it came to women: "Don't bring no bitches to the gig," he said.

"Everybody plays different." We knew what he meant: Whenever a guy brings his girlfriend to a gig, he ends up playing to impress her. Miles wanted us to be completely free in our playing, not worrying about what somebody else might think.

Every once in a while Miles could sense when one of us had a girlfriend in the room. "Where is she?" he'd say. "I know she's here. Too much sugar in the music." And he was always right. I wanted Gigi to hear us play, though, so I told her she could come to a gig but that I couldn't bring her. We'd have to arrive separately, and I wouldn't acknowledge her while I was playing.

One night a few weeks after we started dating Gigi was supposed to come see us play at the Village Vanguard. I tried not to look for her, but of course I couldn't help myself—I scanned the crowd throughout the first set and didn't see her. When I couldn't find her during the second set, either, I wondered what had happened. So during the break, I went to the club's pay phone and dialed her number.

She picked up, and her voice sounded husky, as if she'd been crying. "What happened?" I asked. "I thought you were coming tonight."

"Herbie," she said, "I have to tell you something. We can't see each other anymore. I've gotten engaged to someone else."

I don't know what I expected to hear, but that wasn't even on the list. I had no idea she had been seeing anybody else, but apparently she'd been dating a handsome, wealthy Persian businessman named Hamid, who lived in Paris but also had a place in New York. They would see each other when he came to town, and when he came that weekend, he asked her to marry him—and she said yes. She knew she'd have to tell me tonight that she couldn't see me anymore, and she'd gotten upset. When I called, she was sitting in the bathtub, trying not to cry.

I didn't know what to say. Gigi and I had been seeing a lot of each other, but we hadn't yet slept together or said "I love you." I had to assume she loved this guy, and although I was really disappointed, I certainly didn't want to stand in her way. So I just said, "Well, I wish you all the luck." And I hung up.

As I walked back onstage for the next set, my mind was a jumble. I tried to clear it out so I could play, but one thought kept popping back into my head. Despite feeling upset and disappointed, I realized that I wanted Gigi to be happy, whether that included me or not. If this other guy made her happy, then that's what I wanted for her, because at that moment her happiness meant more to me than mine did. I had never felt that way about anyone before, and the feeling surprised me.

Somehow I made it through the set. Mercifully, the evening was soon over, but as I walked back to the dressing room someone said, "Herbie, you have a phone call." I went to the phone, and it was Gigi. She was crying.

"I broke off the engagement," she said. She told me that as soon as we'd hung up earlier, she had realized her mistake. "I don't love him," she said. "I love you." This was the first time she'd said that to me, and I thought my heart might fly out of my chest. A few weeks later she moved in with me.

IIIIIIIIIII

That same fall Wayne Shorter joined the quintet. I had met Wayne back in 1961, when Donald Byrd invited us both to play on his record *Free Form*. Since then Wayne and I had run into each other from time to time. I knew he was a brilliant musician, but I didn't know him very well personally when he replaced Sam Rivers in September of 1964. Tony Williams and I had been scheming to get him in the band for months because of the way he played.

Wayne was scheduled to join us for a two-night stand at the Hollywood Bowl called "Modern Sounds '64," where the quintet was playing as part of a lineup that included the Gerry Mulligan Quartet, João Gilberto, and Nina Simone. Miles flew Wayne out to Los Angeles, and we had just one rehearsal together before playing that first show. But it didn't matter: From the minute Wayne stepped in, the magic started to flow.

The beauty of Wayne was that he was just *out there,* as both a composer and a player. His mind works differently than anybody else's I know, and he has a playfulness and curiosity that shine through in his music. Wayne was never afraid to break the rules and experiment. He'd do it just for fun, to keep things lively, but then he'd hit on something so brilliant you couldn't imagine how he came up with it.

Once we were all up onstage, just firing away—notes flying everywhere, Tony playing as if he had eight arms. I mean, we were really cooking. We got up to Wayne's solo, and he was about to do what we called strolling, which meant that all the rest of us would drop out and he'd be playing completely alone, with no accompaniment. And suddenly Wayne started playing these weird, ghostly tones, blowing into the horn so you could hear the air going through with just the faintest suggestion of a note. When he started doing that, Tony and I just looked at each other like, *Whoa! Where did that come from?* It was strangely beautiful, almost like a whispering. I'd never heard anything like it.

Miles loved it, of course, because he always wanted us to experiment and push the limits of our playing. He expected all of us to continuously create, without having to lean on him or anyone else. The one thing none of us ever wanted to hear was "Oh, that guy's skating"—when you were playing with Miles, the word "skate" was not in the dictionary. Wayne really responded to that creative autonomy, because the band he'd just left, the Jazz Messengers, was more tightly run. He loved the freedom of being able to push boundaries.

Wayne was a brilliant musician, but he was also just a lot of fun. He didn't talk a whole lot—as he puts it, "If you're the one doing all the talking, you can't learn anything"—but when he did talk, he would crack us up. He's a great mimic, and like a lot of jazz musicians, he loves playing with words. Getting in a car, he'd pipe up, "You get in the front, and the rest of you get in the black." Or instead of going to the "restroom," he'd say primly, "I'm going to the rest of the room." With Wayne, nothing was predictable in either his speech or his playing.

Wayne is kind of like Yoda. He speaks in this whimsical way, but he's also very wise. He's like a Jedi knight! And he loves superheroes—he's totally into fantasy and comics, and he loves to wear Superman T-shirts. Wayne always saw the quintet as a band of superheroes: Miles Davis and the Justice League. There was a standard of behavior we tried to uphold in the band, dressing sharp, playing well, behaving like professionals. In Wayne's whimsical mind, playing by these rules wasn't restrictive or boring; it was merely evidence of our collective superhero qualities.

Wayne is observant about everything, and from that very first rehearsal, or really brainstorming session, with Miles, he liked what he saw:

> We rehearsed that one day, and I was noticing the intelligence level of everyone. I saw the high conversational level, the humor that was going on. It was almost like a club; if you didn't understand what was funny, then you weren't in the club.
>
> Ron Carter would speak very quickly, and Herbie would laugh at something he'd said—but it would just be one word. These guys were always talking and laughing, and they were very proud of what they were doing. The level of playing was so high, it didn't feel like work. It looked like they were in heaven.

Miles loved Wayne, because he'd compose these perfect pieces and then just walk up, hand Miles a sheet of paper, and say, "I wrote something." And Miles never had to touch Wayne's songs, because they were invariably brilliant platforms for our style of playing.

Miles was also intrigued by Wayne. "What does Wayne do in the daytime?" he would say. "How does he spend his time?" Then again,

Miles was kind of nosy about all of us. He always wanted to know what I had in my pockets, because I was always carrying gadgets around. "Where is *Herrrrbie* going with all that stuff? What is he doing with it?" he'd ask Wayne.

I had never outgrown my boyhood love of electronics and mechanical things; if anything, it kept growing the older I got. In high school I had built an amplifier using a Dynaco kit, and from then on I was always curious about how to use new electronic equipment to enhance music. During my time with the quintet, the latest equipment was the German-made UHER portable reel-to-reel tape recorder, so I became obsessed with using it to record our performances, a habit that sometimes drove Miles crazy.

It wasn't that Miles didn't want me to record the music, because he didn't mind that. In fact, whenever we were in the studio making a record, he always insisted that the machines be rolling all the time, because you never knew when we were going to hit on something interesting. He'd get really annoyed if we played something great and it wasn't caught on tape.

What drove Miles crazy was that I always needed a few extra minutes at the beginning of each performance to set up my microphones and recorder. And because I was usually late to shows to begin with, I often wasn't ready when it was time to play. Everybody else would be up onstage prepared to go, and I'd blow in at the last minute and then crawl under the piano to set up my equipment while Miles glared at me.

Once we were starting a set with a song that opened on piano, and I could hear Miles counting off as I was still fumbling around with the recorder. He looked over at the piano, and when my head finally popped up from below, he just said, "Ahhh, shit." Miles used to say that none of our recordings had piano in the beginning, because I was too busy fiddling with my gear. I'm not sure about that, but it's fair to say I was pushing the boundaries not only of music but sometimes of Miles's patience, too.

|||||||||||

One night we were all in the dressing room after a performance at the Village Vanguard. Miles knew a lot of Hollywood people, so it wasn't unusual to have movie stars come see us perform, and that night the actress Mitzi Gaynor was in the audience. Usually the stars would come to the dressing room after the show, but Mitzi hadn't shown up yet.

"Herbie," said Miles, "go find Mitzi. Tell her I said to bring her white ass back here."

"What?" I said. "I can't tell her that!"

Miles shook his head as if I were a misbehaving child. "Tell her those are my words. Say it exactly like that," he said. "Go on!"

I walked reluctantly out to the front of the club, and she was standing right there, talking to a couple of people. I went up and introduced myself.

"Hello, Miss Gaynor. I'm Herbie Hancock," I said. "Miles wanted me to say something to you, but I'm embarrassed to say it."

Mitzi smiled her thousand-watt smile. "Really? What did he say?"

"He said to tell you, 'Get your white ass back here to the dressing room.'"

And Mitzi just smiled and said, "Okay," and then she turned and walked toward the dressing room like this was the most normal invitation she'd ever gotten. It rolled right off her, as Miles must have known it would.

Another time, also at the Village Vanguard, we saw Ava Gardner sitting right up in the front row as we started playing. She was wearing dark glasses, a skirt, and tennis shoes, and Wayne sidled over to me onstage and said, "Hey, Herbie, check out the luggage"—which was what Wayne called a woman's legs. He liked to be able to talk about them without the woman noticing. "Nice luggage," he'd say, and we all knew to look around for a woman in a skirt or shorts.

This happened a lot, because there were beautiful women around Miles Davis all the time. Once when we landed at Los Angeles International Airport, we walked to the curb outside arrivals to find a purple Jaguar XKE waiting. The driver stepped out, and it was this gorgeous blond woman, an actress named Laura Devon. And Miles said, "Ah, my chauffeur is here!" He kissed her, and they got into the car and zoomed off. You can bet the rest of us had checked out her luggage—she was so perfect, she looked like somebody had drawn her.

Another time Liz Taylor and Richard Burton came to Birdland, in New York. They were the hottest couple in Hollywood, and they'd come by before going to another event, so they were both dressed to the nines—but Miles didn't show up that night. That happened occasionally, and it was always a little embarrassing for us, because we knew Miles was the main attraction.

Miles had been struggling with health problems for a while, but that wasn't necessarily why he didn't show up for some gigs. My take was, if Miles didn't feel he could deliver his best on a given night, he just wouldn't turn up, because he'd rather not play at all than play below his standards. He didn't usually miss one-night concert venues, but if we had a weeklong gig at a club somewhere, he'd sometimes skip a night.

Miles had well-known problems with drugs, but as far as I knew, he never missed any of our shows due to that. He had kicked his heroin habit by the time I played with him, and he never went back to it. But Miles was doing cocaine, like pretty much everybody else at that time, including me. In New York in the sixties, finding a musician who wasn't snorting coke was like finding a needle in a haystack. Coke was as easy to get as alcohol; so many people did it socially, it was just around and available. And most people, or at least the ones I knew, didn't overdo it.

Musicians had to be careful about drugs for more than just the obvious reasons. Up until 1967 New York City required anyone who worked in nightclubs to have a "cabaret card," which could be revoked if you got arrested. Many people saw this as a subtly racist policy, as many black musicians were addicts. There were rumors that some of the labels even gave their artists extra cash, perhaps fearing that otherwise they might turn to theft, or hock their horns, to get drug money. So even if a musician did drugs, he took extra care to protect his cabaret card, because losing that meant you'd lose your livelihood, too.

I'd tried smoking weed soon after arriving in New York and didn't like it so much. But the first time I tried cocaine I did like that. While pot made me feel slow and foggy, cocaine gave me energy and sharpened my senses, or so I thought. A lot of musicians felt that coke helped them explore music more deeply, loosen up, not hold anything back, get to the nitty-gritty. I felt that way sometimes, too, but mostly I would do it because it felt good. You couldn't really do any drugs and play onstage with Miles anyway, because the level of musicianship was so high, you had to be on your game to keep up with what the band was doing. You had to be your pure, unaltered self.

For that same reason I never really drank, either, when I played with Miles, even though I did drink socially. And I was able to drink a lot. In New York in the sixties and into the seventies people consumed cocktails like water, and I got to the point where I could mix all kinds of drinks and not get sick—which I thought was great. I built up enough tolerance that I could drink people under the table, and sometimes I'd have a little fun by proving it.

Once, on a tour of Europe in the seventies, a roadie for the band kept bragging to everyone how he could really hold his liquor. He was going on and on, so I finally challenged him to a drinking contest. We got a bottle of Portuguese grappa, a strong grape brandy, and this roadie and I started doing shots. The first five, he was doing all right. But then we got up to about ten . . . and then we kept going . . . and by thirteen or so, this kid just slid off his chair to the floor. They had to carry him out, but I somehow managed to walk out on my own, so I won! I was really drunk, but not too drunk to remember that victory.

The amazing thing was, Wayne had the ability to play music while being ripped. He drank a lot in those days, mostly cognac. We'd call him Cognac Man, which he twisted into Corny Act Man. Unlike the rest of us, he'd drink leading up to a show. He had a system: He'd drink, then sweat it out playing, then drink some more. I never understood how he could play so brilliantly while being stone drunk.

Talking about all this now makes it seem like we drank and did drugs all the time. We didn't, but it's fair to say that a certain level of drug use was pretty much expected among musicians. While I liked coke, I never felt that I was a slave to it. Some guys, if they had a gram at home, they couldn't get through a day without it. I didn't do it every day—I got enough of a high playing with Miles and the guys. Doing coke was something I enjoyed rather than craved.

And occasionally I tried things out of pure curiosity. Like the time I first dropped acid, in 1965.

||||||||||

At the Village Vanguard one night I met a Swedish guy named Björn. Björn had spent a lot of time in Millbrook, New York, which was the town where Timothy Leary had been doing his LSD experiments for a few years. At the time there was a lot of curiosity about acid, which was a legal drug used in psychotherapy and for treating alcoholism. But Leary was also a big proponent of using the drug as a spiritual and mystical tool for raising consciousness.

For months after I met him, Björn kept urging me to try LSD. He was convinced it would open up my creativity as a musician, and he offered to help me with my first trip, to make sure it was done right. I put him off for a while, but eventually I decided to see what the fuss was about. I had a weekend coming up with no gigs, so I told Björn I was ready.

Gigi didn't want me to do it. She wasn't anti-drug, but the idea of my dropping acid scared her. It was a longer high, more unpredictable, and everybody had heard about "bad trips" that caused hallucinations and paranoia. I was a little nervous, too, but how could I pass up the chance to have such a mind-bending experience? Especially since I'd have Björn there to look after me for the ten or so hours I'd be tripping? I told Gigi I was going to do it, and she stayed out of the apartment for the weekend.

Björn came over, and he set everything up as if he were some kind of psychedelic tour guide. "What records would you like to listen to?" he asked me. "You're going to be very high, so I will take care of everything." I picked out about twenty albums, but Björn vetoed a couple of them, including one really far-out record by John Coltrane, who at the time was deep into free jazz. "I think this might be too much for your first trip," Björn told me. Then he pulled out some records of his own that he'd brought: Indian flute music, which he felt might be more appropriate for this journey.

Björn lined up all the records along the living room wall, and then he went into the kitchen to prepare. The LSD was in liquid form, which was the only way it came in those early psychedelic days, and he mixed the right amount into a glass of orange juice. I took a deep breath, said, "Okay, here we go," and drank it.

LSD doesn't hit you right away. It takes a while to get going, but then at some point you realize, "Oh, wait—I'm high!" A couple of hours after drinking the juice, I was *really* high, much more altered than when I did weed or coke. "Björn," I said, "I'm pretty high. This is as high as I've ever been."

And Björn said, "Oh, you're gonna be *much* higher than this."

He was right. Soon the walls started moving, and creatures started appearing on the ceiling. Some of them looked like human beings, but then they'd change, and they were colorful and strange, and I wasn't sure what anything was. And then the apartment somehow became a train, and all the rooms off the hallway were the compartments. But then, when I started walking down the hallway, it suddenly became a jungle. I walked down the hall, cutting my way through the under-brush, and I kept thinking, *Wow, how did all this appear in my apartment?* Because I somehow still knew I was in my apartment, even though I was apparently in a jungle.

I made my way to the piano in the living room, because I thought it might be a cool, creative thing to play while I was tripping. But the keys were twisted into a U shape, so I couldn't figure out how to do it. And then I realized I didn't feel like playing anyway—I just wanted to look around at all the weird creatures and scenes that were morphing on the walls and ceiling.

Björn stayed with me the whole time, just spinning records and sitting quietly for the ten hours or so I was tripping. When it was over, I was glad I'd done it, but it wasn't like I was desperate to do it again. I'd had the experience, and that felt like enough. But then, about six months later, Björn invited me to come up to Millbrook to drop acid there. And I thought, *Well, why not go to the source?*

The Millbrook research was taking place in a big, sprawling com-pound with various barns and houses. As Björn was leading me across the property, we happened to walk by Dr. Leary, so I got to meet him briefly. But he went off to do something else, and Björn took me into a house where three other musicians I knew were already waiting. We were all going to do it together.

This experience was very different from the first one. In my apart-ment I had been mesmerized by the shapes and colors on the walls. But this time, as the acid kicked in, I looked at my arm and realized to my horror that it was covered with insects. It was as if the hair had morphed into these black, crawling bugs, and I couldn't wipe them off.

I'd been warned about bad trips, and I knew I had to keep myself from freaking out. There was no stopping a trip once it started, so if I allowed my fear to take over, there would be hours of misery and terror ahead. So I did what I'd done ever since that day back in high school when my parents wouldn't let me go to a party. Even tripping on acid, I started to take apart my feelings, to mechanically dissect why I felt the way I did.

I know these aren't really insects, I thought. *So why am I seeing them? Why insects?* My whole life I'd always been afraid of bees, so I decided this must be connected. I wasn't allergic to their stings, but for some reason I got really scared when they would buzz around me. I thought, *Maybe I need to face that. Maybe that's what seeing these insects is about.*

"Björn," I said, "I want to go to a place that has a lot of bees." In my altered state I began getting excited about bonding with the bees. *They are creatures of the earth, part of the domain of living species on earth, just like me!* I thought. *They are my brothers! I shouldn't fear them!*

Björn took me outside and sat me on a patch of grass. And sure enough, a few bees drifted by, but I forced myself not to get up and walk away. This was a real breakthrough, because normally if a bee flew anywhere near me, I'd be off like a shot. I couldn't be in the same room with one without my heart starting to beat like crazy.

But somehow, in the middle of what could have been a very bad trip, I decided I was being victimized by my fear—just as years earlier, in high school, I'd felt victimized by my anger over missing that party. And I was determined not to be victimized ever again. Even tripping on LSD, I decided to turn my fear from something harmful into something valuable. And strangely enough, from that day at Millbrook on, I've never been scared of bees. I still don't exactly like being near them, but I can sit calmly if one comes buzzing around. It was just another way I learned to control my emotions.

CHAPTER SEVEN

O f all the songs I've written, the best one, or at least my favorite, came in 1965. And it almost never even got written, because I lost the airplane napkin where I'd jotted it down.

The quintet was heading to California in January to play some gigs and make a new record. Wayne and I sat next to each other on the flight, and as we were talking, I heard a rhythm in my head. I hurried to write it down on a napkin, then stuck it in my pocket, but when we arrived in Los Angeles, I couldn't find that napkin anywhere. Neither Wayne nor I could remember how the rhythm went, so I figured it was lost forever.

We spent three days in Hollywood recording songs for the quintet's new album, *E.S.P.* As always, Miles wanted to keep things fresh, so the first take where we made it all the way through the melody was the one that would go on the record. We recorded Ron Carter's song "Eighty-One," and afterward we went into the booth for the playback. Just as the song was fading out at the end, all of a sudden I heard myself playing the rhythm I'd written on the plane! "Wait!" I said to the sound engineer. "Roll that back—I want to write that down." I had played the rhythm unconsciously, not even realizing it until I listened to the recording afterward.

I didn't originally intend to turn that rhythm into a jazz song—I actually needed it for a TV jingle. At the time I was doing some commercial work for a jingle house called Herman Edel Associates, and they'd hired me to create music for a TV ad for a Yardley men's cologne. The ad was supposed to be set in a sophisticated jazz club, but I knew that if I wrote real jazz, it would be too much for the TV-viewing public. I needed to create a jingle with a rhythm people could follow, something closer to rock than to jazz.

In most rock music there's a backbeat, meaning the accent is on the second and fourth beats. When you're listening to a rock song, those are the beats when you clap. I didn't want to do a straight-up backbeat, but I needed to find a rhythm that was palatable to the average taste, and as soon as that rhythm popped into my head on the plane I knew it would work. It was slightly more complex than a simple backbeat but not so out there that people would get turned off.

When I got back to New York, I started working on the jingle. I wrote the first chord, then the second, then the third . . . and then I got stuck. I couldn't figure out where to go next. I kept playing the first three chords over and over, then trying out different chords for the resolving fourth, but no matter what I tried, nothing seemed to work. I stayed up late into the night, trying to hammer something out, but I just got more and more frustrated. I couldn't seem to answer the question *Where does the song go from here?*

I finally gave up and decided to sleep on it. But when I crawled into bed with Gigi, she said, "Did you finish?"

"No," I said. "I couldn't figure it out. I'll get up in the morning and do it." The finished jingle was due to Herman Edel the next day.

Gigi turned to me and said, "Herbie, get out of bed. You're not going to sleep until this is done. Go! Finish it now!"

I couldn't believe Gigi was throwing me out of bed, but of course she was right—I'd always had a hard time waking up in the morning, much less writing music. So I went back to the piano, frustrated and tired, and tried to think of another way to approach the problem.

At that moment something in my head told me to stop trying so hard and just listen to what the song was telling me. I played those first chords again—and suddenly I got it! The first two chords should also be the *last* two chords. So what would normally be the ending chord—the cadence—would actually be cycling back around to the opening. The song would be structured like a spiral.

This seemed like a simple solution, but at the time you never heard jazz tunes where the chord structure didn't land anywhere but just kept spiraling. Most songs end up settling in a home key, but this one never did. I loved that spiral structure, even though I'd only written it for a jingle.

The agency ended up making some changes, stripping down the drums and changing the bass to something more tango-oriented. But the ad got made, and that might have been the end of the story for that jingle—except that I couldn't get it out of my head.

Throughout my time with Miles I continued to make my own records for Blue Note, and I was scheduled to go into the studio for a new one. I really wanted to turn that jingle's rhythm into a jazz composition for the record, so I decided to reverse the changes the agency had made, taking out the tango elements and putting the drums back in. The song was a little more hard-core after that, with a totally different feel.

In March of 1965 I went into the studio with Ron and Tony and also got George Coleman and trumpeter Freddie Hubbard. We laid down five tracks, and that song was the first. But I wasn't sure what to call it, so on the master we just labeled it "TV Jingle." The song felt important to me, so it was worth searching to get the right title. Blue Note was eager to release the record, but I kept putting them off while I played the song for everybody who came over, asking them what they thought the title should be. But as the weeks kept ticking by, nothing felt right. Then one night my sister, Jean, came over for a visit with a friend of hers.

Jean was in her early twenties now, working for American Airlines in the tariff office. For a short time she had been a flight attendant— one of the first black flight attendants—but when she developed late acne, the airline switched her to a desk job; this was back in the days when a company could hire and fire based on looks. Jean was living and working in New York, so we saw each other a lot.

Anyway, I played the whole record for Jean and her friend, and when it was finished, Jean's friend said, "It kind of reminds me of water." And I thought, *Yeah, it does, doesn't it?* Then she said, "That first song sounds like a voyage. Like a maiden voyage." And I just screamed and clapped my hands. That was it! As soon as the words came out of her mouth, I knew that was the name.

"Maiden Voyage" was a perfect, timeless image. And its ocean-based theme tied the whole record together, giving deeper meaning to other songs on the album, like "Eye of the Hurricane" and "Dolphin Dance." I called the executives at Blue Note and told them the song's title, and they used it for the album title, too. In May of 1965 *Maiden Voyage* was released, and the song, with its unusual spiral structure, ended up becoming a jazz standard.

That song meant a lot to me, and it still does. Whenever I play solo piano, it's my go-to song—if I'm playing only one, that's the one I'll choose. And of course it's also kind of a dedication to Gigi, since she's the one who made me get my ass up out of bed and finish it.

|||||||||||

In December of 1965 the quintet was flying to Chicago for a gig at the Plugged Nickel nightclub. Miles had spent much of the summer and fall recovering from hip surgery in April, then a broken leg in August, but by late fall we were back on track, playing gigs in Philadelphia and Washington, D.C., before heading to Chicago for the holidays.

By now Miles, Ron, Tony, Wayne, and I had been performing in the quintet for more than a year, and we'd gotten so cohesive as a band that it had become easy to play together. We had figured out a formula for making it work, but of course playing by formula was exactly the opposite of what we wanted to do. We needed to put the challenge back in, to figure out ways to take more risks. I had noticed that our playing had gotten a little too comfortable, but on the flight to Chicago it was Tony who started the conversation.

"I've got an idea," he said. "Let's play some anti-music." He wanted us to promise that during our sets at the Plugged Nickel, whatever anybody in the band expected us to play, we would play the opposite. Some people have suggested that Tony was trying to sabotage the band by doing this, but really he was only trying to sabotage our comfort level, to break us open again. It was just another step in trying to push our boundaries as musicians and as a band.

When we walked into the club, I saw that they were set up to record us. "Oh, shit," I said to Tony. "Should we really do this now?" We hadn't said anything to Miles about our experiment, and I was worried we weren't going to sound very good. But Tony, always fearless, said, "Hell yes. Let's do it."

Just before the first set, we told Ron and Wayne—but not Miles—what we were up to. They were both down with it, so from the moment Miles counted off the first song, I started focusing on how I could play against expectation. Whenever a song would build up, getting to a natural peak, the natural inclination would be to push it over the top—but instead I would suddenly bring it down with one quiet note. Tony did the same, building up his playing in volume and intensity, and then, instead of hitting the bass drum, he'd gently tap the cymbal. We did the opposite, too, suddenly ratcheting up the intensity just as a tune was winding down. I couldn't imagine that it sounded very good, but it certainly made us challenge our thinking and our choices.

We knew we were using the audience as guinea pigs for our

experiment, but this was a way to break the habits we had formed—by destroying the structure, then picking up the pieces and building something new. Whenever I glanced out into the audience, I saw what looked like confusion on people's faces. They knew something was happening, but they weren't sure what. So they just kept on drinking cocktails and smoking cigarettes, and we kept on playing as the recorders rolled.

And you know, Miles never said a word about it. He knew better than anyone that something strange was going on, but he never asked us, and we never told him. He just went with it. And he was brilliant! Wayne was, too. I actually felt as if I were fishing throughout those sets—I had some moments here and there, but I didn't shine the way Miles and Wayne did. In fact, at the end of the first night, when the soundman asked us if we wanted to listen, I said, "No way!" I thought it would sound like a disaster. I figured, we'd done it, we'd carved out some new territory, and now it was time to move on.

Seventeen years later, when Columbia released some of the recordings as *Live at the Plugged Nickel,* a friend called me to ask if I'd heard it. "No," I said. "And I don't think I want to hear it." He told me I should, because there was some good stuff on there. But I still resisted.

Finally, a couple of weeks after the record came out, I mustered up the courage to give it a listen. There was so much going on, and it sounded so little like what I remembered, that I was shocked. I really liked it, but I'm not even sure I could explain why. I would call it profound, except that the word "profound," to me, implies something that's deep and elegant. This was not elegant. This was naked and had guts. It was raw. To this day, when I hear recordings from the Plugged Nickel, I'm knocked out by their sheer raw intensity and honesty.

||||||||||

In early 1966 I got a call from Lionel Hampton. He told me that Benny Goodman was doing a couple of gigs and he wanted me to play piano for him.

My first thought was that Benny Goodman was famous for swing music from the '30s. He was a legend, but did it really make sense for me to go backward in that way? But another voice in my head said, *How cool is that!* I knew Benny was a great clarinetist, and I was curious about how I'd respond to his kind of music. I told Miles about the offer, and he just said, "Take it. He's a great player." So I agreed to do it. The band consisted of Benny, who was fifty-seven at the time, eighty-year-old trumpeter Doc Cheatham, guitarist Les Spann, drummer Morey Feld, bassist Al Hall, and the vocalist Annette Saunders.

And I'll tell you something—Benny could *play*. I threw a couple of curves in there, nothing out of context but not your usual rhythms, and he just tore right through them. Every time I'd push a little bit to the edge, Benny would run with it, sometimes doing things I'd never heard a clarinetist do. I had judged him based on the kind of music he usually played, but his scope was much greater than I ever expected. He surprised me, and we had a really great time playing those gigs. It was cool.

I wasn't completely sure how Benny felt about my playing, but a week or so later Lionel Hampton called me again, to try to convince me to quit Miles's band and join Benny's. I was really flattered to get that call, though of course I didn't want to leave the quintet. But the whole experience of playing with Benny and getting that offer was so much more than my young mind had imagined. I was really glad I'd taken the leap despite my misgivings.

In the meantime, back with the quintet, Miles kept pushing me to explore my limits. One day, as we were getting ready to record the album *Miles Smiles,* he rasped, "Herbie, stop using your left hand."

What? I only had two hands, so to stop using one was a pretty drastic step. But Miles must have had his reasons, so I dropped my left hand to my side. Now it would be me playing one line with my right hand, Ron Carter playing another line on bass, and Tony playing the percussion. Normally I used my left hand to impose a harmonic structure on the song, but one-handed I couldn't do that. And that opened up a lot of space within the song, which was exactly what Miles was looking for.

At first my left hand constantly wanted to jump in to cover up space. It was hard to get used to, but playing differently made me hear the song differently, and my right hand responded with new lines. I hadn't even realized it, but I had been staying glued to more standard rhythmic and harmonic placement, because my right hand had been leaning on my left. But now my right hand had all this free space to work with. It was a revelation.

When Miles made that suggestion, I'd thought it was just random. But looking back, I believe he actually could tell that my left hand was holding back my right. Yet he knew that if he said it to me like that, it would have affected my confidence, so he spoke to me in a way that allowed me to figure it out for myself. And he did it, as usual, in very few words.

This was such a liberating experience that even after we recorded *Miles Smiles,* I kept playing one-handed at gigs, my left hand just hanging at my side. There seemed to be no end to the ways in which we could shake things up in that band, and we never got tired of exploring them.

|||||||||||

One weekend Gigi and I drove to Long Island to hang out with some friends. When we got back, I called my phone service and was told that someone from England was trying to reach me. The person had left a number, so I tried calling back, but somehow I never could get through. It was pretty unusual to be getting random calls from Europe, so I was curious as to what it was about.

A couple of days later a secretary at the publishing company 3M Music called. "Oh, we've been trying to reach you, Mr. Hancock," she said. "Mr. Michelangelo Antonioni is doing a movie, and he'd like to know if you'd be interested in doing the score for it."

"Who's he?" I asked. She said that he was a big-shot Italian film director and he was making his first movie in English.

"Are you interested?" she asked, and I told her yes, absolutely. I couldn't believe an Italian director had even heard of me, much less asked me to score his film—I was just a sideman in Miles's band, and sidemen almost never got offered this kind of work. But it turned out that Antonioni was a big jazz fan. He knew my records, and he wanted me, even though I'd never done a movie score before.

So 3M Music bought me a first-class ticket to fly to London for a private screening of the film. I had never flown first-class, and it was *really* nice: tablecloths, beautiful silverware, Beluga caviar, Dom Pérignon champagne, incredible service. I was feeling pretty good by the time I got to the screening, which was to be the first time any of the executives had seen the film. Antonioni had complete artistic control over the movie, so the execs were eager to see how it looked.

I walked into the screening room and saw the tall, slim, elegantly dressed Antonioni. I introduced myself, but we didn't have time to talk before the lights went down and the screening started. Everything was beautifully shot, but I had no idea what I was looking at. There was a series of events involving a hotshot young photographer and some beautiful women, but there didn't seem to be a standard plot or traditional narrative storytelling. There were scenes from London in the swinging '6os—rock and roll, people smoking weed, wild parties. And the end of the movie was puzzling, a very long scene in a park with a bunch of mimes playing imaginary tennis.

I'm sitting there in the dark thinking, *Oh, shit. What is this about?* I didn't understand this movie at all—how in the world could I write music for it? When the lights went up, I did the diplomatic thing, just smiling and nodding my head a lot. The one comfort was that nobody else in the room seemed to have a clue what was going on, either, but we all looked very happy.

The production company got me a suite at the five-star Berkeley

Hotel, near Hyde Park, and I lived there in luxury for the next few weeks. I worked hard, but I had swinging London right outside my door, so I played hard, too. I went to parties with royalty and hung out with a guitar player who knew all the hot places to go. We'd sometimes play sets at parties, surrounded by girls with very nice luggage. I was in love with Gigi, but I was also a twenty-six-year-old musician on the road, so I didn't mind checking out the local "birds," as everybody in London seemed to call them.

In the meantime, I spent hours trying to create the right music for the film, which Antonioni titled *Blow-Up*. Antonioni had told me he only wanted source music, meaning music that has an actual source in the film. So if a character turns on a radio, or is standing in an elevator with music piped in, or is watching a live band in a club, there's music. But I wouldn't be writing any purely atmospheric or background music.

I asked some of the crew members what they thought the movie was about, and I got a lot of different answers. I wanted to ask Antonioni himself, of course, but he was too busy to meet with me. By then I understood that even though the average American moviegoer didn't know Antonioni yet, in Italy he was as revered as Fellini, so I was even more eager to get his thoughts. Finally, a few weeks into my stay, Antonioni invited me to have dinner with him in his suite at the Dorchester Hotel. His English was good, but he brought an interpreter so we could have a more detailed discussion.

I got right to the point. "You know, people on the crew are all coming up with different ideas about what the film is about," I said. "So I want to be sure exactly what you have in mind." I told him a few of the theories I'd heard and asked him which one was right, hoping his answer would guide me in writing the score.

But Antonioni said, "All of them. I just put the events together, and the viewer can make his own interpretation of what it is." I wasn't sure that his answer would help me much, but I did think it was bold of Antonioni to throw his movie so wide open like that.

A minute later Antonioni looked across the table intently and asked me, "'Erbie—what is art?"

I thought, *Well, I'm done for now. The master is asking* me, *What is art?* I was intimidated by Antonioni, because he seemed so fearless and certain in his artistic vision. I had been pretty happy with my progress in writing the score so far, but I had no idea what to say when he asked me this question.

He saw that I was struggling, so he answered for me. "There is no such thing as art," he said. "There is only this painting, this piece of music, that sculpture. And it either resonates with you or it doesn't." He paused for a moment, then added, "There is no such thing as *art*—there are only *works*."

I suddenly understood what he was saying. There was no mono-lithic "art," because no one term could encompass all the varied works that move people. It was pointless to try to create one giant category for them, because people responded differently, or sometimes not at all, to different works. Antonioni was putting power in the hands of the viewer, not the critic or the culture—which tied in perfectly with that first moment when he said every interpretation of his film was correct. In both cases, Antonioni was trying to give power to the audience.

Antonioni creates a film that's provocative, and if it's provocative enough, then there will be many different interpretations of it. That's why, if you see an Antonioni film ten times, you may come away with ten different interpretations of it. When you go to a film and it's all laid out for you, there's nothing to discuss—you walk out of the film, and the film walks out of you. But the end of an Antonioni film is really a beginning, a springboard for further reflection and discussion.

In those two moments Antonioni taught me something profound. He wasn't standing on top of some ivory tower, dictating how people should feel. Instead he was letting inspiration guide him, simply put-ting elements out there for people to create whatever they wanted. This was a brilliant strategy for film, and I realized it also had a direct parallel with music. Sometimes a song is painful, or difficult to swallow. But then if you listen to it again, in another emotional state, it may create a very different impression.

The best music is stimulating, in the sense that it stimulates the *listener's* creativity. It allows the listener to make his or her own interpretation, to be part of the story. It's never easy to let go, but the lesson I took from Antonioni was that, in film and music and art, letting go of control reveals whole new levels for both the artist and the audience. I resolved to try and do that more with my music.

When it was time to record the soundtrack, I had to get suggestions on whom to hire, since I didn't know any jazz musicians in England. We got a trumpet player I'd heard of, but everybody else came by recommendation, and when we started recording, I realized we had a problem. I had been living in New York, playing with the top jazz musicians in the world, and the ones in London weren't quite up to the task. The studio recordings we made in London weren't very good and didn't represent the music I had in my head. I played them for Antonioni, but we both knew they weren't of high enough quality to use in the movie. We needed to record the score again, with better musicians.

The trouble was, because we were filming the movie in England, the film company needed us to use musicians from the British Commonwealth, for tax purposes. So we figured out a little scheme. I told Antonioni I would fly to Canada—part of the British Commonwealth—and record the music there, with Canadian musicians. And I did in fact fly to Toronto and make recordings there, even though I knew already we weren't going to use them. I never told the Canadian guys that, of course, but as soon as I could, I hopped on a flight from Toronto to New York.

In New York I got all the top musicians into the studio as fast as I could—Jack DeJohnette, Ron Carter, Freddie Hubbard, Joe Henderson. We recorded the score, and I put those tapes in the boxes marked

"Canada" and then flew back to London. I handed them over to Antonioni, and as soon as he listened to them, he knew! "Is that Joe Henderson?" he asked, his eyes lighting up. "And Jack DeJohnette?" He was such a huge jazz fan, he could tell who was playing by the sounds of their instruments and the way they played.

I felt bad misleading the Canadian musicians, but in the '60s there really was a vast gap between the quality of American jazz musicianship and that of the rest of the world. In order to give Antonioni the level of music he wanted, I had no choice but to use New York musicians, who fortunately didn't care a thing about getting credit. Eventually, when the *Blow-Up* soundtrack was released, the New York musicians were listed on it, so the secret was out. But for a long time only Antonioni and I knew.

CHAPTER EIGHT

A few years before I joined the Miles Davis Quintet, I heard a record Miles had done with the arranger Gil Evans. It was called *Miles Ahead,* and the first time I listened to it I found myself in tears, the songs and arrangements were so gorgeous. I must have played it five times in a row that first day—it was the most beautiful record I had ever heard. To this day *Miles Ahead* is one of my all-time favorites. I still cry when I listen to it, and I'm not a guy who cries, ever . . . well, not often, anyway.

The genius of Gil Evans was that the sound he created with brass and woodwinds was like that of a full orchestra. He wrote classical references into his arrangements, both traditionally orchestral and harmonically contemporary, and the way he melded them was achingly lovely. Throughout my time with Miles, that influence grew on me.

When it came time to do my next record after *Maiden Voyage,* I wanted to capture the essence of the Gil Evans sound. But instead of doing it with the same instrumentation Gil did, I decided to set myself a challenge, to try something impossible: What was the smallest number of horns I could use and still get the essence of that sound?

I figured I would need at least six horns to capture some of its key colors and nuances, so . . . could I do it with five horns? That would be more difficult, but it still didn't seem like enough of a challenge. What about four? That would be really hard, and it was probably the least number that could actually work. If four was the smallest workable number, then I had to push it one more step, to do the impossible. I decided to use just three horns.

But which three? If there was any hope of creating a rich, orchestral sound, each horn would have to serve as its own section, and all three horns would have to be able to play on either top or bottom— that way I'd have more colors to work with. I picked the alto flute and the fluegelhorn, but I wasn't sure what the third horn should be. Miles said two words, "Bass trombone," which is essentially a regular trombone with a bigger bell and some extra tubing to get lower registers. So that's what I chose.

Now I had the instruments. But what was I getting myself into? I called my friend Joe Zawinul, the great pianist and composer (who later went on to co-found Weather Report with Wayne Shorter), and told him what I was trying to do. "You got any tips?" I asked him. I would need all the tricks and devices I could find to get the fullness of sound I wanted.

In listening to Gil's arrangements, I could hear the bass playing little countermelodies. Gil sometimes doubled these with a tuba, which wasn't typical of big-band writing, but it gave the sound more heft. I wanted to do something similar, but if I had the trombone player double the bass, then I'd have only two other horns to create the rest of the palette. I also noticed that Gil had certain colors that, when standing alone, sounded like a clash of harmonies, but in the flow of the music they didn't clash at all. How did he do it?

I was getting up in my own head about everything, so Joe said, "Herbie, here's what you have to do. First you have to get away from the piano." He told me to write the arrangements without sitting at the piano, just hearing the various instruments in my head. "If you do that," he told me, "you won't be just duplicating your piano lines." I had never written an arrangement that way, so it wasn't going to be easy.

"Next," Joe said, "make every line that each horn plays a singable melody." Normally a composer would write vertical harmonies for the two horns that weren't playing the melody, but Joe's idea was to create melodies for them, too. "Even if the melodies clash vertically with the harmony," Joe said, "the strength of the singable melody will pass right by. The clashes won't sound like clashes—they'll sound like spices to the ear." I wasn't so sure, but Joe just said, "Trust me. It will work."

Writing the arrangements for that record, *Speak Like a Child,* was like solving a puzzle. I used every device I could think of, layering in different melodies, scales, and trills. Most listeners probably never noticed the influence of Gil Evans on that record, but it was very clear to me. I just loved the colors we got out of those three horns, and I began to think that when eventually I started my own band, that was the instrumentation I'd like to have.

Little did I know it, but that day was coming soon.

||||||||||

In May of 1968, two months after *Speak Like a Child* was released, the quintet went into CBS Studios to finish recording our new album, *Miles in the Sky.* On our last day of recording, May 17, I walked into the studio and there was no piano for me to play. At first I didn't say anything, figuring someone would take care of that little oversight. When that didn't happen, I finally said, "Miles, what am I supposed to play?"

"Play that," he said, and nodded toward a Fender Rhodes electric piano in the corner.

Even though I'd always loved electronics and mechanical gadgets, I had no interest in playing electric piano. The conventional attitude, shared by most jazz musicians and particularly by piano players, was that they were cute but not substantial. There was no way they could produce the full, rich sound of a real piano, so why bother with them? They were gimmicks.

So when Miles said he wanted me to play the Fender Rhodes, I wasn't too happy about it. I thought, *You really want me to play this toy?* I walked over, flipped it on, and played a chord. And, to my surprise, I thought it sounded kind of cool. It was prettier than I had anticipated, even if it didn't have the same fullness or depth of an acoustic piano. I played around a little bit and then decided to have some fun by turning up the volume as loud as it would go.

I played a chord, and it was LOUD. And I suddenly realized that if I played this electric piano, Tony wouldn't have to back down from his intensity and volume when I soloed. No matter how hard I hit the keys on an acoustic piano, he always had to pull back so he didn't drown me out. But on the electric piano I could play really loud without even putting any more pressure on the keys—all I had to do was turn a knob. Suddenly I felt excited to play this instrument that I had been so ready to dismiss.

I learned something that day, and not just about the electric piano. I had formed a judgment based on the opinions of others, rather than on my own experience. I had locked the door for no reason at all and almost missed out on an exciting new musical experience because of it. This was one more step in overcoming my musical snobbery, and I vowed not to forget it.

I had actually started listening to electronic music a few years earlier, when Tony Williams turned me on to the German avant-garde composer Karlheinz Stockhausen. Tony had broadened my musical horizons over the years, introducing me to artists like Alban Berg, John Cage, and Paul Hindemith. I was always asking him, "What are you listening to?" because I knew I'd learn something. And one day his answer was to play me Stockhausen's *Gesang der Jünglinge,* one of the first great works of electronic music.

In *Gesang der Jünglinge* Stockhausen used sine waves and clicking noises to form a mesmerizing electronic tableau. When I first heard those sounds, I felt drawn to them, though I didn't really investigate how he'd created them, since I wasn't interested in making electronic music myself. Stockhausen's work was often categorized as classical, but it fell on a continuum of avant-garde music that intrigued me, a continuum that stretched from Stravinsky and Bartók all the way to Jerry Garcia.

One evening in 1966 I was performing with a trio at the Village Vanguard. The club was in a basement, and during a break I was walking up the stairs with another musician when a guy came chasing after me. He said, "There's a musician from the classical scene here who liked the way you played. He wants to meet you." I was always curious to meet classical players, so I said, "Great! Who is it?" And the guy said, "Karlheinz Stockhausen."

I flipped out. I was so excited to meet him that I went running right back down the stairs. We talked for a while, and I told him I was a big fan of his work. He said, "I'm writing a piece using the national anthems of various countries. Would you record the U.S. national anthem for me?" He wanted me to put my version on tape, and he would then manipulate the tape to get the sound he wanted. I was really excited to do it, but between one thing and another I didn't get it done in time. Stockhausen created that piece, called *Hymnen,* over a two-year period, and it premiered in November of 1967.

The late sixties was an exploratory period, and Miles telling me to "play that" Fender Rhodes was part of his own leap into that exploration. *Miles in the Sky* was the first record he made with electric instruments, and he never made another all-acoustic record again. And, thanks to him, I discovered an unexpected love for electronic instruments that would change the way I made music.

|||||||||||

By the summer of 1968 Gigi and I had been together for almost four years. We loved each other, but our relationship hadn't been completely smooth sailing during that time. One of the roughest spots had come a couple of years earlier, in the summer of 1966, when she nearly left me after an incident in Denmark.

The quintet was touring Europe, and Gigi had taken time off from work to come along for part of it. I liked having her with me, but I also wanted to do my own thing sometimes. I had never been abroad before joining Miles, and suddenly we were traveling all over the world, so I wanted to explore and experience everything I could.

One night in Copenhagen a group of Danes invited the band to have drinks after the show. I was always up for that, so we headed out into the night and proceeded to drink our way through the city. I had a pretty high tolerance for alcohol, but the Danish just take it to a different level altogether. I made the mistake of trying to keep up, and by the time I got back to our hotel I was really tanked.

Gigi helped me into the bathroom and started filling the tub, so I could have a bath and pull myself together. But I was too far gone—I threw up all over the place, and she just left the bathroom, disgusted. To my surprise, she went right to the phone by the bed and called the concierge for help booking a plane ticket. "I'm going back to New York, Herbie," she yelled to me in the bathroom. "That's it. I'm done."

She was angry about the state I was in, but she was also angry about the state of our relationship. We had been living together for two years by then, and even though attitudes were changing, most people in the 1960s still frowned on unmarried couples living together. My mother had a very Victorian attitude about it, which she made known. And Gigi felt uncomfortable checking into hotels with me as my girlfriend. She figured that people would notice the absence of a ring on her finger and assume she was either a loose woman or a hooker.

Gigi was also painfully aware that neither my mother nor my sister liked the fact that I had a white girlfriend. A lot of black women felt that way, and some still do. My sister, Jean, would say, right in front of Gigi, "How come all the nice, well-to-do black men end up with white women?" She was resentful, and she made sure Gigi knew it.

I knew that marrying Gigi would make things easier for her, but I was nervous. Because Gigi was European I wasn't sure she really understood what it meant for a white woman to marry a black man in America. A white American girl would have grown up understanding how deeply entrenched American racism was; she would know what to expect. But what would happen when Gigi had to face that ugly underside of American society? She had never seriously dated a black guy before me, so I'd decided it was best to wait a while, to make sure she knew what she was getting into.

But in that hotel room in Copenhagen Gigi decided she'd had enough. When I heard her making arrangements to fly back to New York, I managed to pull myself together enough to come out of the bathroom. "Gigi, come on. Please don't do this," I said to her. She just shook her head, still angry. So then I said, "Let's get married."

It wasn't the most romantic proposal in the world, but Gigi said yes. We called a jeweler the next day, and he came down to the hotel with a tray of rings. We picked out two simple bands and bought them—but even so, I still wasn't quite ready to marry Gigi.

I was twenty-six when we got engaged, and although I knew Gigi was the woman I wanted to spend my life with, I wanted to be free to have more experiences, to not feel tied down yet. Let's put it this way: I wasn't a skirt-chaser, but I did like skirts. Whenever the quintet traveled, I liked to feel that I was allowed a certain degree of freedom.

Gigi struggled with this, and about a year after we got engaged we had a big fight about it. The quintet was about to go on tour, and she and I had it out before I left. I didn't want to hurt her, but I also wasn't ready to make the kind of promises that she needed. The whole time on the road I dreaded coming back to New York. I figured we would fall right back into the same argument, and I didn't know how to resolve it.

When I got back home, I walked into the apartment like I was walking on eggshells. To my surprise, the lights were dimmed and there were candles on the dining room table. My favorite dinner was waiting, and a bottle of very expensive wine. What in the world was this? Was it a peace offering, or was Gigi about to kill me?

Just then Gigi walked in, and she looked absolutely gorgeous. She had a smile on her face, and she walked over and gave me a big hug and a kiss. We sat down, I poured the wine, and I asked her what was going on.

She told me that during the time I was on tour, she'd gone on a little vacation with her friend Maria. While she was away, she had thought about our relationship and the fight we'd had. And she had come to a realization.

"I realized that regardless of whatever else happens, I know you love me," she said. "I trust that to be the truth." I nodded, because it *was* true.

"The second thing I realized was, I have been depending on you for my happiness," she said. She told me she had been relying on me, and on our relationship, to give her purpose. And because I was away so much on tour, she felt empty much of the time. After our fight, she saw that she was putting pressure on our relationship—so much pressure that it was threatening to collapse. "I have to create my own life and be responsible for my own happiness," she said.

I could not believe what I'd just heard. But she meant every word of it. From that day forward she chose to trust in my feelings for her, and she became more independent, and more centered, than I could have imagined. She has such amazing strength of will that she was simply able to change her attitude. Our conversation that day released the pressure from our relationship, and it just got stronger and better from then on.

Gigi taught me something that day. No person is responsible for another person's happiness, and you can't make a person into who you want him or her to be. You have to love her for who she is or look for somebody else. Gigi and I loved each other before that day, but now we were free to love each other for exactly who we were. I looked at her across the table and thought, *Wow, I am a lucky man.* I still think that.

||||||||||

We decided to get married in the summer of 1968. I didn't want a big, expensive wedding, so I said, "Okay, Gigi. You choose. We can either have a big wedding with a bunch of freeloading friends who'll give us gifts we don't want . . ." She was looking at me like I was crazy. "Or," I went on, "we could fly first class to Brazil and live like a king and queen in a beautiful hotel on Copacabana Beach for two weeks."

"Where's my ticket?" she said.

We got married at New York City Hall on August 31, 1968, with my brother, Wayman, as our witness. And then we were off to Rio! We stayed at the Copacabana Palace, a gorgeous Art Deco–style hotel right across from the beach, and on our first night in Brazil we treated ourselves to dinner at the famous Ouro Verde restaurant. We drank champagne and ate oysters, and it was a fantastic night. Until we got back to our hotel.

It must have been the oysters, because I was sick as a dog that whole first night. The next day I didn't feel much better, so the hotel called a doctor for me. I knew that getting a doctor to make a house call would be more expensive than going to the hospital, but the dollar was strong at the time, so how bad could it be?

Well, this doctor apparently knew he'd caught himself a live one. He examined me and said, "You must be very careful. Bacteria could get into your bloodstream, and you could get hepatitis." He insisted on coming back the next day to see me again, and when I asked how much it would cost, he said, "Oh, nothing you can't afford, don't worry."

The doctor came back the next day, and the day after that, and the day after that. Every day he convinced me that I was practically on the brink of death. "Your liver is very swollen," he would say gravely. "You must rest. I will come back tomorrow."

This went on for our entire honeymoon. I spent the whole time in bed or resting on the beach, trying to make sure I didn't get sicker. The doctor kept telling me I was in grave danger. And by the end of our two weeks he had the gall to say, "You are not ready to travel yet. Your liver is too big. You must stay here at least another week." By now he had racked up thousands of dollars in fees from me, and he didn't want to let his cash cow fly on home.

I had gigs with the quintet coming up, and if I didn't get back to New York, I was going to miss them. I called Miles and said, "Listen, man, I got food poisoning, and the doctor here is telling me I shouldn't travel. So I won't be home for another week." Miles, of course, thought I just wanted to have an extra week in Rio with my beautiful new wife, so he wasn't very happy about that. As it turned out, he'd also been suspecting for a while that I was planning to leave the quintet, so now he decided to make sure he had another piano player lined up.

The truth was, I hadn't made any plans to leave the quintet. I had been with Miles for five years, but I was still learning and still really enjoying playing with the guys. Being in the Miles Davis Quintet felt like the gig of a lifetime for a jazz player, so why would I quit? But Miles had noticed the work I had done on *Speak Like a Child* and *Blow-Up,* and he could see that I was developing my own style. I guess he figured it was just a matter of time before I realized I had to branch out, so he decided to beat me to it.

The quintet played a couple of gigs while I was still in Brazil, and Miles hired the hot pianist Chick Corea to take my place. The next time I called Miles, a few days after those gigs, he just said, "Call Jack."

I called Jack Whittemore, Miles's agent, and he said, "You know, Herbie, Miles is aware that you, Wayne, and Tony are all thinking about leaving the band." He went on to explain that if all three of us departed at once, Miles would have to start another band from scratch, since Ron Carter had recently left. But if Miles could replace us one by one, he could integrate each new player into the existing sound and then continue uninterrupted from there. He wanted to take control of the situation.

"Chick played a couple of gigs," Jack said, "and he was good." Not every piano player could step into the Miles Davis Quintet and hold his own, but Chick was more than capable. "Miles wants to bring Chick on while Wayne and Tony are still there," Jack said, "but if you really object, if you really want to stay, Miles will consider it."

Well, I wasn't too happy about getting pushed out of the quintet. On the other hand, I had my pride, and I wasn't about to crawl to Miles and beg him to let me stay. My brain was racing, going through the scenario that Jack had presented me and considering my options. What should I do?

I had been making my own records since 1962, and most of them were doing very well. The new music I was writing didn't really fit the direction that Miles was going in, so it wasn't right for the quintet. And with *Speak Like a Child* I had hit on a combination of instruments and a sound that I really wanted to explore. I suddenly realized that there were all kinds of reasons why it made sense for me to go out on my own, but I had never allowed myself to see that. I might have just stayed in the band forever if Miles hadn't given me that push. Suddenly I was grateful for it.

"Okay, Jack," I said. "Tell Miles I'll leave." I hung up the phone and looked at Gigi.

"That's it," I said. "It's time for me to put my own band together."

CHAPTER NINE

In November of 1968 the Herbie Hancock Sextet made its debut with a three-week engagement at the Village Vanguard. Right from the start other musicians thought I was crazy—why a sextet? As a piano player I could have just hired two guys and gone out with a trio, which would have been much cheaper. The bigger the band, the more guys I had to pay. Even Miles Davis had only a quintet, so who did I think I was, hiring so many players?

But I wanted to continue exploring the three-horn sound I'd been able to develop on *Speak Like a Child,* so I hired saxophonist Clifford Jordan, trumpeter Johnny Coles, and trombonist Garnett Brown, and for the rhythm section I brought in Ron Carter and drummer Pete LaRoca. I knew it would be hard to make money, but thanks to Donald Byrd's advice about publishing, I was getting royalties from "Watermelon Man," which gave me a financial cushion.

During our run at the Vanguard, Ron Carter couldn't make all of the performances because he was playing in a Broadway show. So I brought in the bassist Buster Williams, who'd been playing with the great jazz vocalist Nancy Wilson. Buster was a fantastic musician, and by the end of the gig we were really comfortable playing together, so I asked him to stay on. He was the first piece of the puzzle to fit—the only guy from that very first sextet gig who would continue with me into the Mwandishi era.

I had one more album to do under my contract with Blue Note, so I began making plans to record with the sextet. But I started to realize that even though Blue Note was the preeminent jazz label, and very good at marketing to jazz fans, they really weren't set up to support music that went beyond those boundaries. I wanted to expand further, both musically and in terms of finding an audience, so I decided that after this final record was done, I would try to land a major-label deal.

The last record I did for Blue Note, *The Prisoner,* reflected the beginnings of my new musical directions. It was a concept album focusing on the struggle for civil rights. Like most black Americans, I was shattered by the assassination of Martin Luther King, Jr., in April of 1968 and of Bobby Kennedy two months later. The Black Power movement was growing, and the U.S. sprinters Tommie Smith and John Carlos had raised their fists in a Black Power salute at the 1968 Olympics in Mexico City that summer. Yet although I'd been emotionally invested in the civil rights movement, until now I'd never made any overt moves to get involved in it.

Most of the songs on *The Prisoner* were about Martin Luther King, Jr., including the fourth track, "He Who Lives in Fear." But as serious as its subject matter was, that song, like "Maiden Voyage," had actually started out as an advertising jingle.

I'd been hired to write music for a TV commercial for Silva Thins cigarettes. The ads featured a Mr. Cool–type character, a white guy in dark sunglasses and hip clothes who's always snatching his cigarettes away from the beautiful girls hovering around him. In one ad he even throws the girl out of his sports car, because that's how much he loves those cigarettes. Those ads would never fly today, but the Silva Thins print campaign was even worse, with the tagline "Cigarettes are like women. The best ones are thin and rich." It's no wonder that the late '60s was a time of ferment not only for black empowerment but for women's rights as well.

Anyway, the advertising agency wanted cool, Miles Davis–style music, so I wrote a few bars and recorded it with six horns and a rhythm section. I really loved the sound of that jingle—it was intriguing and mysterious—so I decided to repurpose it as a song. (This was something I did often, as I wrote original music for dozens of ad campaigns over the years, for products like Pillsbury's Space Food Sticks, Standard Oil, Tab soda, and Virginia Slims cigarettes.) The agency didn't much like the idea, but I changed the harmonies, title, and tone and created "He Who Lives in Fear."

The Prisoner didn't sell very well, but it's a record that's close to my heart, as it was the first one I made after leaving Miles and my first step toward a new, freer style of playing. I was soon able to land a new deal with Warner Bros., a big-label deal that I thought would help me in continuing to develop my own style.

Fifteen years had passed since I first learned to improvise by copying George Shearing records. From the beginning, the goal was to move beyond imitation and find my own voice, and I felt that that was finally happening. Miles had been the guiding light to my growth, encouraging all of us in the band to develop our own styles of playing, and during my five and a half years in the quintet I did start to develop my own sound. But it wasn't until I got out on my own that I felt I could really explore it.

Now that I had my own sextet, I started thinking analytically about what actually goes on within a jazz group. At every moment onstage players are making choices, and each choice affects every other member of the group. So each player has to be prepared to change directions at any given moment—just as Miles did when I played that "wrong" chord onstage a few years earlier. Everybody in a jazz ensemble has learned the basic framework of harmony and scales and how they fit. They know the basic song structure of having the rhythm section—piano, bass, and drums—playing together while the horns carry the melody. But apart from those basics, jazz is incredibly broad. There are really uncountable ways of playing it.

For the pianist alone there are so many choices to make: what pitch, how many notes, whether to play a chord or a line. I have ten fingers, and they're in motion almost all the time, so all of those decisions must happen in an instant. I'm reacting to what the rest of the band is playing, but if I'm only reacting, then I'm not really making a choice; I'm just getting hit and being pushed along. *Acting* is making a choice, so all the players must be ready to *act* as well as *react*. The players have to be talented enough, and confident enough, to do both.

I had watched Miles surround himself with amazing musicians and then give them the freedom to act. I wanted to do the same—but I also wanted to push beyond what we'd done in the quintet, into uncharted musical territories. In the quintet we had played with "controlled freedom." Now I was ready to cut loose some of that control, but in the summer of 1969, in the midst of touring and playing and trying to manage all the details of the sextet as well as commercial work and possible new movie work, I needed help doing that. So I made a call to Bill Cosby.

||||||||||

I first met Bill back in the spring of 1963, when I played the gig with Judy Henske at the Village Gate. Bill is a huge jazz fan, and he'd heard that Miles had hired me, so he came up to me after the gig to congratulate me. "Man, you've made it!" he said, clapping me on the back. "I'm so happy for you. I hope I get a break like that someday." Bill had been doing stand-up comedy all over the country, including New York dates at the Bitter End, across the street from the Village Gate, but he hadn't yet made it to the big time.

Two years later, when I was in San Francisco with the quintet, I was standing on a corner near Union Square when a red Mercedes 300SL Gullwing pulled up. To my surprise, Bill Cosby stepped out with a big grin on his face.

"Hey, man!" I said. "Whose car is this?"

"It's mine!"

"No fucking way!" I just started laughing. That car was gorgeous.

"Herbie, you won't believe this," he said. "I just got back from shooting in Hong Kong." He told me he'd been hired to co-star with Robert Culp in a television show called *I Spy*—the first time a black man would be starring in a TV drama. In the two years since I'd seen him, Bill had been on *The Tonight Show,* released a comedy album with Warner Bros., and landed this TV role. He had gotten his big break, all right.

And it just kept getting better for Bill. By the time I was touring with the sextet, in the spring of 1969, he had won three Emmys for *I Spy* and four Grammys for his comedy albums; he'd even charted an R&B song he recorded. *Playboy* magazine ran a long interview with him in May, and as I read it, one other detail caught my eye: Bill had a management company—and I desperately needed a manager.

So I decided I'd give him a call. Even though the sextet wasn't making any money, Bill loved jazz, so I hoped he'd agree to take us on. But when I reached him, he had another idea instead.

"Listen," Bill said, "I want you to write the music for this cartoon special I'm doing. It's about Fat Albert, a kid in Philadelphia." I mean, I didn't even hesitate. A prime-time cartoon starring black characters? Created by a black comedian? This was a really big deal for 1969, so I jumped at Bill's offer.

I figured that if Fat Albert was from Philly, the music should be more R&B than jazz. And because I hadn't been listening to much contemporary R&B, the first thing I did was go to a record store. I bought about fifteen James Brown–type records and then spent a couple of days listening to them over and over again. And then I started writing some music.

We were scheduled to record in Los Angeles, so I asked around to find some funky musicians to add into the mix with the sextet. We went heavy on the electric instruments, with me playing the Fender Rhodes and Buster Williams playing electric bass, and we added Eric Gale on guitar. After we'd laid everything down for the TV show, I asked Bill whether he'd mind if I put some of those songs on an album for Warner Bros. Bill was fine with the idea, so I brought back just the jazz musicians and recorded some of the songs again, leaning more toward R&B flavor than funk. I wanted to have some fun with it, so we called the record *Fat Albert Rotunda*, as a play on "rotund," and the cover art was a drawing of a refrigerator with a bunch of food stuffed inside.

The TV special *Hey, Hey, Hey, It's Fat Albert* aired on November 12, 1969. It was just a one-shot deal, although three years later Bill Cosby would use those same characters to develop the Saturday-morning cartoon series *Fat Albert and the Cosby Kids*, which ran for thirteen years. Our record *Fat Albert Rotunda* sold about seventy-five thousand copies, which wasn't bad for a jazz band but pretty small potatoes for Warner Bros.

I was excited when *Hey, Hey, Hey, It's Fat Albert* aired, but the real excitement had come the day before, when Gigi gave birth to our daughter, Jessica. We had been taking Lamaze classes together, learning all the breathing exercises, and the instructor told us we'd eventually be so familiar with what was going to happen in childbirth that when the time came, it would feel like we'd already been through it. That was true, but still, nothing can compare with what the mother experiences.

When Gigi went into labor, I drove us to Woman's Hospital at St. Luke's, and the nurses got us situated in a delivery room. In the Lamaze class they'd taught us that the partner should deep-breathe along with the mother, to help her stay on track. Unfortunately that can lead to hyperventilation, so you're supposed to have a paper bag with you to breathe into. I was breathing right along with Gigi, trying to help her out, until I got so dizzy, I had to breathe into that paper bag. I didn't pass out, but I was definitely feeling woozy.

Gigi was in the final stage of labor for two hours, which is longer than normal. The doctor told us that our baby was on her back instead of her belly and that if she didn't turn over by herself, they'd have to use forceps to turn her. They gave Gigi a caudal block, which numbed her enough to endure the pain from the use of forceps, then Gigi pushed as hard as she could—and out popped Jessica, all purple. I couldn't tell what was what, and at first I thought the afterbirth was Jessica! You can't really distinguish one thing from another, because everything's pretty much purple, but the nurses cleaned Jessica up, and she started crying.

As I watched my daughter come into this world, I was struck by the realization that this was exactly the same way I had entered it. For a moment I felt as if I were watching my own birth, and it was such a surreal experience, it nearly overwhelmed me. There was something so phenomenal about it, so profound, that I felt bonded to Jessica immediately. It's a bond that has only grown stronger with time.

||||||||||

Shelly's Manne-Hole was a club in Hollywood named after its co-founder, the drummer Shelly Manne. In its first decade all kinds of jazz greats came through that club, including Bill Evans, John Coltrane, Thelonious Monk, and Miles. And in the spring of 1970 the sextet was booked there for a few nights.

Our drummer at the time was Tootie Heath, and as we were doing our sound check before the first show, Tootie's nephew James Forman came down to the club to see us. James was the twenty-three-year-old son of the saxophonist Jimmy Heath, and he was a musician and composer himself. But his main focus now was the cause of black empowerment. He was a member of the militant black nationalist group U.S.

Organization, a rival group to the Black Panthers that was headed by Maulana Karenga and Hakim Jamal, a cousin of Malcolm X's. James had recently discarded what he called his "slave name," and now he went by the Swahili name Mtume.

That afternoon, as we were doing our sound check, Mtume was berating us for not understanding black history and for not doing more to further the cause of black Americans. "You guys have no respect for your heritage," he said. "You need to take a stand. The time is *now.*"

Mtume was on fire for the cause, and his words had an effect on us. From the time I was young I had always made a point not to give in to any victim mentality—but that didn't change the fact that racism existed and affected us all. Sometimes it came in small acts, like the looks Gigi and I would get when we'd check into hotels together. Sometimes it was more serious, like the time I got arrested in Washington, D.C., for jaywalking. I wasn't carrying any kind of ID, and despite the fact that Gigi was, the police hauled me downtown and put me in a jail cell. It took a white friend coming down to the station and apologizing profusely for me before the police would let me go.

But I knew my experiences were mild compared with what others had gone through before me, including my parents, who had grown up in Georgia in the early decades of the 1900s. I had heard stories of Klan rallies and lynchings, and as a child I had seen that photo of the horribly disfigured face of Emmett Till. My feeling had always been, *Who am I to complain?* I was enjoying my life, making music and touring the world. Yet as the Black Power movement grew stronger throughout the late '60s, I felt the stirrings of wanting to do more, if not for me, then for others. Making *The Prisoner* was my first step in trying to get involved. But now, as Mtume spoke so passionately, I realized it was not enough.

Mtume told his uncle Tootie that he was going to give him a Swahili name. Right away, the rest of us in the band said we wanted

Swahili names, too. We didn't know any Swahili, so Mtume came up with names that were appropriate for each of us. Tootie's was Kuumba, which means "creativity," Buster's was Mchezaji, or "skilled player." Mine was Mwandishi, which means "composer" or "writer."

From that point on, the nature of the band started to shift. Technically we were still the Herbie Hancock Sextet, but soon people started calling us the Mwandishi band. We called each other by our Swahili names, and over time we started embracing other visible symbols of the black diaspora. I had never spent much time thinking about my African roots, but all of us became increasingly influenced by African culture, religion, and music. We started wearing dashikis and African talismans, and I began to feel more connected than ever to the civil rights movement and to our shared, collective past as black musicians. This was a powerful transformation, and of course it affected our music.

Mtume was an angry young man, but unlike him, I didn't come to this place out of anger. I wasn't militant and had never been that kind of person. I just realized that because I believed in human rights, and this was the big issue of the day, and it happened to pertain to my own ethnicity, then I needed to be involved in it. This was my way of becoming part of the black civil rights movement, by embracing my identity as a black man, a part of the African diaspora. It was my way of being politically involved without actually getting into the politics of the movement.

Adopting Swahili names helped draw us closer together, and the sextet kept getting tighter. But in the summer of 1970 we were still struggling to book gigs and broaden our audience. I hadn't been able to get a management deal with Bill Cosby's company, and we needed help. So I turned to a guy who'd been a classmate of mine at Grinnell, Lee Weisel, to manage the band.

Lee was a lawyer by training, but he had somehow become the manager for the rock band Iron Butterfly, even though he admitted to not knowing much about music. "Herbie, I'm tone-deaf," he told me. "But I helped these guys get their contract, and now they've got a big hit. I can help you, too."

Iron Butterfly's big hit was a song called "In-a-Gadda-da-Vida," a free-flowing, seventeen-minute jam on their album of the same name. (Rumor had it that the song was actually titled "In the Garden of Eden," but the singer was drunk and slurred the words.) Now that Iron Butterfly was a major draw, Lee thought we might be able to piggy-back onto their success, so he booked us to play on a bill with the band at the Schaefer Music Festival in Central Park.

Boy, was that a stretch. Iron Butterfly was heavy metal before heavy metal, and the audience in Central Park that day was basically a crowd of young white guys wanting to rock out. When a group of black musicians in Afros took the stage, a lot of the audience just started streaming out. Nobody was there to see us, so I tried to think of how we might get the crowd's attention. And the one way I could think of was contrast: We would have to play loud and soft, high and low, fast and slow, long and short.

We played a funked-up version of "Fat Albert Rotunda" and the ballad "Maiden Voyage," but we weren't getting any traction at all. I didn't hear any boos, but I didn't hear much cheering, either. It was a strange afternoon, and frustrating for the guys in the band, who were used to a more attentive audience. Buster in particular was really un-happy. "Why are we even here?" he asked me. "This is just a waste of time."

In a way, Buster was giving voice to a much bigger question: Who were we as a band? The sextet had been in existence for a year and a half now, and its personnel had changed several times. We had made two records, very different from each other. We were taking on a new identity as the Mwandishi band, but what did that really mean? De-veloping the band's voice felt like a puzzle that we hadn't quite figured out yet.

Luckily, just two days after the Central Park show another piece of the puzzle fell into place. And soon after that the whole thing would come together completely.

||||||||||

The Iron Butterfly show was tenor saxophonist Joe Henderson's last one with the band, but we had a gig lined up at the Embassy Room in Baltimore two days later, on August 2. We needed a new reed player fast, so Buster said, "Call Bennie Maupin."

Everybody knew that Bennie was a great musician. He had played with Horace Silver, Lonnie Smith, and McCoy Tyner, and he'd also played on Miles's masterpiece, *Bitches Brew*. And on top of his musical skill, Bennie had a whole arsenal of woodwind instruments: He played every kind of saxophone, plus clarinet, bass clarinet, and flute, and he also played "bastard" instruments like the saxcello and the curved soprano sax. With Bennie we could get all kinds of different textures and colors, far beyond just the sounds of the standard saxophone and clarinet.

I didn't really know Bennie, and we didn't have much time for him to learn the sextet's music before our show, so I told him, "Let's drive down together. I'll talk you through the music in the car." It's about a three-hour drive from New York to Baltimore, and I talked Bennie's ear off. But he remembered *everything*—it was as if he could picture the music in his head as soon as I described it to him. At our gig that night he played like he'd been playing with us for years.

A few weeks after that the final two pieces of the puzzle came along: trombonist Julian Priester and trumpeter Eddie Henderson. Tootie Heath had left earlier in the summer, so our drummer was now Billy Hart. Those three guys, plus Bennie, Buster, and I, would form the Mwandishi band.

The magic of this particular combination was evident the very first night we played together. We had gone to Vancouver for a gig, but we'd never even rehearsed as a unit. Buster, Billy, and I played that first afternoon as a trio while Bennie, Julian, and Eddie stayed in the hotel to go over the music. They were having a cram session just like the one Bennie and I had had on the drive to Baltimore, but none of us knew how we'd sound when we actually played as a group.

That night, for our first set, the six of us started slow, kind of feeling each other out onstage. Very quickly we started to get comfortable . . . and just like that the music started to flow. We started out with "Fat Albert Rotunda," but that wasn't the heart of it. As we moved into "Speak Like a Child," a mellower piece, everybody started to open up, like a flower blossoming. We got freer and freer up there onstage, exploring musical avenues and rhythms with no fear or hesitation, as if we'd been playing together forever.

How was this happening? The six of us had never even played as a group before, but this was turning into one of the most sublime nights of my life. We played for nearly two hours, riding along on this river of gorgeous sound, and when it was over, we just looked at each other in awe. We walked back to the dressing room, and nobody said a word. What was there to say? We had experienced something very deep out there, and words would have felt inadequate.

From that very first night there was a rare, beautiful unity among the six of us—some kind of underlying connection that wasn't apparent before we played, but the minute we started playing, it was there. Now the question was, could we sustain it?

CHAPTER TEN

We took all the gigs we could get in the fall of 1970, and the more we played, the farther out the music got. Everybody in the sextet kept pushing boundaries onstage, and we started doing the same offstage, too.

Bennie was a vegetarian—a rare bird in those days—and once he joined the band, we all followed his lead and started eating vegetarian food. But we were on the road a lot, and it wasn't easy to find restaurants that made dishes without meat. San Francisco was never a problem, because we could just go to the Haight, where the hippies and flower children hung out, and get whatever we needed, but everywhere else it was rough going.

Here's how Bennie remembers that time:

We were into eating a really healthy diet, wheat germ and vitamin B, and a primarily vegetarian diet. We were just incorporating as many things as we felt would be beneficial to our lives.

We could buy certain things and keep them in our hotel rooms. I used to travel with a butane burner, the kind you use for camping. I'd get to the hotel room, and I'd have a bag of brown rice and a big Pyrex bowl, and I'd fix the rice and have it with pickled vegetables. We were all so skinny! We'd all bring our stuff, because we knew it would be difficult—you'd go to restaurants and say, "I'd like a salad," and they'd bring you iceberg lettuce with French dressing and maybe a tomato slice.

At some point I bought a van from the saxophonist Cannonball Adderley, and all of us would cram into it for out-of-town gigs. We'd pack it up with our instruments, luggage, and bags of brown rice and dried seaweed and hit the road for weeks at a time. The six of us spent hours and hours together, onstage and off, and we started developing really strong bonds as a band and as people. Bennie taught us yoga, and we all tried to open our minds to whatever we might encounter on our shared journey.

And it wasn't just our band that was exploring—the whole country was in a state of upheaval and discovery. The combination of the civil rights movement, young people's anger, the Vietnam War, plus the excitement of rock and roll, avant-garde music, the sexual revolution, and psychedelic drugs—all these elements came together in a fantastic alchemy that resulted in far-out music, art, movies, and books. It was a time of beautiful ferment.

Just as with Miles's band, all of us knew it was too much of a high-wire act to play on any kind of pharmaceuticals. On the bandstand we had to be at peak focus, because the music was constantly changing and swirling and unpredictable. I always preferred to play straight, but one time in San Francisco, in the summer of 1970, I popped a tab of acid into my mouth before a show without even thinking. As soon as it dissolved I thought, *Oh, man, what have I done?* I had never played while tripping before—in fact, this was only the fourth time I'd ever taken LSD. So I knew this night was going to be . . . interesting.

Even more interesting was the fact that I still had to drive to the show. My sister, Jean, had moved to Oakland, and I was staying at her apartment. The gig was at the Both/And club, on Divisadero Street in San Francisco, so it was not close by. I borrowed Jean's car and set out for the city, hoping I could get there before the most intense tripping began. But when I got to the Bay Bridge, I started to sweat. All I could think was *Oh, shit. That bridge is reeeally long.*

I drove slowly and talked to myself all the way across, just saying, "You're gonna make it, Herbie. You're gonna make it. Just drive in a straight line." It felt like hours, but when I finally got to the tollbooth on the other side, I thought, *Okay, just give the guy the money and then ask for a receipt. Or, wait—No! Don't ask for a receipt!* Would that seem suspicious? Would it be obvious I was tripping? I was so frozen with paranoia, that tollbooth guy must have thought I was losing my mind.

Somehow I made it to the club and managed to park the car, and when I got inside, the colors and the lights were overwhelming. My feelings of paranoia were growing—I was really convinced something terrible was going to happen. I told the guys I had dropped acid, and none of them could believe it. This was just not a thing I ever did, at a gig or otherwise. But after they got over their shock, at least one person said, "Well, don't leave me behind!" and took acid, too.

I don't remember all that much about the gig, but I do remember that we played one song for nearly an hour before we even found our way to the melody. The six of us were just out there, creating this montage of sound that went in every kind of direction. Sometimes when you drop acid, you hear what I think of as "acid runs": a kind of arpeggio up the scale, with a little trill at the end. That night I kept hearing them, even as the other guys were creating their own amazing palette of sound. The intensity of emotion in the room was profound, and even though I was in my own world, I believe that the audience could feel the emotion, too.

Right from the start of the sextet I had hoped we could move beyond the "control" in "controlled freedom." I wanted to set everybody loose, to explore more deeply the avant-garde side of jazz music. In the beginning we were even more controlled than the quintet had been, partly because we had to find the right personnel and establish a level of comfort and trust together. But now, with these six guys, we were finally arriving at that place. The music was becoming more than just free; at times it felt transcendent.

That was especially true at one surprising gig in November of 1970, at a buttoned-down steak-and-cocktails place in Chicago called the London House.

|||||||||||

The London House was an old-school jazz club on North Michigan Avenue, just a few blocks from the Chicago Harbor. It was the kind of place where mostly older, white audiences showed up in suits and dresses to sip martinis and listen to classic jazz. The music was very good, but it wasn't what you'd call avant-garde. George Shearing and Oscar Peterson and Dave Brubeck played there, and the lineup was usually trios or quartets. The jazz there could be described as calmly exciting, not extremely challenging to the ear.

For whatever reason, London House owner Oscar Marienthal decided to book the Herbie Hancock Sextet for four full weeks, the longest gig I had ever played. I think he thought he was going to get straight-up tunes like "Speak Like a Child," "Maiden Voyage," "Dolphin Dance"—our more melodic, gentler pieces. He didn't realize that the band that had started out so gentle and controlled had evolved into this ferocious beast from outer space.

We were hired to play one short set during the dinner hour and then a longer set later in the evening. I told Oscar, "I really don't think you want us to play during dinner." I couldn't imagine how the clientele would respond to our tripped-out vibe while they dug into their filets mignons. But Oscar insisted, so we played a couple of spacey, funked-up tunes. And that was all it took. He came up to us afterward and said, "Thank you very much, but we'll just have you do the late sets from now on."

We played the first week, and the audiences were just not into us at all. Oscar was irritated, telling us we were playing too loud and "too strange" for his clientele. The guys in the band weren't happy, and they started grumbling about not finishing out the rest of the gig. But I was convinced we could win over the crowds. We had three more weeks to go, and I was determined to turn this thing around.

Meanwhile, there was a guy we met named Jerry who was such a big fan that he came to all the gigs. Jerry was totally into the band, and he hung out with us a lot while we were in Chicago. He was also a self-styled mystic who was into astrology and numerology, and in our state of spiritual exploration we were getting into those kinds of alternative thinking. Everybody wanted to hear what Jerry had to say about the band, so he started looking at our numerology and found out some really cool things.

Jerry discovered that four guys in the band—actually, three players plus our soundman, Billy Bonner (who went by the Swahili name Fundi)—were born on the twenty-ninth of their birth month. And their four birth months represented the four elements, earth, air, fire, and water. Buster and I were both Aries, and Mars is the fourth planet, which was another number four. So the number 429 became the magic number for the band, because it connected with all of us.

This may sound kind of far out, but as soon as Jerry had identified 429 as Mwandishi's number, we started seeing that number *every-where*. I can't tell you how many times we were booked in room 429 in hotels, or I'd look at my watch and it was 4:29, or a cashier would ring up a check that totaled $4.29. It blew our minds how often those numbers appeared—we even made up a logo that incorporated 4, 2, and 9. Something very unusual was coming together within the band, and all of us could feel it.

In our second week at the London House, the audience began to change. Now younger black patrons started coming in from the South Side. Word had gotten out that the sextet was playing different music from the usual London House jazz fare, and people came wanting to hear something far out. The energy in the room was changing, and one night in the middle of that second week it entered the realm of the mystical.

We played the first set, and it was *on*. It was happening. Our friend Jerry had been coming for every show, but he missed the opening set that night. When he arrived, I told him, "Hey, man, it's too bad you missed that first set!" We thought he'd missed out on the magic. But the magic hadn't even started yet.

The second set was even better than the first. We were so tight, so attuned to each other, that it began to feel as if we weren't even playing the music anymore—it felt like the music was playing us, coming down from somewhere above, and we were just the vessels. We were on some other plane, all of us together, but that still wasn't the peak of the evening. Because the third set . . . the third set was transformative.

As we started that set I watched my fingers as I played. To my shock, they seemed to be moving by themselves. I wasn't controlling them; they were just playing of their own accord. Yet everything my fingers played was connecting perfectly to everything Buster was playing, and Bennie was playing, and Billy was playing. As we got deeper into the music we became one big, pulsating creature—all of those guys somehow *became* me, and I became all of them. It was as if we were inside each other, in a way I had never felt before and have never felt since. It was a deeply spiritual experience.

I didn't speak between tunes—we just went from one to the next. And when we finished, the club was absolutely silent. Not a soul moved. I felt totally euphoric, like I was floating on air. And then the applause started. It just rose and rose, the loudest ovation I'd ever heard. People were shouting, laughing, crying.

I tried to stand up from the piano, but I couldn't feel my feet. I looked down, and I swear they were ten feet below me, as if I were floating above my body. I hadn't taken any drugs or had anything to drink that night—none of us had. I couldn't speak, couldn't process what was happening. Somehow I managed to move off the stage and make my way back to the dressing room, still feeling outside my body.

When all six of us were back in the dressing room, we looked at each other in shock. "What just happened?" somebody asked, but none of us could answer that question. We started talking about it, laughing in wonderment and shaking our heads. Then, after about ten minutes, somebody from the club came in and said, "They're still applauding out there. Come out and take a bow."

I said, "I can't, I'm sorry." And I really couldn't, physically—I don't think my legs would have carried me. The audience clapped and clapped for about a half hour, but we never did go back out onstage. We just stayed where we were, trying to process the amazing experience we had all just shared.

Buster remembers a patron in the club being overcome that night:

> We were playing, and someone in the audience near the front just fell out. Just passed right out. After the gig we were over at a friend's house and he was telling us he saw us levitate. "I swear, I saw the band levitate!" he said. "The band left the floor!"

I didn't see the guy in the audience faint, but the person who said he saw us levitate was our friend Jerry. And then Jerry actually had an episode himself, after we left the club and all went to the house of one of my high school friends. Fundi, our soundman, always made tapes of every gig, so we were all really eager to hear what had gone down that night. We sat in Jerry's living room listening to the tape, and even though nobody was having a drink or a smoke or anything, we all felt really high listening to it.

We were all listening intently, and then suddenly Jerry, who'd been sitting in a chair, just keeled over. I mean, he fell right onto the floor, curled up like he was still sitting in the chair. "Jerry!" I said. "Are you okay?" But he was just lying there, as if in a catatonic state. And then, after a minute or so, he came to. He just got up and sat back in his chair as though nothing had happened. Strange!

That London House gig became part of the legend of Mwandishi, but there was another element of it that almost nobody knows.

Whenever we played in Chicago, I would stay with my parents. So after all the crazy experiences of that night, I finally made my way back to their apartment on the South Side. By the time I got there the sun was coming up—it must have been about six in the morning. I fell into bed, exhausted, but an hour or two later the phone rang. My mother answered, and it was for me.

It was the mother of a young lady who had come to all of the Mwandishi band's shows in Vancouver—the place where we'd had that first magical gig, the very first time that Eddie, Julian, Billy, Bennie, Buster, and I played together as a unit. Vancouver was the only other place where we had experienced anything like what we felt at the London House, and this girl had sort of been our muse for that time period. She loved the music of the band, and she came to hear us every single night in Vancouver. She was a beautiful girl, and she played music herself, I believe violin or viola. During the short time we were in Vancouver we hung out a lot with this girl, and all of us in the band grew really close to her. She just had a special way about her.

She was also studying to be a mime, and she'd gotten a scholarship to train with Marcel Marceau that fall. She'd gone to Paris, and we hadn't heard from her since. But now her mother was calling me to let us know that the night before—the night of our transcendent experience at the London House—the girl had died in Paris. She had wanted to run a bath at a friend's apartment, since her own apartment didn't have one, and when the friend told her how to turn on the water heater, she misunderstood how to do it. She turned up the gas but didn't realize she had to light the pilot, too, and she was overcome by the fumes, passed out, and died.

When I told the rest of the guys in the band, we all had the same feeling: that she had been there with us at the London House, and the magic we felt was her farewell. I always think of that night as her night, and her memory touches me still.

||||||||||||

The London House gig was a turning point for the Mwandishi band. We played two more weeks there, and although we didn't have the same out-of-body experience, the music kept getting freer and farther out. We kept listening to the tapes Fundi had made of that magical night, and we still couldn't believe what we heard. It was like we were listening to someone else play, not ourselves. We were mesmerized by the music and listened to it constantly for inspiration.

When the London House gig ended, we drove to Detroit for a stand at the Strata Concert Gallery. Those performances were as magical as the London House shows, and we made tapes there, too. Finally, after the Strata, we were scheduled to appear at the Village Vanguard back in New York. Fundi drove the truck to the club to set up our sound system, and he parked it right out front so he could carry in our equipment. But while he was in the club, someone broke into the truck and stole all the tapes we had inside.

When Fundi told the guys in the band, we all had the same reaction: *Oh, no, no, no!* Equipment you could replace, but those tapes? They were the only ones in existence, and now they were gone! All of us just felt despair that we'd never be able to hear that gig again. We'd felt transported listening to that music—the up-tempo moments were so powerful, and the peaceful moments were undulating, almost meditative. Those tapes were treasures. And now they were gone. Why did this happen? How could this be?

We all agonized for a few days, but I finally had to conclude that losing the tapes was a blessing in disguise. The truth was, we were re-vering what we had done on that one night in November. We were stuck in a time warp, worshipping an event that had passed, and doing that was counter to the very nature of the Mwandishi band. Mwandi-shi was all about exploring, pushing forward into the next moment—what sense did it make for us to listen over and over to an old gig? Wasn't that just hindering our ability to move forward?

In the end, I believe it was good that we couldn't keep listening obsessively to those tapes. Still, for years afterward I thought about them, wondering if they still exist and if whoever took them under-stood what they were. Yet if those tapes suddenly reappeared somehow all these years later, I think I'd be afraid to listen to them. I'd be afraid that they wouldn't sound the same to me, because I'm not the same person I was then. Maybe parts would feel magical and other parts not, which would be a disappointment. I'm a little bit curious, but maybe it's better never hearing them again, because my memory of that night is so perfect and beautiful.

Playing onstage with Mwandishi meant treading a fine line be-tween brilliance and chaos. Everything was intuitive, in the moment. Nothing was planned. We might start with a fragment of a structure, but the sounds we produced on any given day came out of our syn-chronicity on that day—our shared experience. When it worked, it was so, so powerful. When it didn't, it was truthfully kind of a mess. Making music like this was not for the faint of heart, but we kept pressing outward, looking for weird sounds and unexplored paths, always in search of new experiences onstage.

I think of Mwandishi as an R&D band—research and devel-opment, trying new things. It was all about discovery, uncovery, explo-ration, the unknown, looking for the unseen, listening for the unheard. The Mwandishi palette was an intergalactic palette, with emotions and shapes and colors that felt out of this world. Sometimes we didn't even have a beat to hold on to—we would just play moment to moment, going with the temporal flow, relying on intuition to keep ourselves together. Everything was up for grabs as far as creativity was concerned. Everybody accepted whatever anybody else played, and the goal was always to respond without thinking. The music was visceral, emotional, and raw, more so than any music I've played before or since.

We didn't play songs as much as we created a sonic environment. The elements of traditional songs were there—melody, harmony, and rhythm—but we incorporated them in nontraditional ways, using nontraditional instruments. In fact, as the Mwandishi band evolved we started using pretty much anything as an instrument. A table, a lamp, a rock—whatever was on hand, somebody would tap it, slap it, shake it. We were open to any kind of sound from any kind of source.

For a while we got really into flutes. Bennie knew a guy who made all kinds of flutes, and he started collecting them. He had wooden ones, bamboo ones, all sizes from a piccolo to a didgeridoo. And everybody was really into percussion, partly because it sounded good but also because we wanted something to do when the solos were happening. It's a little dull watching five guys standing around onstage while one of them goes off on his solo, so we'd pick up anything we could find and bang on it.

The guys would develop patterns of rhythmic interplay, point and counterpoint, and every night was a new exploration of all the ways we could create music no one had ever heard before—and would never hear again. That was the only rule: never to repeat what you've played before. The goal was always to create, create, create. Buster liked to quote Duke Ellington's reply when someone once asked him, "What's your favorite composition?" Ellington said, "The next one." That's how we all felt, every gig, every day.

CHAPTER ELEVEN

I n the late summer of 1970 a young guy started coming to see us play. His name was David Rubinson, and although he was just twenty-seven, he was already building a reputation as a hitmaker. He had produced records for acts like Santana, Moby Grape, and Taj Mahal, and music executives saw him as having the golden touch, an ability to help artists make commercially viable records.

The time had come for Mwandishi to make a record, and Warner Bros. wanted us to go in a more commercial direction. *Fat Albert Rotunda* was R&B-inflected and easy to listen to, and the executives believed that if we continued that trend, we could sell a lot more records, so they hired David to help us do that. What they didn't realize was that Mwandishi had flown light-years into the future after *Fat Albert Rotunda,* and we had no interest in going back to a more traditional R&B sound.

When David came to see us play and heard the far-out path we were heading down, he knew there was no way he could urge us in another direction. Unlike the Warners executives, David cared more about music than about sales. He loved what he heard when he saw us live, and he wanted to help us express ourselves fully in our music—not make us more commercially palatable. As he said later, "I would no more tell you what kind of record to make than tell you what kind of child to have." Warners had sent David to turn us, but we had turned him instead.

In December of 1970, when we went into the Wally Heider Studios in San Francisco to make our next record, David had distinct ideas about how he wanted to record it:

> What I wanted to do was put Herbie and his band in a hot-house, in a laboratory, and let them create the music they wanted, and then capture it in the studio. So we went into the studio with Mwandishi to record the music the way they played it live. He had this organic band he'd put together, based on collective consciousness, organizing around African cultural roots, and spiritual mutual respect. They were a union.
>
> Herbie was finding his identity—going way back and way forward at the same time. He was blowing down all the walls to the future. The period when I started working with him was an explosive, exploratory period, and those guys in the band, they were all really smart guys. There was no bullshit. That band told each other the truth, all the time.

David wanted to capture that energy on our record, and he believed that having us record live, all together, was the way to do it. But he also had another idea. He was a rock and roll guy, and in rock and roll there was no glass wall between the artist and the production process. Jazz musicians didn't normally get involved in production; we just recorded the cuts and left the rest to the producers, and a few weeks later somebody would hand us the finished product. David knew I was an electronics and engineering guy, so he wanted me to have a crack at the production process, too.

This was a revelation for me. It had never occurred to me that I could take part in production, but as soon as David suggested it I couldn't wait to get my hands dirty. And I loved it! I loved finding effects and sounds, deciding how to arrange the different cuts, and playing around with volume and depth and layers. Just as it had when I started playing electric piano, doing this opened up a whole new world for me.

We released the record, titled *Mwandishi,* in early 1971. There were three songs: "Ostinato (Suite for Angela)," an ode to the black activist Angela Davis; "You'll Know When You Get There"; and "Wandering Spirit Song." We had recorded it as if it were a live performance, with all kinds of percussion and far-out solos, and I felt that it was a step forward for the sextet. We were moving in the direction we wanted to, making music that was as free as we could make it, even in a studio setting.

But not everybody loved it. Warner Bros. had asked for something commercial, but we gave them this whacked-out space record in which the first song had a 15/8 time signature, not something most people can snap their fingers to. *Mwandishi* didn't fit in any of the usual slots. It wasn't a straight-up jazz record, but it wasn't anything else, either. It didn't even fit comfortably on either black radio or white radio. What was Warners supposed to do to try to sell it? I didn't really care, and neither did David, which gave them some heartburn. And we'd give them some more before Mwandishi was done.

|||||||||||

That summer Mwandishi launched our first European tour. From the start it was a disaster in the making.

The tour was arranged by a Danish promoter named Jenny, who was a charming lady but a terrible tour organizer. We flew into Paris, and Jenny told us it would be a two-hour drive to get to our first gig, which was that same night. We figured we'd have plenty of time to make it through customs, rent a van and a car, and get where we were going.

Unfortunately we arrived at Orly airport at noon, which was the lunch break for the customs office. And this being Europe, lunch did not mean a half-hour break—it was closer to two hours. So we all sat there twiddling our thumbs at the airport, waiting for the French customs agents to mosey on back so we could have our passports stamped and get on the road. But when we finally did pile into the van and open one of those giant foldout maps of France, we realized it was more like a six-hour trip to our destination. So we had to drive like bats out of hell that first day just to make our gig.

And this was not a onetime thing. Jenny had routed our tour in the craziest way possible, as if she'd thrown darts at a map of Europe. I mean, we drove from Paris to the north of France, and then back down to the south of France, and then all the way up to Denmark. None of it made any sense. We spent untold hours in the car and van, racing along autobahns and mountain roads just trying to make it to our gigs.

Adding to the absurdity was the fact that Pan Am lost Bennie's suitcase on the way over, so he had only the clothes on his back. Pan Am kept saying they'd find his luggage and get it to him, so Bennie didn't buy any new clothes but just kept washing the ones he had on in hotel sinks all across Europe. We all did our laundry in the sink, but of course we were never in hotels long enough for anything to dry properly, so our clothes started smelling musty. Which was great fun, of course, when we were all cooped up together for hours in the car.

On a lot of those tour dates we were booked to play opposite Wayne Shorter's new band, Weather Report, so they had the same kind of schedule we did. But after about a week they couldn't take it! Wayne and his band flew back home rather than racing all over Europe like we did. I can't blame them, because that schedule tested all of our stamina and patience. But in a strange way it brought us closer, too. Spending that much time together, in those kinds of stressful circumstances, either bonds people together or breaks them apart. Fortunately it bonded Mwandishi together.

Bennie remembers one funny incident from that summer:

> On one of those impossible drives, we played a gig in the south of France and then had to drive all the way up to Denmark. And when we got there, we were under the gun to set up and play. Herbie hooked up his electric piano, and everybody was just totally exhausted—especially Herbie, because he had driven the car. I would drive the van, because our roadie and soundman needed to sleep. We were the ninjas of the jazz world!
>
> We got to the gig in Denmark, and Herbie was playing this long obbligato, an improvised intro to either "Maiden Voyage" or "Toys." And he's playing, and I'm sitting on a chair backstage, looking at him, and I know his expressions by now. And Herbie was asleep! There was no movement of his eyes. He was sound asleep. This went on for a while, and then he woke himself up—jarred himself awake. But he had kept on playing the whole time. He used to be totally sleep-deprived, because he would stay up for hours, days on end.

We did everything we could to save money on that trip, because we had seven guys to pay—the sextet, plus our soundman, Fundi— and I knew the tour was actually costing me money rather than making any. I was still getting residuals from "Watermelon Man" and the jingles I'd written, so the tour was worth it to me. But we cut corners every way we could, sometimes sleeping in people's houses or even in an empty room at whatever club we were playing.

I did make one big purchase, though. I bought us a brand-new $10,000 Miazzi Hollywood sound system, because I wanted Mwandishi to have high-quality sound everywhere we played, rather than just making do with whatever system each club happened to have. And this was the best, coolest portable system I had ever seen. It even had a joystick, which was new technology in the '70s, for moving sound in a four-speaker surround setting.

I was really excited about the system, but the guys thought I was crazy, because now, in addition to all our suitcases and instruments, we'd have to lug a mixer, four big speakers, and other components all over Europe. Most of the time we had a rental van, but we traveled to some gigs by train—and those European trains did not stop for long at each station. As soon as the train started slowing down at our destination, we'd all start throwing our luggage out the windows to the platform, so we'd have our hands free to carry instruments and the sound system in the two minutes the train was stopped. We had to scramble like mad, but miraculously we never lost anything.

Sometimes after we'd spent hours traveling to a club, the management tried not to pay us. For one gig in Italy the manager said he'd pay us after we played, which wasn't standard. I was afraid we'd get stiffed, so we refused to play until we got our money—and then the manager took our instruments and locked them in a room. "You're not getting them back until you promise to go out there and play," he told us. We just sat in the hotel, pissed off, feeling like hostages. I don't even remember how that particular episode got resolved, but that was the one time I was happy to pack up our stuff and get back on the road.

Even when we made it to gigs, got paid, and actually played, we sometimes met with hostile audiences. Like the owners of the London House, some people were apparently expecting to hear mellow versions of "Speak Like a Child" and "Dolphin Dance." European audiences knew me from my days in the Miles Davis Quintet, and they wanted to hear more controlled jazz than what the Mwandishi band was playing. So we'd be up on the stage, really into the music, creating this wild sonic river, and we'd hear people start to boo.

They'd get really upset, as if we had personally betrayed them, but I just told the guys, "Keep playing." People were entitled to their feelings, and I was convinced that the only way to win them was to show them the artistry of where we were now. I'd had similar feelings back when I played with Eric Dolphy's band, because people booed it, too. But even back then, playing in someone else's band, I'd thought I should stand up for what I believed in, as far as music was concerned. That turned out to be a precursor for my experience in Mwandishi.

The funniest part of that tour came at the end, a kind of coda to the craziness. Our final gig was in Paris, and we were scheduled to appear on a TV show to promote it. Bennie still hadn't received his suitcase from Pan Am, so I called the airline and said, "Listen, you've been promising to send this bag for weeks. We're going on television tomorrow, and we're going to tell everybody in France how inept you are." I was really irritated on Bennie's behalf, and as the leader of the group I felt obligated to do something.

Just like that, the suitcase appeared! Pan Am delivered it to Bennie's hotel room, and when he opened it up and saw all the beautiful, hip clothes he'd bought for the tour, he nearly cried. But at that final gig he had a fresh outfit to wear, so at least we were able to finish in style.

||||||||||

That European tour brought us all together, but it also sharpened a difficult dynamic in the band. We were a sextet, and we shared everything. Onstage, every man was as valuable as every other man. But at the same time I was the one responsible for bringing in enough money to pay everybody and for making sure we got to gigs and fulfilled our obligations. I knew the guys weren't making as much money as they wanted—and not as much as they were worth, honestly. But I was already losing money, and I couldn't afford to pay them any more out of my own pocket.

Unlike the other band members, I was married and now had a young child. I was also older than everybody except for Julian. It was only natural that tension started to develop—was the sextet an equal collective, or were the guys hired sidemen for me? Money was a factor in this equation, but it definitely wasn't the only one. This question went to the heart of what Mwandishi was and who we all were to each other.

One incident a few months before our European tour perfectly illustrates that tension. On the morning of February 9, 1971, Gigi, two-year-old Jessica, our dog, Schnuckel, and I were asleep in a hotel in Hermosa Beach, California. The band had been playing a gig at the nearby Lighthouse jazz club, and although my family didn't usually travel with us, they had come this time for obvious reasons—who wouldn't want to leave freezing New York for sunny southern California in February?

Schnuckel suddenly started barking, and a few seconds later the whole room began to shake. It was so violent and unexpected that I couldn't figure out what was happening. How could solid walls sway like that? It was as if they had become butter. I managed to jump out of bed and run to the window, where I could see the sidewalk and pier bucking and swaying. I couldn't speak, but my mind was screaming, *We've got to get out of here!*

The earthquake lasted ten or twelve seconds, but it felt like a whole lot longer. As soon as it stopped I started throwing our stuff into suitcases and packing up to get the hell back to New York. We managed to find a car to the airport, and when we arrived there, I called Buster and said, "Listen, we've booked a flight home. I'm getting Gigi and Jessica out of here." The whole region was a mess of buckled roads and collapsed buildings. The earthquake was a 6.6 on the Richter scale, and it had killed dozens of people and injured hundreds more.

"Well, hold on," Buster said. "What about us?" Of all the guys in the band, Buster was the one who was most willing to speak his mind and butt heads with me. We were both Aries, and we could sometimes go at it, and right at this moment he felt I was abandoning the band.

To me, there was no question that my first obligation was to my family. But like all the other guys, Buster was single, so he didn't have the same frame of reference I did.

"It's every man for himself!" I told him.

"Man, you can't just leave your band!" he said.

"I'm not your daddy!" I said, exasperated. "You guys can take care of yourselves." Buster wasn't too happy with me—I don't think any of the guys were. But to be fair, everybody was pretty freaked out at having just been through a major earthquake, so I didn't think any more about it, though in retrospect it was probably indicative of a larger underlying tension within the band.

|||||||||||

In early 1972, as we started recording Mwandishi's next album, David Rubinson said to me, "You know, in rock music they've been using this new instrument called a synthesizer. You might want to give that a try."

I had heard of synthesizers, but I didn't know much about them. I wasn't a big rock and roll fan, so I hadn't kept up with what was happening in that genre. But David knew. Groups like the Rolling Stones, the Beatles, and the Byrds had started incorporating Moog synthesizer sounds, adding a new, psychedelic layer to their songs. Synthesizers were mostly used as background, but David saw early on that they would fit well within the kind of music Mwandishi was making.

The band was already using devices like the fuzz-wah pedal and the Echoplex, which created a tape echo for electronic instruments, and I had been playing a Fender Rhodes electric piano both onstage and on recordings. I was always hooking up various gadgets to the electric piano, sometimes right before a show. Once, when we were in Boston, I got together with a couple of engineers from MIT, who told me, "Just hook up this box to your piano—it will change the shape of the sound wave!" I loved exploring new sounds.

It was actually very difficult to hook things up to the Rhodes, which is probably why so few bands did it. I had to remove its top to attach the cables, wah-wah pedal, and Echoplex, so the thing looked a little bit like a Frankenstein piano. I didn't mind—who cares what an instrument looks like, as long as it creates the sound you want? But one person who did mind was its inventor, Harold Rhodes.

I had met Harold back when I was with Miles, and at some point he came to see the band play at the Lighthouse in Hermosa Beach. When he walked up to the bandstand and saw all those wires sticking out of its chopped-off top, he said, "Herbie! What have you done to my piano? You've cannibalized it!"

I laughed and said, "Well, I wanted to create some effects, and this was the only way to do it." He still looked horrified, so I said, "You know, you might want to think about making future pianos with inputs and outputs, to make this easier." I probably wasn't the only piano player to have suggested this to Harold, because sure enough, future versions of the Rhodes were designed with jacks, so you could attach different components easily.

Synthesizers took the complexity to a new level altogether. For one thing, the synthesizers of 1972 were nothing like the ones we have today. They weren't digital, so they weren't programmable, meaning you couldn't save anything. And they were really huge, taking up entire walls of studios. They took forever to set up and weren't really portable. But you could create sounds with them that you couldn't create with other instruments, so David thought it would be interesting to lay some synthesizer music over one of the tracks on our new album.

The band was recording at Pacific Recording Studios in San Mateo, and David, who lived in San Francisco, told me, "I know a local guy who plays synthesizers. Let's give him a call." That was how I met Patrick Gleeson.

Pat was an unusual candidate to play on an Mwandishi record. He was a white hippie, not a jazz-funk guy, and instead of a music education he had a Ph.D. in eighteenth-century English literature. David told me straight up that Pat didn't have the musical chops or experience of the other guys in the band, but he'd done a lot of synthesizer programming for various rock bands David had recorded. So we arranged to meet Pat at his studio, Different Fur Trading Company, which was located in a renovated warehouse in the Mission District.

Pat met us at the door, and as he walked us into the studio I saw racks of electronic components lining the walls. This was some complex equipment, and I didn't know the first thing about how it all worked. But I couldn't wait to hear what Pat could do with it.

Mwandishi had recorded a song called "Quasar" for the new album, so David handed Pat a sixteen-track master of the song. Pat put it on, and I told him, "I was thinking we could lay something down right here, at the beginning." So he moved over to his huge Moog modular synthesizer and got to work. After a few minutes of plugging and unplugging cords and turning various knobs, he started laying down some sounds over the track.

I sat back to listen, and what I heard was so hip and majestic, it was just fantastic. Pat's synthesizer added a phenomenal new element to the music, but without MIDI and computers it was fiendishly complicated to produce those sounds. Here's how Pat describes what he did that day:

> I listened to the sonic environment over this short passage and then patched a sound. There was no patch memory then, which meant you had to connect various voltage-controlled audio components together—oscillators with various waveforms, envelope generators, voltage-controlled amplifiers, and various sound modifiers, including frequency and amplitude modulation elements. You adjusted all this stuff until it began to sound like a generalized musical sound.
>
> After about five to seven minutes of patching, I thought I had something Herbie might like to play with. So I began having my

sound engineer cycle back and forth over the passage on tape, fine-tuning the idea.

"Okay," I said to Herbie, "that's the general idea." He asked for some slight modifications, which I did, and then I asked him how he felt about that.

He said, "Did you record it?"

I said, "I was waiting to turn the keyboard over to you." I thought I was just getting the synth ready for him to play, but he said, "No, that's fine—just go ahead and record it," which blew me away.

Pat was surprised, but I didn't know anything about synthesizers and he did, so I figured, why shouldn't he just record them himself? I stayed at his studio for another forty-five minutes, talking through ideas for the rest of the song, and then I said, "I have to leave, but I'll be back with some more tracks. You just keep on going." I wanted him to record more overdubs, which he did—many of which made it onto the record, which was ultimately called *Crossings*.

Over the next couple of weeks I spent more time with Pat, and he laid down overdubs for another song on *Crossings*, called "Water Torture." I asked him a lot of questions about how the equipment worked, and because of my engineering studies at Grinnell I could understand the language. There was no real reason for a piano player to know what resistance and ohms and capacitors were, but I did, so Pat and I were able to talk for hours about how exactly the synthesizers functioned and what kinds of sounds he could draw out of them. The more I learned, the more I wanted synthesizers as a permanent part of Mwandishi's sound.

For the moment, though, my main concern was finishing *Crossings*. I was really happy with the record, which expanded even more on the spaced-out freedom of *Mwandishi*. We had gotten so free, in fact, that it could be confusing for other musicians who tried to play with us.

David Rubinson invited a hot young guitar player named Carlos Santana for one of the tracks, but I had to tell him, "I don't have anything specific for you to play," which threw him off a little bit. Santana wasn't used to that way of making music, so our collaboration didn't work out that time, though we did make some really cool records together from time to time. He has become a dear friend, and we're like family now.

So *Crossings* wasn't for everybody. I loved it, and David Rubinson loved it, but he knew that Warner Bros. would be less than thrilled with the direction we'd gone in. David anticipated that the executives would complain once again about marketability, so he decided to pull off a little ruse, to make a point.

When David walked into his meeting with the marketing executives, he was carrying a reel-to-reel tape. At this type of meeting, this would typically be the master for the new record. David threaded it into a tape machine, and when he pressed PLAY, the room was filled with the sounds of some really out-there jazz fusion. The executives sat quietly, listening.

After ten minutes or so David pressed PAUSE. "Well, what do you think?" he asked the room.

It's great stuff, they all said—but how in the world are we supposed to sell it? Just as with *Mwandishi,* they were afraid the music fell too much between the cracks to become commercially successful.

"Well, what you've just heard is not actually Herbie's new record," David told them. "It's the B side of Miles Davis's *Bitches Brew,* which is number nine on the charts right now." That little trick made David's point perfectly: How could they claim that this type of music wasn't marketable when *Bitches Brew* had sold so many copies? There was obviously a market for it, despite the executives' preconceptions. David then played excerpts from *Crossings* for them, and they all pledged to work hard to sell it. But David could already sense that this might be the last record Mwandishi made for Warner Bros.

The Warners executives weren't the only ones who were skeptical about *Crossings*. Lee Weisel was still managing us, and he didn't really know what to do with this kind of music, or with us. I appreciated everything he'd done for us, but after *Crossings* came out, I asked David Rubinson if he would take over managing the band in addition to producing our records. David wasn't an experienced manager, but he understood and respected what Mwandishi was trying to do, so it made sense to bring him on in that new role.

Around that same time, I decided there was another person I wanted to bring permanently into the band: Pat Gleeson.

In 1972 it was a radical move to add synthesizers to a jazz record. But that was nothing compared to hiring a full-time synthesizer player to travel with the band—and especially hiring a guy like Pat for a band like Mwandishi.

First of all, Pat would be a long-haired, gray-bearded white guy in a band of black men with Swahili names and dashikis. Second, adding him meant that one more person would be taking a cut of whatever income we made. Third, the other guys had never played with Pat, and some of them were skeptical about whether synthesizers even qualified as musical instruments at all. And fourth, it would be no small feat to lug synth equipment from gig to gig and then create the right sounds onstage every night using handfuls of patch cords.

But I just really dug the sounds that Pat added to the music. So in the spring of 1972 I invited him to join us.

There was one funny moment we shared in the beginning, soon after *Crossings* came out. We were all hanging out at David Rubinson's house in San Francisco, and my sister, Jean, was there, too. She had a copy of *Crossings* in her hand and was reading off everybody's Swahili name—Mwandishi, Mchezaji, Mwile, Pepo Mtoto, Jabali, Mganga . . . and then she turned to Pat. "So what are we gonna call you?" she asked.

Pat just shrugged. What could he say? He was a white dude in a black band, and besides that, he didn't know any Swahili.

Jean laughed. "I know!" she said. "We'll call you *Bwana!*"—the white-hunter name in safari movies from the '30s. Everybody cracked up, though Pat looked over to me first to make sure I was laughing, too.

‖‖‖‖‖‖‖‖

Pat knew he couldn't carry around his giant Moog synthesizer, so he tried to find a more portable version that would work. A company called ARP was making a smaller synthesizer, the 2600, but even that was still pretty big and not very easy to use. There was still no memory, so Pat had to create sounds from scratch every time he used it. And there were so many ways of doing that, he had to keep track of dozens of patch cords at a time, remembering where to insert them to create certain effects. Here's how Pat describes it:

> I've got a back panel. And on that back panel there are some very basic audio things. There are oscillators, which make pitch—that's all they do, just pitch, high and low. I've got filters, which can filter out the top of the band, or high-pass can filter out the low.
>
> I've got a thing called a "sample and hold generator," which can be used to apply different voltages either to make a rhythmic pattern in a filter or to make a pitch pattern in an oscillator. I mean, there's a limited number of things I can do, but I can also take them and put them together in weird ways. Then I also had a wah-wah pedal, which I used a lot. And I also had a very noisy Echoplex.
>
> So with those, at every instance when the band was playing something, at the moment they were playing I would—I won't even say decide. I would just know that I was going to take *this* patch cord and go into *there,* and then go into *there,* and this would get me started; it would be enough for the first ten seconds of sound.

And while that ten seconds was sounding, I could patch something else up and complicate the sound, and then when that musical gesture for the rest of the band had come to an end, then I could no longer use that patch—I'd have to start again.

In the course of an evening, I probably changed patches two to three hundred times. I had about twenty-five patch cords, and when I went with the group, I thought I would color-code the patch cords to help me. But there wasn't even time to think about that: You just grab a cord, you put it into an oscillator, and you're on your way.

The guys in the band were used to exploration, but this was a pretty radical change. Not all of them loved it, but I did. Adding synthesizers opened up whole new territories for us to explore. Pat would sometimes tell me, "Herbie, I don't always know what sound is going to come out," and I'd say, "Don't worry, because I don't always know what a chord is going to sound like when I play it, either." And it was true! I had a general idea, but mostly I just knew that whatever sound came out, we would make it work somehow.

We had a saying in the band, "Everything is everything." Everything was part of a whole, all of it melding together, playing off each other, coming together as one. When Bennie started a solo on the bass clarinet, Pat would echo it with his synthesizer or bridge it back into what the band was doing. Then Eddie might pick up the thread, playing off what Pat was doing. Everything was everything, and everyone was everyone.

Onstage we were learning from each other and reaching new heights all the time. And offstage one of the guys in the band was about to teach me something that would change my life forever.

CHAPTER TWELVE

One Thursday night in the summer of 1972 Mwandishi played a gig in Seattle. When it was over, we heard about some parties that were happening, so we all took off into the night to have some fun. The band didn't always party after gigs, but on this night we hit the town hard. We went to as many different places as we could, and by the time we straggled back to our hotel the sun had not only risen—it was already beginning to set again. I was totally spent, but we had only a couple of hours before we had to get to our Friday-night gig.

I fell into bed and slept for those two hours, and when I woke up, my head was hurting and my mouth was dry. Oh, man, I did not feel like going to play, but I had to somehow find the energy. When the other guys came downstairs, they looked about as rough as I felt. But we managed to drag ourselves to the club, and because it was a Friday night, it was already packed. The audience was ready for a show, even if we weren't quite ready to give them one.

As we came out of the dressing room and made our way to the stage I felt as if I were rising from a coffin, like a vampire. My body and mind and soul were just shut down, and when I looked out at all those people, with all that energy pulsing out of them, it was too much for me. I didn't have enough juice to start the way I normally might, opening with a strong piano intro, and for whatever reason I also decided not to open with the drums. I looked over at Buster, our bassist, and said, "Toys."

"Toys" was a medium-tempo tune off *Speak Like a Child,* and instead of starting with me, it starts with the upright bass, the softest, gentlest instrument in the band. I figured we'd let Buster ease us in, and I hoped we'd be able to find some energy somewhere.

Buster started playing, and what came out of him was amazing. Astounding! I was hearing notes fly all over the place, and wondering how in the world he could do all that on a four-stringed instrument. At one point I saw him do three different activities at the same time: The fingers on his left hand were somehow moving up and down simultaneously while two other fingers were trilling. His hand looked like some kind of crazy spider, crawling up and down the neck of the bass.

He finished up one progression, then paused for a moment and looked at his strings. I saw him nod, like "hmm," and then he did the whole thing over again! I was flipping out, and so was everybody in the club. I could feel my energy rising, could feel myself waking up. I let Buster go for ten minutes or more, even though normally that intro would go for only a couple of minutes. Then, when the rest of the band joined in, the place exploded.

We had come onto the stage half-asleep, but Buster had lit a fire under us. The rest of that night was so beautiful, one of those gigs where everything just comes together. Afterward people came up to the stage, some of them crying, reaching out to shake our hands, to touch us, to hug us. A woman told me, "We didn't just hear this music. We *experienced* this music." I'd never heard anybody say that before, but it was true. All of us in that room had just shared a spiritual experience, and Buster was the spark that made it happen.

When we got back to the dressing room, I grabbed Buster and

said, "Where did that come from? Whatever made you play bass like that, I want some of it!"

His eyes were so bright, it was like he was lit from within. He said, "Herbie, I've been chanting for a way to tell you about this." And he started telling me about this Buddhist philosophy he'd just started practicing. During those two hours when the rest of us were sleeping off the previous night's partying, Buster had been awake in his room, chanting the words *Nam Myoho Renge Kyo* over and over. He hadn't slept at all, but when it came time for the gig, he had more energy than all the rest of us put together.

Now, this wasn't actually the first time Buster had tried to tell us about chanting. About six months earlier his sister had come to a gig in Philadelphia, and he'd brought her into the dressing room after the show. "Hey, Toni," he said to her, "do that cool thing you showed me." And she started chanting. She chanted *Nam Myoho Renge Kyo* several times, and then she opened up a little book and went into some other kind of chant.

We were all mesmerized by what she was doing, mostly because of the sound and rhythm of it. I was thinking, *Yeah, this is cool!* because it was a rhythm I hadn't heard before. Everybody in the band was always searching for new sounds, and this was definitely new and unusual. It was actually kind of hypnotic. But at the time I just thought it was something interesting we might explore for our music. It didn't particularly register as a spiritual exercise.

I hadn't thought about chanting since that day in Philadelphia, but now that I knew Buster was doing it, and especially now that I'd seen the energy and focus it gave him, I was really intrigued. The truth is, if Buster had just told me about Buddhism, I would probably have just said, "Hey, great! Whatever works for you, man." I doubt that conversation would have spurred me to explore it myself. But seeing firsthand what chanting did for him musically onstage—well, that got my attention.

Buster invited me to come to a Buddhist meeting the next night, and I told him I would. I needed to find out more about this phenomenon.

|||||||||||

From the time I was young I considered myself to be somewhat spiritual. Even though my experiences in the churches of South Side Chicago hadn't turned me into a churchgoer, I was always interested in different religions. I had never found what I was looking for in the Western religious tradition, though, so in the '70s, like a lot of Americans, I began exploring Eastern religions.

In fact, everybody in the band did, especially after that otherworldly experience at our London House gig. In our spare time we'd hit the bookstores in various cities, reading up on all kinds of belief systems, from Transcendental Meditation to Sufism to Eastern mysticism and even the occult. We all wanted to discover whether we could somehow conjure up again what we'd felt that night onstage.

We were eager to find a way to connect like that more often, and finding a spiritual path seemed the way to do it, because the music itself felt so spiritual. While it was often wild and angry, relentless and visceral, at other times, when it was peaceful and calm, it had a strange, almost mystical beauty. In those moments we felt a power greater than ourselves, and we all spent a lot of time exploring what that power might be.

I did a lot of reading in the course of that search, but I always ended up with more questions than answers. It seemed to me that most of the books I read would be tough for ordinary human beings to understand, as a lot of them were written in a very intellectual way, which bothered me. If only intellectuals could understand a religion, then what was in it for everybody else? I was searching for a belief system that applied to everybody and could be understood by everybody.

When Buster started telling me about his Buddhist philosophy, a practice of Nichiren Buddhism adopted by Soka Gakkai International (SGI), a lay Buddhist organization, the first thing I noticed was how much it resonated with beliefs I already had. He told me that the purpose of chanting those words, *Nam Myoho Renge Kyo*, was to fuse your life with the mystic law of cause and effect through sound. That surprised me, because cause and effect is a basic principle of science. Throughout my life, whenever I had taken apart a situation like it was a clock, what I was really doing was looking for cause and effect, for deeper ways of understanding events. So if that was also a tenet of Buddhism, then I was definitely interested in hearing more.

But at the same time I wasn't sure about this idea that chanting certain words could actually cause something to happen. That sounded a little far-fetched. If Buddhism required me to believe that, out of the blue, I wasn't sure I could make the leap.

"Oh, don't worry," said Buster. "Chanting *Nam Myoho Renge Kyo* works whether you believe in it or not."

What? Now, this definitely didn't sound like any religion I'd ever heard of. Every other religion I knew of depended on blind faith, and some of them required elaborate displays of it. But here's what Buddhism did sound like: science. Because the law of gravity works whether you believe in it or not. And the laws of thermodynamics work whether you believe in them or not. Why would religion be weaker than natural laws? Shouldn't it be even *stronger*? Then why should religion require a person's belief for it to actually work?

Buster repeated, "Listen, this works whether you believe it or not—so you have nothing to lose by trying it." And that made perfect sense to me. I liked the fact that, in Buddhism, human beings have the capacity to create their own destiny. They are not dependent on an external higher power to fix things; by chanting *Nam Myoho Renge Kyo*, people could seize control of their own lives.

I had one more question for Buster: "Do you have to stop believing in other things to become a Buddhist?"

"No," he said. "You don't have to stop believing in anything you already believe in. If you just do this practice, the truth will reveal itself." He told me that simply chanting those four words would help me achieve what I really wanted to achieve, because Nichiren Buddhism isn't just theory; it contains documentary proof and real evidence of its validity in our daily lives. Followers of Nichiren Buddhism believe that when chanting helps people gain or achieve something in life, it provides a tangible affirmation of an intangible inner transformation—called Actual Proof—to themselves and to others of the power in their lives unleashed by their Buddhist practice.

I decided it was worth a try. At this point, I was searching for a way to have more nights when I was "on" musically, and if Buddhism could help me do that, I was ready to start. So I told Buster I would join him at the meeting.

||||||||||

Pretty much my whole adult life I'd been functioning on "jazz musician time," which meant I rarely got to places on time and sometimes ran an hour late. Buster had told me where the meeting was and that it started at seven. Sometime around eight I made it to the address he had given me.

When I got there, I found myself in front of a big apartment building. The front door was locked, and Buster had forgotten to tell me the apartment number, so I had no way to get buzzed in. I stood there for a few minutes, not sure what to do. Then I thought, *Well, Buster said chanting really works. Might as well try it now.* I said *Nam Myoho Renge Kyo*—or something close to it, anyway—a couple of times, and just then a guy came up behind me and unlocked the door! He went in before I realized what was happening, though, and the door clicked shut behind him. I was still stuck outside.

I kept saying the words, and soon another man came to the door, this time from the inside. He opened it up and peered around, as if he were looking for someone, and when he went back in, I grabbed the door before it could latch shut. At least I was inside the building, but I still didn't know which apartment the meeting was being held in.

As I stood there in the hall I heard this faint sound, like bees buzzing. I started following the sound, down the hallway and around a corner, and just as I stepped to the door where it was coming from the sound stopped. I knocked, and when the door opened, I saw a group of people sitting cross-legged on the floor. They had just at that moment finished their chanting and were wrapping up the meeting.

I apologized for being late, but everybody welcomed me warmly. Some people had to go, but a few stayed to talk to me about the practice, and their experiences, and what had happened in their lives as a result of it. We talked for fifteen or twenty minutes and then somebody said, "Okay, let's chant three times, and then we'll split."

At the front of the room was a wooden cabinet with its doors swung open. Inside the cabinet was a scroll with Chinese writing on it. "That's the Gohonzon," somebody explained. "When you chant, keep your eyes open and look at it." This was a serious-looking scroll, with its calligraphic Chinese lettering and that beautiful wood cabinet. I thought, *Okay, this is no joke. This is not something to be played around with.*

We chanted *Nam Myoho Renge Kyo* three times, and I kept my eyes trained on that scroll. The whole thing took about a minute, but I felt transported. I felt high! This was so unexpected—nobody had told me what it actually felt like to chant. I just thought it would be a simple recitation, a moment to get through. But my body, my mind, and my soul responded to it in a way I had never imagined.

The following week I attended another meeting. We were still in Seattle, because it was a ten-day gig, so some of the same people were there. I managed to arrive on time, so I got to hear *Gongyo*, which is the recitation of parts of two chapters of the Lotus Sutra. This was what Buster's sister had chanted a few months earlier in Philadelphia.

The minute everybody started chanting it I was drawn deeply into the rhythm. I tried to follow along in a little book someone handed me, and even though I had trouble with the Japanese words, it was so exhilarating to chant together with this group of people that I didn't want it to end.

I still wasn't sure what exactly Buddhism held for me, but I wanted to pursue it further and see what would happen. Like Buster had said, what did I have to lose? And I might just have something to gain.

||||||||||

Gigi and I both loved New York, but now that we had Jessica, I started thinking about moving our family out to Los Angeles. The weather was gorgeous all year round, and unlike in Manhattan, we could actually have a yard and maybe even a pool. A lot of the record companies were based there, and David Rubinson was in San Francisco. And you could actually park in L.A.! In Manhattan we could never find parking. We'd double-park and then listen for people honking in the morning, so we'd know to go move the car.

"Let's move to L.A.," I said to Gigi.

"No way!" she replied without any hesitation. New York was the only U.S. city she'd ever lived in, and it was perfect for her work and her lifestyle. She had no interest at all in moving.

"Come on, let's just try it for a year," I said. "If you really don't like it, we'll come back to New York." Gigi fought the idea for months but finally gave in. We found a renter for our apartment, but even as Gigi was packing she was still pissed off about the move, throwing stuff into boxes and yelling, "I don't know anyone in L.A.! All my friends are here!" She was so convinced this would be a mistake that we left most of our furniture in New York, in case we decided to come back.

I wasn't sure how long this experiment would last, so we rented a little house on Dorrington Avenue in West Hollywood. And our first week there, as Gigi watched three-year-old Jessica run around naked in the backyard in the middle of December, she changed her mind. In New York at that time of year Jessica would have been bundled up in six layers, plus a hat and mittens. I was away for a gig, but Gigi called me on the road and said, "Okay. Let's buy a house."

We looked at a few places over the next month or so, and in the end we had to decide between one in Laurel Canyon and one on Doheny Drive, just north of the Sunset Strip. The Laurel Canyon house was beautiful, in perfect condition, and ready for us to move in. The Doheny one was really neglected, with musty carpeting and contact wallpaper, and it smelled like cat pee. But there was something about that second house—it definitely had possibilities, if we had the patience to fix it up.

We couldn't decide between them, so I went up to the second floor of the house on Doheny Drive and sat down to chant. I had been practicing Nichiren Buddhism since those meetings in Seattle, chanting twice a day, doing morning and evening prayers. I had also gotten into the habit of chanting whenever I needed clarity, as it always seemed to clear my head and help me see situations in a new light. I chanted for about ten minutes, and even though that room was in terrible condition, being there just felt really right. I went back downstairs and said to Gigi, "I want it to be this house."

Gigi was respectful of my chanting and of my opinions, but she knew how much work it would take to fix the place up, so she wasn't quite convinced. "Let's flip a coin," she said. We did, and the Doheny house won. We bought that house for $72,000 and have lived there ever since. And to this day I still chant on the second floor.

In the six months I'd been practicing I had also begun studying and learning more about Nichiren Buddhism and its history. It was founded by the thirteenth-century Japanese monk Nichiren Daishonin, who concluded that the Lotus Sutra, which was taught thousands of years ago by Shakyamuni, the historical Buddha, was his highest teaching and contained the essence of all his sutras, or teachings.

Nichiren revealed that the essence of the Lotus Sutra is hidden in its title, *Myoho Renge Kyo*, literally "the wonderful law of the Lotus Sutra." On a deeper level it means "The Mystic Law of Cause and Effect through Sound," the one universal law contained in the life of the universe itself. The Daishonin inserted the word *Nam*, which means devotion or dedication of one's life, to this universal law.

Nam Myoho Renge Kyo: These may sound like four random words, but in a way you can compare saying them to saying a person's name. If someone says the word "Jessica" to me, it's not just a word; it brings to mind an image of my daughter, and of everything she means to me. When someone speaks my daughter's name, it releases feelings and emotions in me. Likewise, when we chant *Nam Myoho Renge Kyo*, we're not just saying idle words; we're invoking the meaning of those words from our life, the law of the universe within all life. When we chant those words, we are awakening the Universal Law within, the awakening of our own inherent Buddha nature, our true self. By chanting *Nam Myoho Renge Kyo*, we are *polishing our life*, aligning ourselves with the rhythm of the universe.

Nichiren Daishonin said that this should be taught life to life. Doing this practice is the practice of *polishing our life* just as we are. When this transformation awakens our highest condition of life—our Buddha nature—synchronizing with the life of the universe, it brings forth a state of compassion, wisdom, and courage from within. This in turn fuels our desire to move ourselves and others toward an indestructible happiness that cannot be defeated by suffering of any kind.

Now, I know that this all sounds pretty far out. But at a more basic level, Buddhism taught me a very important lesson about human life and human beings: It showed me how to turn adversity into opportunity. We believe that obstacles are a means for our growth.

When he first told me about chanting, Buster said, "You practice for yourself, and you practice for others." Buddhism is a compassionate practice. It's about respecting and caring for others, sharing the practice as a means to relieve them of their sufferings. Shakyamuni said, "How can I help people to find the Buddha way?" The Daishonin taught the true intent of the historical Buddha's teachings.

That emphasis on *others* really struck me. I had never spent a lot of time thinking about how to help other people. I wasn't a bad guy, but I had never been a particularly empathetic person, either. I pretty much focused on music, and that was that. But hearing Buster talk about focusing on other people and helping to make their lives better really affected me.

Ever since I was seven years old, music had been the number one thing in my life. If anyone asked me how I would describe myself, I would have said without hesitation, "I'm a musician." But as I got deeper into the practice of Buddhism, a new realization began to form inside me. I began thinking of myself as a human being first, removing any sense of separation between myself and others.

I started to see music differently, too. Before, I played music for the sake of playing music; my focus was on tunes, harmony, rhythm, and melody. Now I began trading my musician's ear for the larger purpose of using music to address issues in our daily lives. My desire turned to seeking ways to create music to serve humanity, to contribute something empowering and potentially transformative to the people of the world.

At the time I first started practicing Buddhism, though, my live music was attracting primarily a small number of hardcore avant-garde jazz fans. How could I expand that audience, providing a doorway to their appreciation of the new direction of our music? I began chanting about it.

||||||||||

After doing three records with Warner Bros.—*Fat Albert Rotunda,* *Mwandishi,* and *Crossings*—I knew we weren't cutting it with them. WB was a big label, and our records just hadn't been reaching a wide-enough audience. And instead of moving in a more commercial direction, Mwandishi's music was just getting weirder and more far out.

With each new record David Rubinson was like Houdini, pulling rabbits out of a hat to convince the executives that we had sales potential. My reputation as an artist was still intact, but for commercial reasons we knew it was only a matter of time before Warners dropped me. So David said, "Let's make a move before that happens." He knew it would be easier to get me in at another label if I didn't have the taint of being released by Warners.

Bruce Lundvall was the vice president of Columbia Records, and fortunately he was a huge jazz fan. He pitched Clive Davis, the president of the label, to sign me. I'm not sure whether Clive was all that keen on the idea, but Bruce really went to bat for me. We agreed to a deal, and David told Warner Bros. we were making the switch. I suspect they were relieved, since they seemed eager to move away from this new nexus of funk, jazz, and rock. In fact, around that same time they also let go of another band that, like Mwandishi, was pushing boundaries but hadn't yet found a wide audience: Earth, Wind & Fire. It wouldn't be long before they wouldn't be feeling quite so relieved about losing either of us.

For the new record, which we called *Sextant*, we still had only three songs. But this time I changed up how they were constructed. I wanted there to be more contrast, more compelling arrangements, to draw in more listeners. And for the first time we had synthesizers throughout the whole record. The songs and arrangements were complicated, so we rehearsed for months before going into the studio. One song, "Hidden Shadows," had a time signature that changed from bar to bar, over four bars, and then repeated, so we practiced it over and over again until we got to the point where we could just feel it without having to count in our heads. I wanted to use that pattern as the platform and then construct the solo improvisations on top of that, but it's hard to improvise when you have to focus on counting the beats.

After weeks of rehearsal we finally got it down to where we could play it in our sleep. Then we started playing it faster and faster. We'd be doing improvisations and not even have to think about where the patterns were, but then they'd end up with a *bap!* from the drummer, signaling the end of the pattern. And then it felt so second nature that we started adding more percussion, wood blocks and shakers. It was a beautiful structure of sound.

The whole record was like that, which I hoped would appeal to a wider audience. Mwandishi incorporated different kinds of beats, some of them African based, some of them backbeats. At this point our music still required pretty active listening, but there were other avant-garde jazz bands way farther out than we were that had no real beats at all, just raw free jazz. Compared to them, we were more mainstream. But even though I had high hopes for *Sextant*, it still didn't reach the kind of sales the record label was hoping for. I began to wonder if it was possible to break through that ceiling we seemed to have reached without compromising myself as an artist.

And then I found some inspiration from a very surprising source: the Pointer Sisters.

CHAPTER
THIRTEEN

The Pointer Sisters burst out in the spring of 1973 with a self-titled debut album and a single, "Yes We Can Can," that went to number 11 on the pop chart. This wouldn't have meant much of anything to Mwandishi, except that David Rubinson was now managing the Pointers, too, and their success gave him an idea.

David had been trying to get our music played on black college radio stations, but that hadn't led to significantly higher album sales. We were still playing small clubs and niche venues, so David decided to shake things up. He arranged for Mwandishi to appear at a week-long stand at the Troubadour Club on Santa Monica Boulevard—with the Pointer Sisters opening for us.

If it had seemed strange for Mwandishi to play with Iron Butterfly two years earlier, this felt even weirder. The Pointer Sisters sang throwback harmonies blending jazz, bebop, disco, and R&B, and they wore 1940s hairdos and thrift-store styles as part of their act. We were a group of serious guys in dashikis and Afros, playing high-wire improvised electronic music where people sometimes couldn't even find the beat. Any way you looked at it, this was one strange bill.

We were booked to play at the Troubadour two shows a night for a week, and on that first night the lines went around the block and way down the street—it was as if everybody in L.A. wanted to come to this show. David had hired P.R. people to get the word out, and the club was filled to capacity with jazz fans, agents, executives, actors, and other musicians. It was a scene.

The Pointer Sisters came out and did a half-hour set, and they just killed it. People had never seen anything like them! Here was this group of women cracking up and having a great time, one of them actually roller-skating around on that tiny Troubadour stage. Their music borrowed from the past, but it had a contemporary twist, so they were able to reach across all kinds of barriers. The Pointer Sisters were electric, and everybody in that building felt it. At the end of their set, they came offstage still laughing and carrying on as everybody was stomping and yelling for more.

Seeing the effect they had on the crowd just about turned my head inside out. The Pointer Sisters were *fun*. They were out there showing people a good time, lifting everybody's spirits with their light, happy vibe. When Mwandishi took the stage, the vibe was very different, because although our stuff was great, it was serious. This gig put one thing into clear perspective for me: The audience at a Pointer Sisters show could let loose and have some fun, but the audience at an Mwandishi gig had to do some work.

And that work extended into listening at home, too. When people put on a Pointer Sisters record, they could either sit and listen or do things around the house—cook dinner or finish some housework or any kind of activity, really. If you put on a Mwandishi record, you couldn't really do anything else but sit and listen, because you had to be concentrating to take it in. This wasn't music you could just have on in the background.

I started thinking, *Who's got time for all that? People have things to do!* We were putting out records with just three songs on them—three long songs that changed tempos and time signatures and keys and everything else. We were requiring a tremendous amount of attention and patience from our listeners, both live and on the records. No wonder our audience was limited.

That gig with the Pointer Sisters got me thinking in a different direction. I told David, "I want to reach people like that." I loved Mwandishi's music, and we had certainly been able to touch people with it. But I was beginning to understand why it was so hard to reach beyond the serious jazz fans who dug our style of playing. If we could find a way to incorporate the kind of excitement the Pointer Sisters brought without compromising who we were as a band, we might finally be able to break through.

Part of the Pointer Sisters' appeal was their stage act, of course— the hairdos and costumes and roller-skating. But I had spent five formative years playing with Miles Davis, who wasn't one for jumping around and acting out onstage, so I wasn't interested in theatrics. We always let the music speak for itself, and I wanted to continue doing that.

What can we do with what we have? That was the question marinating in the back of my mind. I kept thinking about how we could redesign our music to make it more accessible, and just as I had before our gig with Iron Butterfly, I thought about contrast: loud to soft, high to low, simple to complex. I didn't believe we needed a radical change, but there had to be something we could do, musically, to get the attention of a broader audience.

I talked to the guys in the band about my thoughts, but most of them were stewing over the fact that we'd played on a bill with the Pointer Sisters in the first place. They felt that Mwandishi's music was "real" in a way that the Pointer Sisters' pop stylings weren't—but to my mind, this was just the same kind of musical snobbery that I'd exhibited when I first started with Miles. The Pointer Sisters were great at what they were doing, and rather than judging them, I wanted to learn from them. I was ready to move in a new direction, but not everybody else was, and that difference of opinion deepened cracks that had already formed in the band.

|||||||||

It was around the time of the Troubadour gig that the guys in the band rebelled: They wanted to get paid more money, and they wanted to be put on salaries.

I understood where they were coming from. By now we had been playing together for several years, and they'd never had any raises. We always split the take from each gig, but paying seven guys, plus our soundman, Fundi, meant there wasn't much to spread around. Every member of the band was an amazing musician, and not only did they all put a lot into the music, but they had to pack up and carry all their own gear and the sound equipment, too.

I didn't know all the details of the band's financial situation, because David Rubinson handled the numbers. But because I paid all the expenses, I was pretty sure Mwandishi had been costing me money over the years. The guys seemed to think I was profiting from the band, so I asked David to run the numbers on what was coming in and going out, and we scheduled a meeting with everyone to discuss it.

Before that, I made them a proposal: "I will level with you about what we're making, and if you want to split everything down the middle, we can agree to do that," I said. "But if we're losing money, then everybody will have to chip in equally to cover it." Nobody wanted to promise to cover losses, so that conversation didn't go very far. What it did was crystallize the difference between how I saw the band and how the band saw itself.

The typical setup for a jazz band is that there's a leader and there are sidemen. The guys wanted to be paid as sidemen, at a level that matched their skills. But I saw the Mwandishi band as a collective: When we made money, we all made money, and when we didn't, we didn't. We were in it together. Otherwise I couldn't sustain it with that number of people.

David pulled the information together, and we all met at my accountant's office in New York, where most of the band members still lived. The numbers made it obvious that between all the expenses of flights, hotels, gas, rental cars, and food, I was losing a lot of money just keeping Mwandishi going. Not only was I playing for free; I was actually paying to play in my own band.

Now, I didn't actually mind this, because I was still getting income from "Watermelon Man" and commercial work. I did have a family to support, but it wasn't as if Gigi and I were living hand to mouth. Besides that, I honestly believed that playing this music, at this time, was necessary. The Mwandishi band was a beautiful experiment in expanding musical boundaries, and if it cost money to explore that, I was willing to take the hit.

On the other hand, I didn't want to lose more than I already was losing. It didn't make sense for me to lay out more in salaries for everybody, especially when we had no plan for how the band might actually become profitable. But the guys were still insistent that they needed to get paid more. In their minds I was the bandleader, and if I wanted to hire musicians of their caliber, I needed to pay for them. If there wasn't enough money coming in, that was my problem, not theirs.

The guys started refusing to do interviews to promote our gigs unless they got paid for their time. They took the position that if they weren't on salaries and their income was based on splitting up the proceeds from gigs, then the gigs were the only things they'd do. The amazing sense of camaraderie that had sustained us through that disastrous Europe trip was really fraying.

But in the end it wasn't money issues that broke up the Mwandishi band. Ultimately it was the music.

From that initial gig in Vancouver when Eddie, Julian, Billy, Bennie, Buster, and I all played together for the first time, through the amazing London House experience, through Buster's "Toys" gig, Mwandishi was capable of conjuring a truly magical musical experience. There were times we shared so much empathy and connection onstage that it really did feel spiritual. At our peak those experiences happened regularly. But when Mwandishi was off—when we didn't connect—the experience wasn't pleasant, and what we were playing just sounded like noise, even to us.

By the summer of 1973 we never knew if a gig was going to work or not. Any band has peaks and valleys, and while the peaks we continued to experience were high, the valleys were starting to feel uncertain and tiring. And we seemed to be ending up in the valleys more often than ever before.

Also, while the Mwandishi band had reflected the spirit of the times, those times were changing. As rock music had grown in popularity people's musical tastes had turned to less demanding music, and a lot of jazz musicians were taking note. Jazz had become so complex, with the rise of free jazz and other avant-garde styles, that people were eager to embrace the simpler, more boy-next-door style of rock and roll. Anybody could relate to rock music, whereas jazz came from a more selective artistic standpoint.

But rock grew out of the blues, after all, and used electric instruments, both of which jazz drew upon. And because jazz musicians are curious by nature, many players began experimenting with jazz-rock fusion, from Wayne Shorter's Weather Report to Tony Williams's Lifetime to Chick Corea's Return to Forever. It looked as if fusion would be the next wave in the jazz world.

All of these developments were percolating in my mind, but I still wasn't sure what to do; the one thing I did know was that I didn't want to feel so untethered anymore. When I started the sextet, I was eager to become untethered musically, and when we first did, it was thrilling. But Mwandishi's music became so spacey, and so far out, that after a while it got exhausting. Now I wanted to make music that was more rhythmic, music that would connect me back to the earth. I wasn't sure exactly what that music would sound like, but it was time to explore.

In the meantime, I got a call about a movie. Ever since doing *Blow-Up* in 1966, I had wanted to write more soundtracks, but the only film I'd gotten since then was the TV movie *Hey, Hey, Hey, It's Fat Albert.* So I was really excited when a producer got in touch to tell me about a new movie called *The Spook Who Sat by the Door.* And I was even more excited that it was being made by an African American production company.

The story, which was based on a controversial novel by Sam Greenlee, follows the first black CIA agent, a guy named Dan Freeman. The CIA trains Freeman as a spy, but unbeknownst to them, he's actually a black nationalist. After he leaves the CIA, he turns around and uses his training to lead a black nationalist revolution. The title is brilliant, as it has several meanings: "Spook" is a nickname for spies, but it can also be a slur against black people. And the "spook who sat by the door," in the sixties and seventies, meant the black secretary who was hired to sit near a company's front door, to show everybody who came in that the company didn't discriminate.

The producers didn't have much money, but I didn't care—I really wanted to do the music for this film. I wrote songs that were heavy on electric instruments and synthesizers, which excited me and reinforced my feeling that it was time to move on. The movie came out in 1973, and that soundtrack was the last recording I did with the Mwandishi band.

||||||||||

After Gigi and I moved to Los Angeles, I started going to Buddhist meetings just about every night. During the meetings people would offer testimonials, talking about the amazing things their practice of Buddhism had brought—everything from a new job to a new car to finding a spouse. People were eager to share the good things that were happening to them, the outward and visible signs of Actual Proof.

But in those first few weeks I found myself thinking, *Well, I already have those things.* I couldn't really relate to what people were saying, because I already had a wife, a house, a daughter, loving parents, and enough money to put food on the table and pay my bills. If the practice of Buddhism was about filling some kind of void in your life, did I really need it? Still, something kept me going to those meetings and kept me practicing and studying through that time of doubt. Even though I had so much good in my life, I knew there might be something missing that I just wasn't aware of yet.

A couple of weeks went by, and I kept practicing. Then one day something changed. Rather than feeling outside of what other people were saying at the meetings, I was feeling their joy, as if I were sharing their experiences with them. At that moment I knew there was more to this Buddhism than what I could see on the surface. I realized that what I'd thought was the Actual Proof—those tangible things people talked about—was really just the outward evidence of a deep inner transformation. I finally understood that the *transformation* was what Actual Proof was all about.

Practicing Buddhism created that transformation in me, too, though it took many years to unfold. In the beginning of my practice all I knew was what I read and what I learned through other people's experiences. I chanted and studied, but it's not so easy to immediately grasp lessons that have been handed down from a thirteenth-century Japanese monk. Fortunately the president of SGI, Daisaku Ikeda, has provided books and lectures that translate Daishonin's writings into concepts that are applicable in today's world.

President Ikeda, who joined SGI the same year I started playing piano—in 1947—is an amazing writer, lecturer, poet, and peace activist. He is a preeminent educator, having established the Soka school system and Soka universities in Japan and the United States, and he has received more than three hundred honorary degrees. I can honestly say that his example as a human being helped me understand life in a way I hadn't before. He became my mentor, a concept I wasn't even aware of until I started studying his writings.

Growing up in Chicago, I always thought the American dream was about pulling yourself up by your bootstraps, succeeding through your own hard work and effort. The term "mentor," meaning someone who guides you to realize your own potential, was new to me, but as I learned about it I realized to my surprise that I'd already had a mentor in music: Miles Davis. I had never thought of him as a mentor, but as I reflected on his behavior as a musician and a teacher, what he represented to me musically, and how he affected my own vision of music, my eyes were opened to the concept.

Miles was my mentor for music, and President Ikeda was becoming my life mentor. The more I studied and learned, the more I saw President Ikeda's dreams as similar to my own: I want people to become awakened, to be more compassionate, to respect one another. To exhibit wisdom on a global scale. Yet, as I said, all these realizations didn't happen at once; they took many years to develop. But it all started with those first few weeks in Los Angeles, as I began to understand what the practice and chanting were really about.

When I first started chanting, I focused on the survival of Mwandishi. A year later, as Mwandishi was unraveling, I started focusing on what was coming next. The problem was, I knew more about what I *didn't* want to do than what I *did*. I didn't want to give up the freedom we had developed, but I wanted to ground myself—to look at some other musical territory rather than up into the sky all the time. But what was that territory?

I had a lot of questions swirling in my head, and very few answers. So I did what I'd learned in my practice: I chanted for a specific answer. *What do I want to do musically?* I spent hours at my Gohonzon, seeking an answer to this question and trying to keep my mind open for some kind of direction.

And then, one day as I was chanting, I heard it.

I want to thank you . . . falettinme . . . be mice elf . . . agin.

It was that great funky groove by Sly and the Family Stone ringing in my ears as I chanted! I kept going, but the song stayed right where it was, playing over and over as if it had been planted in my head. Then suddenly I saw an image of me sitting with Sly Stone's band, playing this funky music with him. And I loved it!

But then the image changed, and it was *my* band playing that funky stuff, and Sly Stone was playing with me—and that felt strange and uncomfortable. That upset me, because my discomfort felt like an expression of jazz snobbery, where funk was somehow lower on the food chain. Meaning, while I didn't mind playing funky music with Sly's band, I didn't want that to be *my* band. It was more of the same old musical elitism I had been fighting against, in both myself and in others, and here it was popping up in my subconscious.

So, just as I'd done all those years ago with "Watermelon Man," I decided to ask myself a few simple questions: Was there anything wrong with funky music? No. Was it somehow worse to play funk with my own band than with someone else's? No. Then why was I feeling dismissive of the idea? I had certainly been listening to a lot of funk music, including Sly Stone. And funk was related to jazz, and it was related to the black experience as a whole. I had to face my own prejudice—or as Buddhist practice says, face the negativity of my fundamental darkness—and defeat it.

And that's the moment I decided to start a funk band.

Switching to funk felt like a big gamble, because even though I liked listening to it, I had no idea if I could make it happen myself, to my standards. I had actually tried once before, recording some funky tunes back in the '60s for Blue Note, but that had been a disaster. I was too far removed from that sound, and the songs never really came together, so the record never even got released. I didn't want to make a record that combined jazz and funk—I wanted pure funk. Because I wasn't a funk musician and I hadn't really played with funk musicians, there was no guarantee that would work out. But the message had been clear, so I decided this was a risk worth taking. It was time to funk out.

And that meant it was time to disband Mwandishi. I knew that most of the guys wouldn't be interested in this new musical direction, partly because they were in the thrall of that same musical elitism I had felt. Going from Mwandishi to a funk band probably wouldn't seem like progress to them as much as a regression.

Also, regardless of how they might feel about funk, people don't like change in general. It's just human nature: It's easy to become comfortable with what works and feel "if it ain't broke, don't fix it." Audiences in Europe had booed Mwandishi because they didn't want change. Critics and fans had freaked out when Bob Dylan went electric, because they didn't want change. One of the hardest things to do in life is to judge events for what they actually are, rather than giving in to the discomfort we naturally feel at losing something familiar.

Human beings start out with a youthful spirit that lends itself to exploration, but over time we lose that. We find our comfort zone, and we don't want to leave it. Change means subjecting yourself to challenge, scrutiny, self-criticism, and disappointment, so it's hard to embrace, especially if you like where you are.

So most of the guys in Mwandishi were pretty upset when I told them I was breaking up the band. But it just made more sense to me to start fresh. I'd be going in a new direction, playing a different kind of music, and I wanted to bring in some new energy. Besides that, I was still thinking about that Pointer Sisters show, and I knew the new band would need a different kind of stage presence.

I decided to take a practical approach: If I wanted to do a funky record, I needed some funky players, because that style fell more toward the entertainment side of music than the art side. Jazz was a "listening music," while rock and funk were performative. Rock and funk audiences were used to a more animated visual presentation, and pure jazz musicians tend to be very cool when they play—eyes closed, not moving much.

The most animated person in Mwandishi was our reed player, Bennie Maupin. More important, he seemed the most open to change. As it turned out, he'd been paying close attention to the same musical shifts that I had. Like me, he was going home after Mwandishi gigs and listening to a completely different kind of music—Luther Vandross and Stevie Wonder and Marvin Gaye and of course Sly Stone. Bennie was really into exploring new musical directions, so I invited him to be in the new band.

I asked around about other players and ended up hiring drummer Harvey Mason, the brilliant Latin/African percussionist Bill Summers, and bassist Paul Jackson, who, unlike Buster, played the electric bass as his primary instrument. I had learned enough from Pat Gleeson to take on playing synthesizers myself, so they would definitely be part of our new sound. But the band's overall instrumental makeup— a four-player rhythm section plus one horn—was totally different from Mwandishi.

The five of us hit the ground running, but where exactly we were going, none of us knew.

CHAPTER
FOURTEEN

Back in 1965, when I turned that Yardley cologne jingle into the song "Maiden Voyage," I discovered something cool about writing music. I had been completely stuck, unable to figure out the song's progression, and nothing I tried sounded right. But then I finally stopped trying to *write* and just *listened*. And that's when the song revealed what it wanted to be.

Eight years later, as I began making music with my new group, something similar was happening. My intention had been to start a straight-up funk band, but when the five of us began playing together in the summer of 1973, the music was telling me otherwise. Our tunes just wouldn't stay in the straight-funk box; we kept getting into this gray area between jazz and funk. At first I pushed back. But I realized pretty quickly that I was better off listening to what the music was trying to tell me than trying to control it.

Anyway, the music we were making was too much fun to try to shove it into some kind of box. We were going in a lighter, more carefree direction than Mwandishi, having fun playing musical games, playing around with the rhythms. Paul Jackson was an unusual funk bass player, because he never liked to play the same bass line twice, so during improvised solos he responded to what the other guys played. I thought I'd hired a funk bassist, but as I found out later, he had actually started as an upright jazz bass player.

Our drummer, Harvey Mason, brought his jazz chops to the music, too, creating new rhythms that were almost the opposite of what you might expect. This was especially true on the first song we started working on, a tune called "Home Grown."

We got together to bounce around ideas, and I started out writing a bass line, playing it on the Minimoog synthesizer. Then Paul started playing an accompanying figure up high on his bass. We didn't have a guitar, which was unusual for a funk band, but I had decided I could instead just play guitarlike figures on a Clavinet, which has keys like a piano but is a plucked instrument like a harpsichord. I'd heard Stevie Wonder and Parliament Funkadelic's Bernie Worrell playing a Clavinet, and I really liked the sound. So in a burst of zeal or maybe naïveté, I thought, *We don't need a guitar!*—which is probably another reason we ended up moving away from a straight-up funk sound.

After I wrote the Minimoog bass line for "Home Grown," I played it for David Rubinson. Now, David was not only a producer and manager, but he was also a drummer. He listened to the line and said, "Why don't you add a little syncopation?" This was just a minor shift, but it changed the whole feel of the song. David never got credit for it on the record, but that syncopated bass line ended up becoming the defining line in the piece, which we later renamed "Chameleon."

While the bass line was the main attraction, partly because it opens the song, Harvey Mason's drum line was also really original. The pulse was funky, and it opened up a lot of territory, both harmonically and rhythmically. Most drum lines sound like *boom-kak-boom-kak,* but Harvey's was almost backward-sounding to that. It was a great, funky beat, and between it and the bass line, "Chameleon" started us off with a fantastic creative platform.

If Mwandishi had worked with an intergalactic palette, this new band was working with an earthy one. The guys were capable of stretching out as Mwandishi did, but now our melodies had a sense of familiarity, so even though the band was stretching, the listeners didn't have to. We played around with the harmonies and rhythms, but the untrained ear could still follow the music. And we'd sneak enough stuff in there so that the trained ear had a good time, too.

I loved this direction we were heading in, and I couldn't wait to create more new songs. But then Harvey Mason said, "You know, 'Watermelon Man' has been around for ten years now. What if we did a new arrangement of it for this record?" I just about flipped out. Right away my brain started racing with ideas of how we could update the sound of that song.

"I have a few ideas," Harvey told me. "In fact, I just thought of one in the shower the other day!" He suggested adding a stop-time element to the arrangement, which was a nice way to funk it up. And then Bill Summers, who had a doctorate in ethnomusicology with an emphasis on African music, had another suggestion. He had studied a form of African Pygmy music called Hindewhu, and he wanted to incorporate elements of that style into the song.

I had actually heard Hindewhu on a record put out by the Folkways label, and I really liked it. "Let's do it," I said to Bill, and he got to work. He poured water into a beer bottle, and then he made a pattern by singing a note, then blowing across the bottle mouth to produce another note, then singing another note. It was such a cool pattern, and I also loved the fact that it didn't sound exactly like the Folkways record but was Bill's own creative twist. And then he took it a step further, overdubbing countermelodies against that pattern, also with the beer bottle. That became the intro for the new version of "Watermelon Man."

As we worked out the songs for our new record we were turning into a new kind of band: a jazz-funk fusion band. I hadn't intended to go down that road at all, but that's where the music was leading us.

And it was exciting, because even though jazz-rock had appeared on the scene, there weren't really any instrumental jazz-funk bands, so this was a new niche. Our songs sounded different from anything else I was hearing out there, but we didn't know how audiences would react to them. So we decided to find out.

Normally a band will make a record and then play in clubs and concerts to support it. But I decided to do the opposite. We spent a few weeks playing our new songs in clubs all over the San Francisco Bay Area—the Haight, Mill Valley, Berkeley—to see how people responded. We played in dance clubs and more intimate venues, for all kinds of crowds, and everybody just flipped out! People were dancing, laughing, and having fun, just completely letting loose as we played. It was a party, and people loved the groove.

Playing live helped us figure out what was working and what wasn't, so we were able to refine the songs before recording them. But equally important, those shows created a buzz, where people were talking about our funky new sound and getting excited about the record before we'd even made it. By the time we headed into the studio, we knew where we wanted to go. Now we just needed to figure out what to call the record.

||||||||||

I was still chanting for hours each day, with all the zeal of a new convert, and I began focusing on the question *What should the title of the record be?*

I wanted something primitive and earthy but with an intellectual component—a smart title that would get people thinking. *Crossings* and *Sextant* both incorporated African imagery on their covers, and I definitely wanted the jungle in the title. And—oh, yes—it wouldn't be bad if the title had a sexual meaning, too. This was the '70s, after all, and we were a band of young guys. This was a lot to ask for a title, but as I was chanting, it suddenly hit me: *Head Hunters.* As soon as that phrase popped into my mind, I started laughing. It was the perfect title, with the perfect triple entendre—the jungle, the intellectual, and the sex.

We recorded the main sessions of "Chameleon" at Wally Heider Studios, and I used one of Pat Gleeson's synthesizers to play that funky bass line. A lot of people assumed that Paul Jackson was playing it, but he was actually playing the rhythm guitar accompaniment, far up the neck of his bass. I wanted to do something different, to surprise people.

After we recorded the piece, I started to think that the bass line I'd laid down wasn't punchy enough, so I decided to rerecord it, programming the Minimoog so the notes were shorter. The next day I took the tape to David Rubinson, but when he played that new bass line as an overdub, he forgot to turn off the original track. "Hold on, David," I told him. "Both tracks are playing." We didn't need both those bass lines . . . but they actually sounded kind of cool together.

Normally it's impossible to have stereo bass, because the lower the frequency, the more difficulty the ear has in perceiving direction. That's why you can put subwoofers in any part of the room: Your ear can't tell where low-frequency sounds are coming from. It's only when pitch gets higher that your ear starts to perceive directionality more clearly. Consequently, nobody ever records stereo bass.

But listening to those two tracks, I got an idea. "Hey, David, since those bass lines weren't recorded together, they won't be exactly the same sound," I said. "Could that function like stereo bass?"

"Theoretically," he said. "Let's try it."

So we put one bass line on the left side and one on the right—and just like that, we had stereo bass! We decided to use both on the record, but they weren't quite in sync, so I had to go back to Different Fur and fix the timing. They still weren't perfectly in sync, but it was better that way, because if they had been, they would have canceled each other out.

When we were done, I thought we had a beautiful record, but as usual, David had a hard time convincing the studio executives at Columbia that we had a product they could sell.

Here's how David remembers it:

When I turned in the *Head Hunters* album, it was met with very little enthusiasm by the record company. The only person who liked it was the college-outreach guy. The R&B side didn't want anything to do with it. The white jazz guys didn't want anything to do with it. It was fascinating! The music industry doesn't know what to do with those who don't fit into a particular slot.

But Herbie was in tune with the people, and so the people found it.

A few weeks after the record came out, David called me.

"Hi, Herbie," he said. "Quick question for you. How many copies of *Head Hunters* do you think we sold this week?"

"I don't know," I told him. "A thousand? Two thousand?" I figured sales were probably similar to what they'd been for *Crossings* and *Sextant*.

"Nope," he said. "*Seventy-eight* thousand." I sat there for a moment, stunned. And then we both started laughing.

"Just this week?" I asked. I couldn't believe it. I could not in my wildest dreams have imagined selling anywhere near that number of records in a single week.

"You're going to have a platinum record," David told me. And I still couldn't get my head around it.

When I'd first started practicing Buddhism, I had spent hours upon hours chanting to save Mwandishi, unaware that I was shackling myself trying to maintain my personal status quo. But the minute I opened up my heart and mind and soul to going in whatever direction I was led, *Head Hunters* happened. There was a beautiful life lesson to be learned in that: the power of letting go.

After trying for so long, we were finally breaking through to new audiences, including big numbers at traditionally black colleges and universities. That trend really started in Washington, D.C., thanks to the work of Columbia promo man Vernon Slaughter and a friend from my high school days in Chicago named Alden Lawson, who was working at the Howard University radio station. Those two turned D.C.'s black students on to *Head Hunters,* and Alden spread the word to other universities, too. He had contacts at most of the black colleges, and he made calls all over the place to make sure everybody knew about this new jazz-funk sound. Black colleges went crazy for our music, and from there it just exploded all over the country.

We started touring to support the record, but I still couldn't really take in what was happening. We played one East Coast show opposite Santana, in a pretty big arena, and the place was packed, completely sold out. As I was getting ready to walk onstage, I turned to David and said, "Wow, Santana sure brought them out tonight."

David looked at me and smiled. "That's not Santana," he said. "That's you."

I laughed. "You think these people came to see *me*?"

"Herbie, you have a big hit record now," he told me. "They're here to see *you.*" I just shook my head. It really was like a dream.

We kept on touring, kept on playing, kept on selling records. And because most of the guys in the band were also SGI members, we did a lot of chanting together.

Here's how Bennie remembers that time:

> We played every nook and cranny we could find—we were just out there! It was such an interesting time for us, because we were chanting furiously all the time, going to visit Buddhist community centers, and we had a hit record on the charts. We were just having fun, enjoying it a lot. And so were the audiences.

The music we created was right on the mark, because it resonated with everybody, across the board. The timing was right, and our attitude about the music was right, right on down to the promotion of it. This was an explosion of creativity and innovation in a direction no one had ever gone in before. It was our time.

It was magic, and the original recording reflects that magic. We were able to create an instrumental group palette, a combination of jazz and funk with some very specific rhythmic elements that people could feel.

It did feel like magic, especially when the record kept on selling and selling. Within six months *Head Hunters* went gold. And it just kept on going, eventually passing Dave Brubeck's classic *Take Five* to become the biggest-selling jazz album of all time. Today that top spot is held by Miles Davis's *Kind of Blue,* which was released back in 1959 and still keeps selling. But for a while, at least, *Head Hunters* was at the very top—to my surprise, and maybe a lot of other people's, too.

||||||||||

The band, which was now being called the Headhunters, toured throughout 1974, and it was a completely new experience for me. The audiences were much bigger, and they weren't necessarily jazz fans. A lot of them didn't even know my earlier music but just wanted to hear the cuts from *Head Hunters.* We were a jazz-funk outfit now, and I was stepping out from the piano to play giant synthesizers. We had an electric, funky sound, and unlike the audiences for Mwandishi, these audiences weren't necessarily looking for something new and challenging every night—they just wanted us to play songs as they'd heard them on the record. Paul Jackson was originally a jazz bassist, so he wanted to improvise, and he would play a different pattern for every gig. I finally had to say to him, "Paul, you have to play the bass line on the record, or people are going to riot." Neither of us was used to that.

Another big difference was that at Mwandishi shows people sat almost reverentially in the audience. But at Headhunters shows they would *dance*. Our drummer, Harvey Mason, didn't come with us on tour, so I hired a guy named Mike Clark to step in. Mike was from Oakland, and he played with this particular kind of beat—the Oakland Stroke, they called it. It's a jazzy funk beat, and as soon as Mike stepped in, I knew, *This is going to be cool*. Mike got people up on their feet.

I was really excited to be reaching so many new listeners, but not everybody was enthusiastic. The critics started grumbling that I had turned my back on jazz, or that I was a sellout.

That's the thing about commercial success: It can instantly change how people see a record or a book or an artwork, because people make assumptions about the artist's motivation. They assume he's creating with an eye toward making money, rather than fulfilling an artistic vision. But while it was true that I wanted our music to reach more people, *Head Hunters* was also a natural next step after the Mwandishi records, especially given the movement toward fusion that was happening with bands like Tony Williams Lifetime and Weather Report.

But as *Head Hunters* climbed higher on the charts, some critics really started reacting negatively to it. The tone of this review, by Lee Underwood, was typical of the worst ones:

> Mr. Communicate-With-A-Wider-Audience, Herbie Hancock, opened to a full house recently, again pleasing the funkers while disappointing the more cerebrally oriented connoisseurs. At its worst, Hancock's music is commercial trash; at its best, it is almost as schizoid as Frank Zappa's offerings.

My older brother, Wayman, and me, dressed for success in the early 1940s.

By the time I started high school, I'd been taking piano lessons for six years. But it wasn't until sophomore year that I discovered that people my age could play jazz.

My parents, Wayman and Winnie Hancock, with my brother and me in front of my dad's grocery store on the South Side of Chicago, 1940. People called my mother "high-strung," but years later, her condition would be given a name: bipolar disorder.

My sister, Jean, was three years younger than me, but she was smart and sharp-tongued and could even be intimidating.

With my mother at Grinnell College. I enrolled in the fall of 1956, at age sixteen, but I spent more time studying music than my engineering courses.

Me in the early 1960s, right about the time I first met Miles Davis.
When he asked me to play something on his little spinet piano,
I nervously played a few bars of "Stella by Starlight." To my relief,
he rasped, "Nice touch."

Standing astride a Manhattan street in 1964, in a photo used on the
cover of my third album, *Inventions and Dimensions*.

Miles Davis, Ron Carter, Wayne Shorter, and Tony Williams, with me on piano at left. We never rehearsed, and Miles never gave us notes on our playing. He'd just say something like, "Don't play the butter notes," and let us figure out what he meant.

Gigi and I married at New York City Hall in the summer of 1968, five years after we started dating. I knew I loved her, but I was a young jazz musician and hadn't been ready to settle down.

With Gigi and our daughter, Jessica, in the early 1970s. Jessica was a beautiful baby, though it took her a couple of years to finally grow some hair. During the Mwandishi period, I had enough to spare.

After leaving the Miles Davis Quintet, I started my own sextet. In the early '70s, we took Swahili names—mine was Mwandishi, meaning "composer"—and the music started to get pretty far out. From left to right: Buster Williams, Bennie Maupin, Eddie Henderson, Julian Priester, and me.

In 1972, we added synthesizers to Mwandishi, bringing a white hippie Ph.D. named Pat Gleeson into the mix. From left to right: Patrick Gleeson, Bennie Maupin, me, and Buster Williams.

Music technology of the 1970s and '80s was still pretty limited, but Bryan Bell helped us find ways around the limitations. He could improvise on equipment the way musicians improvised on their instruments.

In this photo for the *Sunlight* album, I'm surrounded by eleven keyboards, which is a lot for a guy with only two hands. Shortly after this, we finally figured out how to control multiple synths from one keyboard.

Jamming with the great Carlos Santana in the '80s.

The first time I was asked to play with Joni Mitchell, in 1979, I made the mistake of assuming she only did folk music. She's one of the most versatile and skilled musicians I've ever played with.

At the same time I was pushing the limits of electric music, I still loved exploring traditional jazz sounds. In 1977, Chick Corea and I did a stripped-down tour: just two guys and two pianos.

Me with my beloved 1963 Cobra, the first car I ever bought—right after Donald Byrd talked me out of buying a station wagon.

After the untethered space music of Mwandishi, I decided to come back to earth. I started a funk band that became known as the Headhunters. This is the touring band (clockwise from top left): Bill Summers, Paul Jackson, Bennie Maupin, Mike Clark, and me.

V.S.O.P. was meant to be a Very Special Onetime Performance at the 1976 Newport Jazz Festival. But people liked hearing classic jazz so much, we decided to keep it going (left to right): Tony Williams, me, Wayne Shorter, Ron Carter, and Freddie Hubbard.

On stage with the very cool robots that Jim Whiting designed for Godley & Creme's "Rockit" video.

Winning my first Grammy, in 1984, for "Rockit." The first time I heard scratching, on Malcolm McLaren's "Buffalo Gals," I knew I wanted to use it on a record. From left to right: Bernard Fowler, Grand Mixer DXT (formerly D.ST), Anton Fier, JT Lewis, me, Wayne Brathwaite, and Jeff Bova.

On the set of *Round Midnight* with the great director Bertrand Tavernier, who made the risky decision to film the music scenes live rather than taping the music in a studio setting.

With my mom on Oscar night. I loved doing the music for *Round Midnight*, but I never imagined I'd be nominated, much less win.

Switching to clavitar meant I could stand out front on stage like a rock star.

I've been playing with Wayne Shorter for fifty-three years now, and I'd gladly play for fifty-three more. He's more than just an amazing, creative, gifted musician—he's my best friend.

In the 1970s and '80s, Stevie Wonder and I got into an amiable competition, with each of us trying to buy Serial No. 1 of whatever new electric instrument came down the pike. Stevie's a creative genius, and a good friend.

With Quincy Jones and the Montreux Jazz Festival founder Claude Nobs. I met Quincy back when he was a young trumpeter in the early '60s, and in the '80s I approached him about starting a partnership.

When I played "Rhapsody in Blue" with Lang Lang at the 50th Grammy Awards, it was the first time I'd played a serious classical piece in public since college.

With my sister, Jean, and brother, Wayman, in the 1980s. My relationship with Jean grew complicated when she told me she wanted to become a professional singer; then, just a few years after this photo was taken, she died in a shocking accident.

With Gigi and my parents at Vice President Gore's house in 1998.

In my home studio. From the days of cutting and splicing tape to making music with iPads, I always get excited to see what's coming next.

More than forty years after I started practicing Buddhism, I still chant every day.

Gigi, Jessica, and me. My family has always supported me through good and bad—even when the bad got worse than anyone expected.

The notion that I'd gone in a new and different direction because I knew I'd make more money was funny to me. How could I possibly have known our jazz-funk experiment would be that popular? There was no guarantee I'd gain any listeners at all—and there was a real risk that I'd lose part of the audience I already had! The idea that I had some master plan for making a big commercial hit was just not logical.

Over the coming years, as I got even deeper into electronic music, these critics would get even louder. But it didn't change my course. I had to be true to myself, and this was the music I wanted to pursue. Anybody who ever played with Miles Davis learned that you can't worry about what the critics think. You have to make the music your heart tells you to make.

A couple of years after *Head Hunters* came out, an interviewer with *Contemporary Keyboard* magazine asked me why so many people objected to electric keyboards. Here's what I said—and it still holds true for any kind of change, or progress, that people naturally resist:

People back in the early 1900s used to say the same thing about the car: Why are you driving around in an electric car when you should be riding a horse? TV, movies, all those things faced that. People are unable to change sometimes. Those very same people might be saying something completely different in five years.

People don't have to give anything up by having an open attitude. When they have a closed attitude, they aren't even allowing for the fact that perhaps the technique of playing these electric instruments is going to improve over the years. It's very difficult to play with nuances on some synthesizers. But that's not necessarily going to be true tomorrow. I started playing piano when I was seven. Just think what it's going to be like when you get people starting to play synthesizer when they are seven.

In the meantime, I just kept making the music I felt in my heart and playing those bigger and bigger venues. Pretty soon there would be a whole new wave of electric instruments for me to explore.

||||||||||

In the midst of all the *Head Hunters* excitement I got a call to do another movie. This one was about a New York City architect, played by Charles Bronson, whose wife is murdered and his daughter raped by a gang of thugs. He goes on a wild vigilante streak, killing muggers and punks all over the city. Called *Death Wish,* it's a dark and violent film, a reminder of how dangerous New York was in the 1970s.

The director, Michael Winner, didn't know my music, but one of the actresses in the movie was a big jazz fan. Over lunch one day he asked her who he should hire to do the score, and she said, "Herbie Hancock." Then she told him to go out and buy the *Head Hunters* album. Michael liked what he heard, so I was hired.

I was really deep into synthesizers by now, and I wanted to use them in the movie. Nobody had really done that before, and especially not in combination with orchestral instruments, but I decided to combine those elements to add a new twist to a classic sound.

The rape scene happens early on, and I decided to use the synthesizer to create an ominous undercurrent of sound. The synth drones a low note, and I added orchestral sounds on top of it—the plucking of strings, the sound of a bow against wood. It was more sound effect than music, though it did have melodic overtones. I felt that would match the mood of the scene better than straightforward music.

I experimented in other ways, too. For one scene in the subway I asked the drummer to give me a particular beat, but then in the studio I decided I wanted to play it backward. Today you can just press a button and get that effect, but in 1974 I had to take the tape and physically play it backward through the machine to get that sound. It was time-consuming, but there was something about that reverse beat that felt eerie and foreboding.

In one famous scene Bronson pours handfuls of quarters into a sock to make a weapon. He starts swinging it around inside his house, getting wilder and more manic—and suddenly the sock smacks into the wall and bursts, spilling the quarters everywhere. It's a weird scene, and I wanted music that would capture the character's complex emotions. So I decided to borrow from a piece that I've always loved, Stravinsky's *Rite of Spring*. The piece I wrote doesn't have exactly the same chord structure, but it is evocative of Stravinsky, though I'd be surprised if many moviegoers ever made that connection.

I had about six or seven weeks to do the whole score, which isn't much time to write, orchestrate, and record forty minutes of music. Making it worse was that fact that I'm a terrible procrastinator. When I have a deadline, I often wait to write until it's almost too late—and then I just pick something in a hurry and start there. That's pretty much always been the way I work, even though it results in panic toward the end of each project. It also leads to a lot of sleepless nights, as I race to get everything done in a wild rush.

Toward the end of composing for *Death Wish* I was just completely wiped out. I pulled a couple of all-nighters in a row, but with the deadline just a few days away I still needed to write one of the most important parts: a piece for an emotional scene where Bronson's character is recalling his murdered wife, Joanna. The piece would be called "Joanna's Theme," and Michael Winner was really anxious for me to nail it. I was anxious, too, as this scene was the movie's emotional core. Michael kept saying, "Do you have anything yet? When are we going to have 'Joanna's Theme'?" I don't know who was more nervous about it, him or me, but between us we were a wreck.

I kept going around and around, trying to figure out a line that would embody the emotion of that scene. And finally, at the last moment, I came up with a melody and a chord structure that sounded haunting and heart-wrenching. I wrote out the parts and then hurried to get into the studio with the orchestra to record it.

I didn't know anything about conducting, but I stepped in front of the musicians and tried to guide them through the piece. When we finished, I knew we had it! But would Michael agree? We really didn't have time to try anything else, but there was no guarantee that he'd feel the same way I did. I walked into the booth to listen to the take, and Michael came in, too. As the engineer played it back I looked over to see Michael's response—and he had tears in his eyes.

That was such an amazing moment for me. I had done it! I had finished the music, and the director loved it. I had worked so hard over the past six weeks, it just felt as if a mountain had been lifted from my shoulders. I went home feeling relieved and happy, but even I didn't realize how emotionally overwrought I had become until I went into the bathroom and suddenly burst into tears. I had been completely dry-eyed when Michael was in the sound booth crying, but now that I was home and knew it was over, I was crying, too. Tears of joy.

||||||||||

Now that *Head Hunters* was a big commercial success, Columbia couldn't wait for us to put out our next album. In the summer of 1974 we started recording the record that became *Thrust,* using the same lineup as on *Head Hunters* except for one change: We brought on the Oakland Stroke drummer Mike Clark permanently, replacing Harvey Mason.

I always tried to do something new on each album, and for *Thrust* I wanted to create a song that showcased the drummer. On most jazz and funk songs the horns or piano carry the melody, and it's easy to construct a song around an improvised solo. But could a song be constructed around the drums? I decided to take it on as a challenge, a puzzle I needed to figure out.

I started thinking about how rhythm might be the main feature of a song. I considered the various parts of a drum kit, but there had to be a way to go beyond that. Suddenly it hit me that there was one kind of rhythm that takes center stage: tap dancing.

Tap dancing uses a device called stop time, which is essentially a way of alternating accented beats with silence, changing up the rhythm of a song. I knew I could simply write a song that incorporated stop time, but then, in the spirit of Miles, I thought, *Why not make it harder?* What if I took an existing song, something slow and melodic, and turned it into an up-tempo, stop-time showcase for drums?

Now I was excited. I knew the perfect song to rewrite, a ballad I'd done for *The Spook Who Sat by the Door*. I completely reconstructed it, using rhythmic phrases based not just on straight-up 4/4 time but with five beats or three beats or seven beats interspersed. To make it even more challenging, I worked in something we called displacement, where we would take a phrase or musical element that would naturally fall in one place and move it slightly forward or backward in the song.

I decided to name the tune "Actual Proof"—the Buddhist concept of a concrete example of the practice working in your life. It's a cornerstone of Nichiren Buddhist belief, the visible evidence that it's working and a motivation to continue practicing. I had started incorporating some elements of Buddhism into my album covers, and this would be another one.

The complex rhythms of "Actual Proof" were a challenge to the listener, but they were a challenge to the musicians, too. One time when we were in the studio, I heard Paul Jackson working something out on his bass. A couple of minutes later I said, "Okay, let's do 'Actual Proof.'" The engineers started recording, but when I counted off, Paul jumped in with a completely different bass line from the one we'd been playing on the road.

"Whoa! Whoa!" I said. "Paul, what was that? It messes with the arrangement. You know we have to keep the same bass line—we can't just keep changing it up like that."

"Yeah, man, I know," he said. "I'm sorry. I'm sorry."

But then I laughed, because that bass line he'd played was slick! I said, "Listen, that bass line was so *bad,* let's do it! It's better than the one we've been doing." The only thing was, it was so convoluted, I wasn't sure where the first beat came in, so I wasn't sure how to count it. "Okay, Paul—where is one?" I asked.

When Paul explained it to me, it was not where I had thought at all. I said, "No way! Are you kidding me?" And he said, "I'm not kidding!" And he counted it for me.

It took me a while, but I figured out a whole different pattern underneath Paul's bass. And that's what we ended up recording. It was a killer bass line, but that's how Paul was; he could come up with things nobody else could. To this day musicians who want to play "Actual Proof" will ask me how the rhythm works. When I tell them, they say, "No way! No way!"—just as I did. No matter how many new electric instruments we brought in, the coolest part of any song was always seeing the human brain create patterns and rhythms nobody had ever heard before.

CHAPTER FIFTEEN

One morning about a year after *Thrust* came out, the doorbell rang at our house on Doheny. I was still in my pajamas, but I went to see who it was. When I opened the door, a young guy was standing there.

"Hi, Herbie," he said. "It's Bryan Bell."

I had no idea who Bryan Bell was or why he was standing at my door. He started talking about sound mixing and guitars and synthesizers, but I still couldn't figure out what this was about. Then he pointed at my AC Cobra, which was sitting in the driveway, and asked about it. I said, "Oh, yeah. That's my car, but it's not running right now."

"Do you have any tools?" he said. "I can fix cars." I brought him a toolbox, he popped the hood and fiddled around for a few minutes, and suddenly the car was fixed. I didn't know what he'd done, but this kid obviously knew his mechanics. I said, "Well, let's take it out for a ride, then." So we got in the car, and I opened it up on Sunset Boulevard, racing at about eighty miles an hour toward Beverly Hills, and as Bryan and I talked, he reminded me that we had met about six months earlier.

Bryan had been the soundman for John McLaughlin's Maha-vishnu Orchestra, which had opened for some of the Headhunters' shows on our Northeast tour. I had noticed that the sound quality for McLaughlin's band was really sharp, so I'd asked to meet the sound guy. Apparently when I was introduced to Bryan, I had told him to look me up if he was ever looking for another gig. So now here he was. He was leaving the Mahavishnu Orchestra, he explained, and he'd come all the way from his home in Portland, Oregon, to Los Angeles just to knock on my door.

After we talked for a while, I said to him, "Listen, you want to stay here in my guesthouse a few days? I just converted my garage into a studio, so we can work on some stuff there, see how it goes." And that was the beginning of a partnership that would last through the next eight years and nearly twenty albums.

Bryan was just twenty-one when we met, but he had an amazing aptitude for electronics. He loved music, and he loved figuring out creative ways to use electronic equipment to enhance it. I already had a great and knowledgeable keyboard tech, Will Alexander, and a soundman, Craig Fruin, so at first Bryan just provided sound equip-ment. But before long Will started spending more time with another client of his, Keith Emerson of Emerson, Lake & Palmer, so Bryan began revamping our band gear, first for recording and then for tour-ing. And that's where his genius started to shine through. He was able to customize equipment in a way that not only changed how we recorded and performed but also changed the sound of the band.

In the spring of 1976, as we were getting ready to record the album *Secrets,* Bryan started fiddling, customizing everything to enhance the Headhunters' particular sound. He replaced the keyboard mixer, got new amps for everybody in the band and new speakers for me, and then configured everything to enhance the stereo sound for when we were onstage. Bryan was always bursting with theories on how to im-prove our sound, and he was always up for a challenge.

I would say, "Bryan, I want to make the synthesizer do this new thing" or "Can we make these two components communicate with each other?" and he would answer, "Well, that's never been done before, but let's see if I can figure it out."

Bryan was always ordering new parts and gadgets, and when they'd arrive, I'd take the instructions and start reading, but he would just immediately jump in and start messing around. He'd explain how certain components changed the band's sound, describing the physics behind them. We spoke the same language because of my engineering background, but Bryan took things to a whole new level. He could improvise on equipment the way musicians improvised on their instruments.

Here's how Bryan described the way we worked:

> It was the most simpatico relationship, where together we were able to make something greater than the sum of its parts. Herbie's a great artist, and I'm a good engineer and a good thinker, but together we did stuff that nobody else could do, and that was very special and rewarding.
>
> Herbie would say, "Hey! Let's do this!" and I would think, *Okay, this will be two years of my life, every spare minute, a hundred hours a week. Because he's right, this needs to be built, and we should have it first.* Herbie always loved to present something that nobody's heard or seen.

Bryan worked with us on the *Secrets* album, and he also came with the band on tour in the summer of 1976. We traveled all across Europe, playing jazz festivals at soccer stadiums and bullfighting arenas, and by then he was acting as my keyboard tech and the house mixer, too. It's unusual to find an engineer who's good at both studio recordings and live shows, but Bryan could do both. He was just really good at figuring out ways to overcome the limitations of equipment.

But just before we went on that European tour, Bryan and I got a glimpse of the musical future, one that would have far fewer limitations than the analog age we were then living in.

||||||||||

We recorded *Secrets* in San Francisco, and I arranged for Bryan to stay at the Zen Center while we were there. I had a friend who worked with the center's abbot, Richard Baker, who was referred to as Baker Roshi—"Roshi" being the word for "Zen master." The dormitory rooms were full, so Baker Roshi fixed Bryan up in the guesthouse, which was used by California governor Jerry Brown when he came there to meditate.

Bryan was really happy to be at the Zen Center, because he could meditate and chant there, and Baker Roshi's staff fed him great vegetarian food and even bought clothes for him. Bryan told me it was "like being in the pope's summer home." One night Baker Roshi came to Bryan and said, "What are you and Herbie doing tomorrow?" Bryan told him we were recording in the afternoon, but the morning was free. And Baker Roshi said, "Great. Xerox needs you."

He told Bryan that a friend of his at the Xerox Palo Alto Research Center (Xerox PARC) had invented something cool and wanted our help. At this time Xerox PARC was like the center of the universe for technology. Xerox was a huge corporation, with tons of money for R&D, and because the Silicon Valley revolution hadn't happened yet, there wasn't a lot of competition from tech start-ups. Xerox PARC had the smartest, most forward-thinking scientists and researchers, and new patents spewed out of them every year like they were coming out of a fire hose.

Baker Roshi explained to Bryan that his scientist friend needed me to come play some piece of new technological equipment. "Are you both U.S. citizens?" he asked. "Do you have your passports? You'll need them to get in." Luckily we did have them, since the Headhunters were going abroad on tour as soon as we finished the record. But what was this all about?

Bryan called and told me what was up, and the next morning we made our way to the Xerox PARC building at the Stanford Research Park. The first thing they asked us to do was sign a nondisclosure agreement. This wasn't too unusual, except for the length of time it covered: We had to promise not to reveal what we were about to see for five full years. I mean, whatever we were about to experience, it was serious business. Bryan and I handed over our passports and signed a bunch of paperwork, and finally we were taken into a small conference room.

A guy about my age came in to greet us, and he introduced himself as Alan Kay. "I'm sure you're wondering what this is about," he said. "We've created a personal computer."

His invention was called the Dynabook, and it was a tablet-size computer, which was completely unheard of then. A couple of other "personal computers" had been released in 1975, including the Altair 8800 and the IBM 5100, which was billed as a "portable computer," though I'm not sure who actually considered it portable, since it weighed fifty-five pounds.

Alan was trying to perfect certain elements—what we'd now call applications—of the Dynabook. He told us he wanted to show us a few, and that he needed my help for one in particular that had to do with music. He also said that Bryan and I would see all of this separately, because the researchers wanted us each to have our own experience and reactions to it.

Well, I couldn't wait to see what this "personal computer" looked like, especially if it had a musical application. Alan led me through a labyrinth of hallways and into a dark room with several lighted workstations. He explained what each one did: One was for painting, one for writing, one for animating. And one was for a synthesizer-type application that you could use to play previously recorded sounds.

For this application the scientists had gotten recordings of each instrument in the London Philharmonic playing every note on the scale. The computer used a prototype version of a sampling keyboard, so you could choose which instrument it would play and then play those notes by pressing the keys. That was really cool, but not nearly as cool as what Alan showed me next.

Because it was a computer and had a hard drive, the Dynabook could also record what I'd just played—and then play it back for me. I had never seen anything like that before, and it was immediately obvious how that capability would change how music was made forever. I had never seen digital audio before, only tapes. The idea that this little box could automatically remember and then instantly play back anything I put into it was mind-boggling.

I thought about Pat Gleeson, furiously plugging all those patch cords into the synthesizer to create sounds from scratch. And about having to physically loop tape backward to get the drum sound I wanted for *Death Wish*. And about all those hours spent in production, when engineers used a razor blade to cut tape and then splice it back together, worrying that the blade might slip a millimeter in the wrong direction. This invention was going to change absolutely everything about how music was created. And I couldn't tell anyone about it—for five years!

After Bryan and I each gave the researchers our thoughts on the Dynabook, they brought us back together in the conference room. Alan started telling us about how he expected this technology to evolve, and it was like hearing something out of science fiction. He talked about portable devices, running on batteries, using wireless connectivity, with far larger memory than the sixty-four kilobytes of RAM that came with the IBM 5100. And Alan had actually invented the Dynabook as an educational tool for kids, so he was aiming for all this new technology to be simple enough for a four-year-old to use.

What we had just seen was, in a sense, the first iPad. Alan Kay was one of the pioneers of both object-oriented programming and the graphical user interface and went on to work with Steve Jobs and Steve Wozniak at Apple in the 1980s. He really is one of the fathers of modern-day computing, and I still can't believe I was lucky enough to see some of his inventions in their early stages.

|||||||||||

In the spring of 1976 David Rubinson got a call from the founder of the Newport Jazz Festival, George Wein. I had played that festival many times over the years, and George wanted to book the Headhunters for the next one, in June. I was happy to do it, but David had another idea.

"You know," he said, "maybe it's time not to be so accessible to promoters. You have a hit record now. We should be a little more exclusive." Since *Head Hunters* came out, we'd been playing bigger arenas, not only in the United States but also in Japan and Europe, which have really devoted jazz audiences. We had attained a new level of success, but David knew George would probably offer us the same fee we'd always gotten to play the festival. David felt that if we agreed to play Newport again, just as we always had, we'd be taken for granted not only by George but by the audience as well.

But David also knew it wasn't a good idea to just turn down an important jazz impresario like George Wein. So he came up with an idea. "Let's make a proposal that George will never agree to," David said. "That way we're not the ones saying no. He is."

David knew that George had wanted to feature a tribute to Miles Davis for that year's festival, but that after some hemming and hawing, Miles had decided he didn't want to do it. So David called George and said, "Why not do a Herbie Hancock retrospective?" He proposed covering the three major phases of my career: the Miles Davis Quintet, Mwandishi, and the Headhunters.

George was bound to say no to that. He'd never done retrospectives on any jazz artists before, not Duke Ellington or John Coltrane or Charlie Parker or Miles, so why would he agree to do one for me? I was still in my thirties, so my body of work wasn't nearly as expansive as that of many other artists.

The only problem was, George said yes. He got really excited, especially about the idea of having three separate bands appear at the retrospective. The first would be a reunion of the Miles Davis Quintet, the second would be a reunion of Mwandishi, and the third would be the Headhunters. These three bands were so different, it would be a feat just to get them onstage, with all their different lineups, instrumentation, and styles.

I knew we could get the guys from Mwandishi, and of course the Headhunters were ready to play. But the question was, would Miles agree to participate? I decided to ask him first, before the other guys in the quintet, knowing that if he consented, this reunion would be a truly incredible night of jazz for everybody involved.

I called Miles and told him about the retrospective, and I asked him if he'd be willing to play with the quintet onstage. And to my surprise, he actually said yes. I think he was excited about the prospect of playing with Wayne, Ron, and Tony again. Once Miles agreed, I approached the other guys, and of course they all signed on. But somehow I already had a feeling that this might be too good to be true. I told the guys, "You know, Miles might change his mind, so I can't vouch for whether he'll go through with this or not." They each said they'd do it regardless, but I really did hope Miles would do it.

After I got the other guys on board, I called Miles back to reconfirm.

"Herrrrbie," he said, "I've been thinking. What would that be like, me playing for my own sideman? You were my sideman, and now I'm going to come be yours?" As much as he might have liked to play with everybody, doing it as part of a Herbie Hancock retrospective just didn't feel right to him.

"Okay, Miles," I told him. I was disappointed, but I understood. And I already knew whom to ask to take his place: Freddie Hubbard. Freddie was not only a great trumpet player, one of very few who were capable of stepping into what had been Miles Davis's place on a stage, but he and I also had a long history together. Freddie had played on many of my Blue Note records, including my very first one in 1962, *Takin' Off.* He had helped establish my career, so it felt right to invite him to play with us—and not just be a substitute for Miles.

Without Miles, we obviously couldn't call the group the Miles Davis Quintet. But what *should* we call it? After tossing around a bunch of different possibilities, we came up with V.S.O.P. I've always loved titles with double meanings, and V.S.O.P. had two that were perfect. First, it's a grade of cognac (Very Superior Old Pale), which is a brandy that has been aged a certain length of time. The more the cognac ages, the better it tastes—which is the perfect metaphor for an artist's retrospective. I was only thirty-six that summer, which is not really that old when you look at it now. But I had been around for a while, and so I liked the idea of improving with age.

And V.S.O.P. could also stand for Very Special Onetime Performance, which is what this particular reunion was intended to be. When I managed to pull together the guys from the quintet, I thought, *Let's make this special, a onetime thing—either you saw it or you didn't, but either way it will never happen again.*

So now we had our lineup for Newport: V.S.O.P., Mwandishi, and then the Headhunters. And that's when I started to realize how incredibly difficult it was going to be to do this concert. Three bands, three rehearsals, three set changes . . . and each band's style was light-years away from the others'. It wasn't difficult for me to play acoustic jazz or hard bop or fusion or funk. But to do one right after the other, with different lineups and almost no time to recalibrate my brain between performances? This was going to be an adventure.

In fact, it turned out to be the hardest concert I ever played. I was sweating my ass off, trying to focus on whatever style we were playing, and then, between sets, making sure we had the right personnel and equipment up on the stage. We had less than twenty minutes between each band's appearance, which really isn't much time to wrap your brain around the shift from something like "Maiden Voyage" to Mwandishi's far-out space music.

With V.S.O.P. we fell right back into the groove of playing together. But trying to re-create the magic of Mwandishi was pretty much impossible. When that band was still together, we were incredibly attuned to each other both onstage and off. But there was no way we could instantly recapture that synchronicity. It was like asking a group of circus performers who hadn't practiced in a year to suddenly do a trapeze act; where we used to be able to catch each other effortlessly, we were now just trying hard not to crash to the ground. Here's how Buster remembers it:

> We got together to rehearse the Mwandishi band. It was fun, nothing but laughing and talking, telling stories and reminiscing and hugging. And then we tried to play some music.
>
> Trying to re-create what we had in that band was the most difficult thing I had ever done. It was almost impossible. We had some flashes, and there were a few moments of brilliance, but I don't think any of us were satisfied at the end of that performance.
>
> You know, it's like trying to re-create the first time you had a climax. It's never the same! But that's what we were trying to do. I think that performance made us all know that Mwandishi was a moment in time that was a treasure, something to be revered, not messed with. Let's use it as a spiritual impetus for us to go on,

go forward, and create beauty, but that particular thing just couldn't be done again.

Of the three groups that played, the one that got the most attention was V.S.O.P. People hadn't heard that sound since we'd played with Miles, and they just went crazy. A lot of the jazz players from the sixties, including Tony and Wayne and Ron, had gone on to form fusion bands, so there were fewer major groups around playing pure, top-level acoustic jazz. The serious jazz fans at Newport just ate it up.

So many people loved it that we started getting interest from promoters about taking that quintet on the road. And I thought, *Well, why not?* We could go on a onetime V.S.O.P. tour, right? If it was only a single tour, it would still be a Very Special Onetime Performance— an exclusive event for jazz lovers. So that's what we did.

We toured all over Europe, and thousands of jazz fans turned out. People were just really excited to hear this style of music again, and the five of us were loving playing it. As much as I wanted to explore electronic music, I was enjoying playing a completely different style of music with V.S.O.P.

In fact, we were all having so much fun, we eventually gave in and decided that V.S.O.P. wasn't going to be a onetime thing after all. We kept touring throughout the next few years, even as I continued to delve deeper into electronic music with the Headhunters. I was still really focused on the future of music, but I decided it wouldn't hurt to dive back into the past in a new, more seasoned way. It somehow made the past become new again.

Along those same lines, Chick Corea and I decided to do a tour together in 1977, just two guys and two acoustic pianos. I had known Chick for years, and of course he was the pianist I replaced briefly in Mongo Santamaria's band, and who later replaced me in the Miles Davis Quintet. Chick and I had a lot of the same influences, and I loved his style, but at first I wasn't sure whether our two-piano collaboration would work out. There was only one way to find out, and that was for us to get together and see whether we could make the magic happen.

At the time Chick was living in the Los Feliz neighborhood of Los Angeles, in a home that had two grand pianos. I drove to his house one afternoon, and at first we just sat and talked about what pieces we might like to play together. After a while we finally took our seats at the pianos, and Chick counted off a tune we both knew. I don't remember what song it was, but it was something easy, so we could just fool around a little bit and see how things went.

We began by being very polite to each other—I didn't want to get in his way, and he didn't want to get in mine. But little by little we started warming up, taking it to the next level. And about five minutes in we were just flying all over the place, playing off each other and having a great time. And then we picked another tune, and we started to improvise an intro, just vibing off each other, and we both started cracking up. We were laughing, playing back and forth, and about halfway through that song we stopped and I said, "Okay, this is not going to be a problem."

We started to make a list of songs for the tour, but neither of us actually knew any of the other's songs. Chick and I were both composers and bandleaders, which meant we did our own stuff. So that first list had songs like a piece from Bartók's *Mikrokosmos* and the standard "Someday My Prince Will Come." We worked up a few numbers, but for the rest we decided to more or less wing it, wanting to save some of the improvisatory fun for the audience.

The great thing about Chick's playing is how whimsical and loose it is. There's a real playfulness to him that shines through in his music, and the titles of his pieces often refer to fantasy and whimsy. Those qualities shine through in his personality, too, which made touring and playing with him a joy. He's very open to everything, and he has a spiritual side, too, having been a Scientologist for many years.

And as much as he and I enjoyed playing together, the audiences seemed to enjoy hearing us. We toured through seven countries, and the crowds really went nuts. I can remember performing five encores after our show in Montreux—and by the last encore we weren't even playing piano anymore, just standing up at the front of the stage, making sounds and faces at each other in a rhythmic way, riffing on the great chemistry we shared.

Touring with Chick and with V.S.O.P. was a fun and challenging acoustic complement to working with the Headhunters—but electronic music was where my heart was leading me. I couldn't wait to find out what was coming next.

CHAPTER SIXTEEN

My mother had tried to instill a love of classical music and culture in her kids, but that didn't mean she was stuck in the past. She considered herself progressive and open to new ideas, and despite the fact that she was in her sixties now, she wanted to be the hip mom.

My parents weren't exactly staunch Christians, and my mother only occasionally attended church. So when I told them that I was practicing Buddhism, she seemed intrigued and asked me several questions about it. My dad wasn't as interested—maybe he figured it was just a phase. It seemed as if everybody in America was exploring alternative religions in the '70s, from Scientology to Transcendental Meditation to the Moonies, and a lot of people would dabble in one thing or another and then move on.

But my mother saw that I had become a dedicated practitioner of Buddhism, so when I asked her if I could put an altar and my Gohonzon in their apartment when I came to town, she didn't hesitate. I noticed her watching me sometimes, so one day I just asked her, "Would you like to chant with me?" And she said yes.

After that we chanted together whenever I was in Chicago,

including Gongyo, a simple but profound ceremony performed twice a day, and before long she started chanting on her own. I'm always happy whenever anyone starts practicing Buddhism, but I was particularly pleased about my mother, who'd had such a hard time with her bipolar disorder over the years—not that we knew there was a name for her mood swings. No one had thought her behavior was caused by an actual illness, because that just wasn't part of the vocabulary. But sometime in the late 1970s she was finally diagnosed as suffering from manic depression, as it was then called. She started taking medication, and although that helped, she was still having trouble with her moods.

It was my sister, Jean, who recognized that my mother's condition seemed worse when she was at home in Chicago. Jean had recently moved to Los Angeles, and she asked me, "What if Mom moves out to L.A. for a while and sees a psychiatrist here?" Our hope was that spending some time on her own, in addition to psychiatric care, might improve her condition. So my mom packed some clothes and came out to L.A. for what we thought might be a six-month stay. While she was here, she and I chanted together, and she got connected to the community of SGI Buddhists in L.A. I was really happy about this development, but my sister wasn't as enthusiastic.

In fact, Jean had a pretty negative attitude about my practice of Buddhism. We had gotten along well as kids, apart from the occasional squabble, but as we got older we seemed to get into arguments more often. Like my mother, my sister knew how to cut with her words, and she wasn't afraid to do so. She didn't object to Buddhism itself, but she had an attitude about the fact that I was practicing it. "You call yourself a Buddhist," she'd snap at me, "but you behave like you're the only person in the world."

My sister seemed to have complicated feelings about me, and in particular about my success. Maybe she felt that things had come too easily for me; I'm not sure. But I know that things definitely hadn't come easily for her. She was a brilliant young black woman in a world that didn't appreciate either her race or her gender.

Jean was the smartest person I ever met, but she had to fight for every ounce of respect she got. After leaving American Airlines, she'd taken a job working for IBM in the San Francisco Bay Area, and she was actually one of three women who developed IBM's first automated teller machine. This was a top-secret project while she was working on it, but even after ATMs were being installed on every street corner, she still never got credit for it.

She had an engineer's mind, as I do, and she got good jobs working in data processing and programming. But she really wanted to be a singer. And that was the other thing that caused strife between us: Jean felt I wasn't supportive of her dream to sing professionally.

Jean respected me as a musician and wanted my approval of her musical ambitions. Maybe she even hoped I would help her get a leg up in the music business. But I had been around some of the best singers in the world, and even though Jean had a nice voice, her pitch control wasn't the greatest, and I couldn't ignore that. So I didn't take the steps she apparently had hoped I would take, and consequently her feelings were hurt.

At some point in the late 1970s Jean got frustrated that I hadn't done more to help her. Whenever she would ask, I would kind of hem and haw, but finally she backed me against a wall. "Herbie, tell me the truth," she said. "Do you think I can ever make a career out of singing?"

I tried to be diplomatic, saying that as a pianist I wasn't a good judge of vocal ability. But my sister was too smart, and too good of a debater, to let me get away with that. "Simple question, Herbie," she said. "Yes or no."

So I told her the truth. "No," I said. "I don't think so." She looked as if she'd been slapped in the face. I wished the conversation could have gone another way, but that was how I felt, and I wasn't going to lie to her—I've never felt comfortable lying. But Jean was very, very hurt by my reply. I think she just felt completely cut down, and she never asked me about singing again.

When I think about that conversation now, I wish I hadn't been so blunt. There are plenty of singers who know how to deliver a song, even if their pitch isn't the greatest. Jean was a good singer, and she had a lot of heart, so who was I to say she couldn't do it professionally? She might have ultimately found that out for herself, but that would have been a whole lot better than her feeling that her brother had cut down her dream. I'm not the kind of person who spends time regretting, and I understand why I answered her the way I did. But I wish I could have found a way to respond that hadn't hurt her so much.

My sister did end up finding her place in music, but not as a singer: She wrote songs that were recorded by Earth Wind & Fire, Booker T. & the MGs, and Nnenna Freelon. She also wrote lyrics for some of my songs. But our relationship was never the same after that conversation. I honestly didn't spend a lot of time thinking about it, because I figured things would just play themselves out over time. Neither of us could have known it, but Jean didn't have much time left.

In the years since I started practicing Buddhism, I've come to certain realizations about myself. One is that in my life I've had a tendency toward selfish behavior. I didn't want to lie to Jean because I felt that it wasn't the right thing to do, but in protecting my own needs, I hurt her. I didn't have to be so rigid in judging her abilities—she would have loved it if I had found a way to encourage her efforts. Instead, I did what I felt I needed to do, but it was primarily, if unconsciously, for my own sake.

A few years after that conversation with Jean, my mother came with me to a Buddhist meeting. At these gatherings people would often stand up and speak about an experience they'd had, or a lesson they'd learned as a result of their Buddhist practice. I stood up and talked about discovering that there was a deep-seated selfish nature in me, which I hadn't been aware of until my practice of Buddhism revealed it to me. And you know, most of the people there said things like "Really, Herbie? You don't seem selfish." They were all very supportive.

But out of the corner of my eye I could see my mother nodding her head. She knew it was true.

As human beings we are often good at hiding, or not recognizing, our weaknesses. But my mother knew me better than anybody, and she confirmed what I suspected about myself. Ever since then that tendency toward selfishness is something I've tried to be aware of and to overcome.

I should add one more thing about that conversation with my sister. Ironically, around the same time I was telling her I didn't think she could make it as a singer, I was about to become a lead vocalist myself. I wasn't really a professional-quality singer, either—but a new piece of equipment would make it possible for me to sing lead. It would also take me another step further into electronic music.

||||||||||

One day in 1977 I looked around my studio and realized I had a problem. I called in Bryan Bell and said, "Man, we have to do something!" I had at least twenty-five synthesizers and so many keyboards that they were stacked together on their sides like planks.

Bryan just looked around the room and exhaled a big sigh. He knew what I was about to say.

"I want to have a setup where I can play any synthesizer in this room—with just three keyboards," I told him. This had never been done before; normally you'd need more keyboards, because they weren't equipped to switch back and forth easily among multiple synthesizers.

Now, the interesting thing about Bryan was, he never said, "This can't be done," when I asked him to do something. He might dampen my enthusiasm by saying, "Okay, but it will take two years and four million dollars," but he knew that if he simply told me something wasn't possible, I wouldn't let it rest. It's my Buddhist nature—if somebody tells me, "This has never been done before, and it may be impossible," my first response is to say, "Well, then, there's a perfect opportunity for victory!" Buddhism is about finding ways to turn obstacles to your advantage. As Bryan liked to joke, "There are no excuses when you have a Buddhist boss."

Bryan needed help figuring this one out, so he called a high school friend of his named Keith Lofstrom. Keith is a computer genius, the kind of guy who builds his own computer chips and rewrites operating systems for fun. He didn't learn to drive a car until he was in his thirties, but he got his pilot's license at fifteen, because planes are cooler than cars. Keith is an interesting cat, and he has a brilliant technical mind.

With Keith's help, Bryan figured out how to build a matrix of three keyboards, with a manual patch bay, that could control all the synthesizers I had. But in order for this to work, all the equipment had to be in an open-standards architecture, which meant we could plug different brands into each other and they would communicate. We thought this was brilliant, but not everybody liked the idea—particularly the synthesizer manufacturers. Open standards was an idea before its time, and companies had no interest in sharing technologies.

Bryan found this out quickly when he made a couple of calls to synthesizer companies to explain what we were doing:

> I call up Bob Moog, and I say, "Hey, Bob, this is Bryan from Herbie Hancock." And he says, "Oh, yeah, I love Herbie Hancock! How you doing? What are you up to?"
>
> And I say, "Well, I'm going to hook my Moog into my Oberheim so Herbie can have the perfect sound." And Bob goes, "Hmph, just buy more Moogs," and hangs up on me. Which was unlike Bob, who in the past had always been very supportive.

This was not my idea of openness, right? And so I call Tom Oberheim, the inventor of the Oberheim synthesizer. And I say, "Hey, Tom, how are you doing?" He says, "Hey, what are you up to?" I say, "I'm working for Herbie Hancock." And he says, "Oh, I love what Herbie and Joe Zawinul do with my instruments. What's up?" I tell him, "I want to hook up my Moog into my Oberheim so Herbie can have the perfect sound."

And Tom says, "I will void your warranty if you do that."

And this gave us great pause, because these were $10,000 synthesizers that were just two weeks old. You've got to be very serious if you're going to take the risk of drilling into them, knowing you don't have a warranty. But that was the synthesizer manufacturers' attitude at the time—they just didn't get it.

Warranty or no warranty, we had to try this, so we went ahead and made the modifications. And finally I was able to play multiple synthesizers without having to be surrounded by multiple keyboards. I mean, if you look at the back cover of the *Sunlight* album, there's a picture of me surrounded by eleven keyboards. That's a lot for a guy with only two hands! But step by step we were using new technology to streamline the way I made music.

||||||||||

A few months after that I saw an ad in a keyboard magazine for a piece of equipment I'd never tried before. It was called a vocoder, which was shorthand for "voice encoder." Originally developed in the 1920s and 1930s for scrambling and encoding speech communications, the vocoder was later picked up by musicians and vocalists because it could make other sounds mimic the human voice. The ad announced that the Sennheiser company was putting on a demo in a studio in L.A. for anybody who was interested.

I called David Rubinson and said, "Let's check this out." I wasn't aware of this at the time, but a few bands had started experimenting with vocoders, including Kraftwerk, the Alan Parsons Project, and Pink Floyd, though for the most part they used it for background vocal effects. I had written some lyrics for a new song, and I wondered whether we could program the vocoder for lead vocals. It wasn't really intended for that kind of use, so nobody had done it before—which is of course why I wanted to do it. I always wanted to be the first to try something new.

We went to the demo, and I got so excited by the possibilities that I bought one on the spot. This was a leap of faith, because those Sennheiser vocoders cost about $10,000, which was a small fortune in 1978. And if I was really serious about integrating it into my music, I'd have to buy two, to have a backup in case something went wrong with one on the road.

The vocoder was essentially a black box with rows of knobs and inputs where I could plug in my synthesizers, keyboards, and microphones. I brought it into the studio and handed it to Bryan Bell. "I want to use this for lead vocals," I told him. "Can we do that?" I knew it wouldn't be as easy as plugging a microphone into the box, but I wasn't sure exactly how complicated it would be.

Bryan went to work on the problem with David Rubinson's engineer, Fred Catero, an amazing producer and recording engineer who had worked with everybody from Janis Joplin to Santana to Sly Stone. He'd also engineered *Mwandishi, Crossings, Sextant,* and *Head Hunters* for me, among many other records. Fred was brilliant in the studio, and I knew that if anyone could figure this thing out, Fred and Bryan could.

For two weeks, night and day, they fiddled and tested, adding compression, white noise, and equalization to the microphone and synthesizer. They learned that the vibrato in a singing voice is actually three kinds of vibrato—the modulation of volume, pitch, and filter—all of which I would need to control on the synthesizer. It was like solving a complicated puzzle, but by the end of the second week they had managed to configure the vocoder to sound human enough for a lead vocal.

When they demonstrated the effect to me, I loved it. I'd written lyrics for only one song, but the vocoder just sounded so hip that I wanted to get lyrics for the other songs, too—to do a whole album with vocoder lead vocals. This was going to be cool.

In all the years I'd been performing onstage I was always hidden behind a piano or various keyboards. It was easy for a horn or guitar player to stand front and center, but drums and piano were always in the back or to the side. But now I would be singing lead in addition to playing synthesizer, so I said to Bryan, "I need to be up front."

This presented a whole new set of challenges, because keyboards weren't really portable at that time, so I had to be wherever they were—unless Bryan could figure out how to create a portable keyboard with its own vocoder switcher, so I could turn the effect on and off. It was a typical Bryan assignment: Hey, can you do the impossible? And can you have it finished in a couple of weeks?

Here's how Bryan remembers it:

> I told Herbie, "The only way you can be down front onstage is if we make a portable keyboard, and then we have to include all these special controls on it, to control and switch different vibratos."
>
> We had to be able to switch the signals for the vocoder from the portable keyboard, too, because Herbie had to use the microphone to talk to the audience. There was a mic-only mode and a synth-only mode, so he could solo the synthesizer parts, and then there was a vocoder mode, which took the mic and the synthesizer and put them into the vocoder.
>
> We had about four weeks. The record was done, the tour was booked, and it was "Oh, crap! Now we have to build the world's

first portable keyboard, which hasn't been done; build the first vocoder switcher, which hasn't been done; and by the way, while we're at it, put in a remote control for the switcher." We just threw in all the technology we could.

This was five years before MIDI [musical instrument digital interface, which revolutionized the world of music by enabling digital interconnection among equipment]. We were doing a lot of the basic architecture of MIDI from the beginning of Herbie's system, and it just kept getting deeper and deeper as we went.

Once Bryan figured out the vocoder and created a portable keyboard, there was another problem to sort out: If I was planning to move around between my keyboards and the front of the stage, where would my microphone be? Bryan took a headset microphone and attached it to my glasses using a wire tie, and then he used a wireless guitar transmitter for audio—and that's how he made one of the first wireless headset microphones ever used for lead vocals.

Like everything Bryan and I developed, these were brand-new technologies. We could have tried to patent or sell them, but that's not why we were inventing things—we just wanted to find new ways to create cool sounds and play them seamlessly onstage. Both Bryan and I were happy to share these breakthroughs, and we were also happy to switch as soon as somebody else created something better. Here's how Bryan describes it:

> As soon as a portable keyboard came out that was made of fiberglass instead of wood, or that used a five-conductor cord instead of a fifty-conductor cable, we went, "Hallelujah! This is groovy! I can get rid of mine and have this, which is faster or lighter or more ergonomic." Anytime there was a new commercial product that was better than our custom one, we just took our stuff out of service and moved on.

I was always putting Bryan under crazy deadlines, but he managed to figure out all these modifications just in time for our European tour in 1978, in support of the new record, *Sunlight*. I couldn't wait to try them out.

For the first time I was front and center in shows—and I loved it! Suddenly I was up there like a rock star, playing my portable keyboard and singing lead. And particularly during our shows in the United Kingdom there always seemed to be beautiful girls in the front row, dancing and singing along. The single "I Thought It Was You" didn't make much of a ripple in America, but it was a hit in Britain, and everybody at the shows seemed to know the lyrics. I'd be singing, *Just a glance from behind / happened by chance or design,* and I'd look out and see half the audience singing along. Of all the records I'd done, this was the first where most of the songs had lyrics, and performing them onstage was unlike anything I'd ever experienced before.

The funny thing was, as much as the English audiences loved *Sunlight,* the audiences in Germany hated it even more. They apparently still wanted Herbie Hancock, acoustic piano player, but instead there I was with my portable synthesizer, singing some disco-inflected songs through this strange device, making electronic music that bore almost no resemblance to jazz as far as they were concerned. The Germans went crazy, booing and sometimes walking out.

Those audiences seemed to believe that the artist should be doing whatever *they* wanted him to do, even if it meant staying stuck in the past. But there was so much new and exciting electronic technology— and so much more on the way—that there was only one way to go, as far as I was concerned: into the future.

|||||||||||

In 1979 Bryan and I decided it was time to get a personal computer. We knew everything was moving to digital, and this was the logical next step, but PCs were so new that we didn't know much about the various brands. So Bryan called his friend Keith Lofstrom again, to ask his opinion.

"What should we get," he asked Keith, "a Commodore Pet, a TRS-80, or an Apple II?"

Keith said, "Get the Apple II. They've got the interface figured out, and it's open architecture—they have slots, so you can make your own stuff." He also told us that Apple was about to release its Apple II+, which had a whopping 48 kilobytes of memory, up from 32K in the Apple II.

So Bryan and I got in the Cobra, drove down to a little mom-and-pop place in Santa Monica, and bought two Apple II+ computers, which basically looked like flat beige typewriters. One was for us, and one was for Fred Catero, who'd handed me his credit card and said, "Herbie, whatever you're getting is cool, so get me one, too."

I was excited to see what we could do with our new Apple II+, but first Bryan wanted to show me something that had nothing to do with music. At the store he'd also bought me a 100-baud modem, and when we got back to the studio, he hooked everything up: the modem, the computer, a TV monitor, and a telephone line. The modem came with a subscription to something called The Source, so Bryan dialed up, using the modem, and connected to the service.

"Okay, now what?" I asked, looking at the black screen with some glowing numbers and letters. Bryan started flipping through the booklet to figure out how we could connect to the "chat" function.

He started reading off instructions to me, and I typed in commands until we somehow got connected with another user. I typed "Hi," on the screen, and whoever it was typed "Hi" back.

I typed, "We just got an Apple II! This is my first time chatting." And whoever it was typed back, "Congratulations! My name is Fritz."

This was cool! I had no idea who or where this guy Fritz was, but here we were, just chatting with each other over our computers. What an amazing invention! We kept typing, this slow back-and-forth of green letters on a black screen, and Fritz asked me what I did for a living. I typed that I was a piano player. "Do you have any records?" he asked. I typed, "Yes, about twenty of them. What do you do?"

He wrote, "I make beer. Kind of like you with your records—I make a lot of beer." And then he typed, "Actually, I'm the owner of the Anchor Brewing Company."

Wow! This blew my mind, that the owner of Anchor Steam beer and I could randomly meet over the computer. The idea that he was up in San Francisco, typing away, and I was sitting in my studio in L.A., and we were getting to know each other—it was like science fiction. I was laughing at how amazing it was, but pretty soon Bryan got a serious look on his face. He said, "Oh, my god, Herbie—if recording is going to be all digital, and we can communicate digitally by computers, you know what that means? It means one day we'll be able to sell music over our computers." This was in 1979! But Bryan saw it as clear as day, even then.

That was a long way in the future, of course—because as advanced as these new computers were, they were still pretty primitive. Floppy discs were available only as an external accessory, if at all, so some of the first personal computers had no storage device save for the small internal memory. If you wanted to buy a program, you had to order it by mail, and digital data was usually stored on cassette tapes. You had to hook up a cassette player to your computer and play tapes to transfer information. And you'd better have a pretty high-quality player, because otherwise the data might be compromised.

After Bryan and I had fiddled around on The Source for a while, we turned to the big question: How could we use this new machine to make music?

At first I thought I would use it mainly to write music. The computer had audio, so I thought I could develop different sounds and then play them back. Beyond that, I wasn't really sure what to do with it. We knew the Apple II+ had lots of capabilities, but computers hadn't really been used for making music before, so we'd be making stuff up on the fly. And neither of us knew how to speak the computer's language, Applesoft BASIC. But Apple had included a programming manual with the computer, so Bryan decided to teach himself.

He created a piece of software called Cosmic Keyboards, which created pages for each song that we could store on the computer: a page for lyrics; one for chords; one naming all the instruments used, how they should be hooked up, what cables they needed, what the settings were, what programs they used. His goal was to create a computer-based system for tracking all the data for each song, complete with diagrams. Nothing like that existed yet.

But that was only the first step—Bryan had much more ambitious plans. He felt that all the automated parts of our setup were too slow, so he actually started thinking he would build his own 16-bit master computer, just to speed up our processing. The Apple II+ would still be the terminal, but Bryan wanted to build a program that would enable us to do more things in less time.

I thought he was crazy. "Bryan, you've never even written code for the Apple II," I reminded him.

"Well, I have this book," he said. "I'll learn how." He'd bury his head in the programming book and then start typing things in, essentially hacking this brand-new Apple II+. We'd be in the recording studio, and he'd disappear in between takes to mess around with his programming, with his Applesoft BASIC book open at his side.

Bryan was fearless, making stuff up as he went along. He not only built that 16-bit master computer, he also added the first disc drive on a synthesizer keyboard and, with Keith Lofstrom, built the first automated patch bay for music. His inventions and modifications helped me write more music than I ever had before, and between 1979 and 1981 I released six albums: *Directstep, The Piano, Feets Don't Fail Me Now, Monster, Mr. Hands,* and *Magic Windows.*

Most of our technical advances were used for the Headhunters, since V.S.O.P. and my duets with Chick Corea were entirely acoustic. But it was at a V.S.O.P. show in Japan in 1979 where we saw the next great vision of where music technology was heading.

I was still touring with V.S.O.P. in between Headhunters tours, and the band was particularly popular in Japan. Wayne, Ron, Tony, Freddie, and I went on tour there in 1979, and as we were setting up to play and record a live album at Denen Coliseum in Tokyo, the great Sony recording engineer Tomo Suzuki came up to talk to me. "We have a top-secret product that we are revealing for you today," he said. And he showed me a little box with a three-inch silver disc.

"What does it do?" I asked.

He said, "It plays back digital audio." Now, I hadn't seen digital audio recording since being shown the Dynabook three years earlier, so this certainly got my attention. He said, "Herbie, we are going to record your concert today with a digital device, instead of audiotape. Then we're going to make something called a mini-compact disc." This was Sony's music product of the future, intended to replace vinyl albums and cassette tapes, and we were getting a first glimpse of it.

Sony knew I was an electronics guy, so they wanted to give me the honor of being the first concert they recorded on this new technology. CDs as we know them didn't come out commercially until early 1985, so nobody knew yet what Sony was up to, which meant that Bryan and I were once again witness to a pivotal moment in the history of technology. But even though we didn't have to promise not to tell anybody about it for five years, I'm not sure people would have believed us anyway. That's how fast everything was moving.

CHAPTER

SEVENTEEN

I n the late 1970s, as equipment got better and more advanced, Stevie Wonder and I got into a little competition. We'd see a prototype for a new kind of synthesizer, and we'd both tell the manufacturer, "I'll buy two right now if you'll give me Serial No. 1!" Each of us wanted to be the first guy to own whatever cool new thing was coming down the pike. I always bought two, to have a spare on the road, and Stevie bought two because he was building a museum-worthy collection.

In 1979 an Australian company called Fairlight put out a new kind of synthesizer, one you played by drawing waveforms on a screen with a light pen. I read about it in a keyboard magazine, and that light pen sounded like the coolest thing around, so I got in touch with the company and asked if I could see a demo. Fairlight had just one rep in the United States, and he was in Pennsylvania. He was scheduled to come to L.A. to show it to Stevie Wonder, but I convinced him to come to my house first.

These synthesizers cost around $25,000 each, which was beyond my price range, but I knew a couple of other guys who might be interested. I invited Quincy Jones and Geordie Hormel over to watch the demo with me. By 1979 Quincy was already a legend. He'd been nominated four times for an Academy Award, had won five Grammys, and had just won an Emmy for his work on the miniseries *Roots*. Geordie was an heir to the Hormel Foods fortune, and his passion was composing music. He owned a recording studio and had written music for such TV shows as *Lassie, The Fugitive,* and *The Adventures of Rin Tin Tin.*

The rep showed up at my house in a Winnebago van that had synthesizers set up inside, so we stretched extension cords into my house to power them. When he showed us how they worked, I was mesmerized. The notion of drawing directly onto a screen, rather than flipping switches and patching in cords, was a radical idea at that time. With the Fairlight light pen you could draw a line where the horizontal axis was for pitch and a vertical for volume, but then you had to type in some technical wording to set the tempo. It was fascinating to watch, though not exactly what you'd call user-friendly just yet.

When the demo was finished, Quincy asked, "So how much are these things?" The rep told him the price, and Quincy just smiled and shook his head. But Geordie, who looked like a hippie with his long hair and granny glasses, reached into the pocket of his overalls and took out a wad of cash. "I'll take two," he said. I thought that rep's eyes were going to pop out of his head.

I didn't buy a Fairlight that day, but eventually I got two of them. My arsenal of electronic instruments just kept growing, and with computers now in the mix, the possibilities of how to make music seemed limitless. The first record we made after I got the Apple II+ was *Monster;* here's the listing in *Monster's* liner notes of what instruments I played:

Herbie Hancock: piano, E-MU Polyphonic keyboard, Clavitar, Waves Minimoog, Prophet-5, Oberheim 8 Voice, Yamaha CS-80, ARP 2600, Hohner D6 Clavinet, Rhodes 88 Suitcase piano, Steiner EVI, Sennheiser Vocoder, WLM Organ, Linn-Moffett Drum, Modified Apple II Plus Microcomputer, Roland CR-70.

To anybody not familiar with electronic music, this must just look like alphabet soup. The fact that I was playing so many different kinds of electronic instruments definitely irritated some jazz purists, who didn't like that I was moving further and further away from classic jazz. They feared that with so many musicians branching out into fusion and other genres, classic jazz was in danger of dying out. After all, if even the guys who had played with Miles Davis—Ron Carter, Tony Williams, Wayne Shorter, me—were moving away from traditional forms of jazz, what hope was there for the genre? Even Miles himself was moving away from that sound, pushing further into jazz-rock fusion. So, despite the fact that I was continuing to play acoustic music with V.S.O.P., people were still getting worked up over the Headhunters, electronic music, and the supposed death of jazz.

One of the most vocal critics was someone I started touring with in 1981—a guy who, at the tender age of nineteen, had bestowed upon himself the mission of saving jazz.

||||||||||||

Ever since the Newport retrospective in 1976, I had been touring off and on with V.S.O.P. The lineup had stayed the same—Tony, Ron, Wayne, Freddie Hubbard, and me. But I'd started getting frustrated with Freddie. He was a brilliant trumpet player, but he functioned on his own timetable, and more than once he came to shows so late that he left the rest of us hanging. As I said, I'm a guy who runs late a lot of the time myself, so if I was noticing it, it was *bad*.

Once, in Cleveland, Freddie was so late that he actually had to get a police escort to race from the airport to the venue. He came rolling in a couple of hours after our start time, but instead of apologizing, he seemed to have the attitude "Okay, I'm here now, so everything's cool." I'd known Freddie a long time, and we were good friends. But like me, he's an Aries, and Aries people have a hard time apologizing, always finding excuses for mistakes. I recognize that trait in myself, and I struggle with it. But Freddie had it down to a science, and he seemed to have no desire to change.

It got to the point where I didn't want to work with Freddie anymore, but we had a V.S.O.P. tour coming up, and I already knew Wayne Shorter couldn't come because of a prior commitment. When people are expecting a quintet, it might be okay to give them a quartet, but not a trio. I needed to find a replacement for one or both of those guys.

Right about that time I got a call from a Columbia A&R man named George Butler. "Herbie, we have this new artist we're excited about," he told me. "He's from New Orleans, a trumpet player, and he's just phenomenal. His name is Wynton Marsalis." Columbia was in the process of planning Wynton's first record, and they wanted me to work with him, since I had a track record of selling jazz albums as both a musician and a producer.

"I'll send you a recording he did with his teacher in New Orleans, a double trumpet concerto," George told me. "Give it a listen, and let me know what you think."

Well, I listened to that recording, and it about knocked me flat. How was a teenage kid playing like this? Wynton had amazing skills, well beyond his years. And that gave me an idea: Why not ask him to join Ron, Tony, and me for the V.S.O.P. tour? That way I could replace Freddie, Wynton would get some seasoning, and V.S.O.P. would get a little pop from having a trumpet prodigy on the road with us.

The only problem was, Wynton was pretty young for us to take him out on a tour like this. Ron, Tony, and I had been around the block a few times, and we knew each other really well. We were at a different stage of our careers, and our lives, than this young kid. Sure, it would be cool and interesting to play with Wynton, but did we really want to bring a teenager straight out of the gate on a multicountry tour?

Also, Ron in particular was really protective of V.S.O.P.'s legacy with Miles Davis. Whoever played trumpet with V.S.O.P. was literally stepping into Miles's shoes—was that something we should just hand over to a nineteen-year-old? Tony was less bothered by that, maybe because he had been just seventeen when he joined Miles. Ron had a point, but I thought that in trying to protect the legacy of the quintet, he might ultimately do more harm than good.

"Look, man," I said to him. "We can hold on to this and keep it for ourselves, but when we die, it will die along with us. Or we can share it with the younger generation, and they will carry it on beyond us." If jazz is about anything, it's about being open and sharing. We had been so lucky to play with Miles all those years, and Miles had generously shared his knowledge and experience with us. How could we now turn around and shut out another young player, refusing to share our knowledge and experience with him?

Ron understood, so even though he hadn't heard Wynton's recording, he said, "All right, Herbie. Let's bring him in."

Some young guys might have been intimidated, going on tour with players from Miles Davis's quintet. And because Wayne wasn't coming, Wynton would be the only horn, which was an even bigger responsibility. But from the very first show Wynton killed. He didn't seem nervous at all onstage, and the audiences loved him.

Wynton had grown up in New Orleans, and he had a little bit of the showman about him. He was a great player, but then he'd add flourishes to the ends of his solos, adding a little razzle-dazzle to garner applause. Ron, Tony, and I had come up with Miles, who never did that kind of thing, so we didn't love that part of Wynton's performing. I found myself wishing he would just play, but I figured that maybe he was nervous and he'd tone it down over time. So, as Miles had done with us, I never said anything directly to Wynton about his playing.

That said, Wynton, even at nineteen, was quick to criticize other musicians. Because he was so young he got a lot of attention and did a lot of interviews, and he was more than willing to share his negative opinions about some of the jazz greats who had come before him. I couldn't understand it—why would a celebrated young player feel the need to tear others down? But Wynton considered himself a jazz purist, and anybody who didn't meet his standards would feel the sting of his words.

A couple of times, after I heard about Wynton's harsh assessments of other players, I said to him, "What are you doing, man? Jazz music has a hard enough time finding an audience. We should be helping each other out, not tearing each other down." And Wynton would say, "Yeah, I know. I'm sorry! I got carried away." To hear him apologize afterward, you'd think he really just couldn't control his tongue. I heard that one time he called Miles to apologize for having criticized him in the press. Miles, who was so often gracious to younger players, said, "Oh, man, don't worry about that shit. I did the same thing to Dizzy." Miles was being kind to Wynton, because he had in fact never done that to Dizzy Gillespie.

A few years later, though, Wynton pushed Miles too far—and he did so in public, at the Vancouver International Jazz Festival. Miles came onstage with his band at the time, which was heavy into electric music. Right in the middle of their set, Wynton walked out onto the stage, trumpet in hand, completely uninvited. It looked like he wanted to challenge Miles to some kind of musical duel, but Miles wasn't having any of that. He tried to wave Wynton off, but when Wynton didn't leave, Miles stopped the band.

Wynton was an amazing player, but that kind of competitiveness was, to me, his weakness. From a very young age he behaved with a kind of entitlement, and he never seemed content to let players play and keep to his own business. He seemed driven to make comparisons all the time, to put down whoever wasn't playing at a level or in a style he approved of.

But we all have our weaknesses, and if I'm honest about it, I had some of the same failings Wynton did. I had been a jazz elitist for many years, turning my nose up at rock and pop music until Tony Williams and Miles taught me otherwise. I'd also turned my nose up at electric pianos until Miles taught me otherwise. Nobody's perfect, and it's certainly not fair for me to sit here and criticize a guy for criticizing other people.

The truth is, Wynton's positive contributions to jazz have far outweighed anything negative he's done. Wynton reenergized jazz for a lot of young musicians, and he's brought thousands of new fans to jazz through his talent and charisma. He co-founded Jazz at Lincoln Center, he created television and radio shows educating people about jazz, and he's even written books on the subject. He's full of positive energy for the music he loves, and he's doing more than just about anybody else to make sure it thrives.

When I think about why, with all that positive energy, Wynton might have felt the need to tear others down, I remember a strange incident that happened when we were on tour in Japan. It was the second V.S.O.P. tour with Wynton, and Wayne Shorter was able to come on this trip, so we had a full quintet. Late one night after a show, Wayne called me in my hotel room.

"Hey, Herbie," he said. "I think we should go to Wynton's room. Something strange is happening." I asked what was up, and Wayne just said, "He seems really depressed. I'm a little bit worried about him."

We went to Wynton's room and knocked on the door. He opened it to let us in, and I saw that his window was open. This was a little strange—you don't normally open a window in those high-rise hotels. I didn't say anything, though, and once we were in the room Wynton went over and sat on the windowsill.

"You okay?" I asked him. He didn't say anything at first, and he wouldn't look at me but just stared out the window for a bit. I wasn't sure what to do, but finally he spoke.

"I hear something in your playing, and Wayne's playing, and Ron's and Tony's—I hear something that I don't have," he said.

"Come on, man," I said. "What are you talking about?" I wasn't just trying to make him feel better—I genuinely believed that Wynton was a gifted trumpet player. What did he think we had that he didn't? I wanted to help him out of his funk, but I was also really curious.

"I just think something's missing in my playing," he said.

I thought about the fact that Wynton felt compelled to add those little razzle-dazzle moments onstage, and I wondered whether he did that to compensate for whatever deficit he felt he had. I wanted to ask him about that, but how could I? He and I had never had a conversation about those moments, because I hadn't wanted to step on his toes. Especially in a young player, you have to be really careful not to stifle creativity or style but encourage the person to just play. Wynton was obviously really down on himself, and I wanted to be careful not to make the situation worse.

"Wynton, I don't know what you're hearing," I told him. "But you're playing great. You're playing with heart." I urged him not to beat himself up and reminded him that none of us ever stopped trying to play better. In my head, though, I kept wondering—what was in this young man's life that made him so uncertain of himself? So uncertain, in fact, that he felt he had to tear down others to boost himself up?

I never did find out exactly what set Wynton off that night, because we never talked about it again. It was the only time I ever saw him express that kind of vulnerability, but I never forgot it.

There's one other story from that V.S.O.P. tour that's worth telling. Wynton had decided to bring his brother Branford to Japan. Branford was an up-and-coming saxophone player, but of course we had the great Wayne Shorter playing with us. We were scheduled to record a live album on that tour, and Wynton was pushing hard for us to include Branford on two songs on the record. He was the one who'd taught Branford how to play jazz, and he wanted to give him this opportunity.

Now, this was a pretty bold move, having the new guy in the band ask if his brother could replace one of the greatest saxophonists of all time, and not surprisingly some others in the band and crew thought this was a bad idea. *He won't be as good as Wayne! It's going to hurt the record! It's going to hurt Wayne's feelings!*

But when I went to Wayne to ask what he thought about it, he just chuckled.

"Okay, explain this to me one more time," he said. "There's Wynton's brother, who he loves, and Wynton wants to let him play. And I'll still get paid the same, and I still get my song on the record, and I don't have to work as much." Wayne just looked at me, deadpan. "Why does everybody think this is bad for me? I'm not getting it."

I laughed and said, "Well, because you're the sax player, and he's not."

"One more time," Wayne said, slowly. "Why is this bad for me?"

And that was quintessential Wayne Shorter. Branford ended up playing on two songs on that album, and Wayne just told him, "Have a great time! I'm here if you need me!" He was nothing but happy for Branford, who went on to launch a great jazz career of his own.

||||||||||

We had nicknamed Bryan Bell's friend Keith Lofstrom "The Universal Patch Cord," because he could plug anything into anything else and make it work. But Keith's wizardry extended beyond music. He designed and made computer chips at home, and wrote software and built hardware for all kinds of applications. To a gadget freak like me, Keith was a kind of superhero. So in early 1981, when Bryan told me, that Keith was on a team that was helping to design software for the brand-new space shuttle, *Columbia,* I flipped out.

Ever since I was a boy in Chicago I was fascinated by the idea of space travel. I may not have paid a lot of attention to the news when I was in New York in the sixties, but I definitely paid attention when Soviet and U.S. astronauts started going into orbit, and when Neil

Armstrong set foot on the moon in 1969 it blew my mind. The idea that now, with a space shuttle, we could just fly into space and then return? This was the future coming to life.

So when Bryan told me that Keith could get us passes to watch the first space shuttle launch in person, I was as excited as a little kid. I couldn't believe I was going to get to watch, close up, as this amazing vehicle soared into space. The launch was set for April 10, 1981, at Kennedy Space Center. Bryan and I flew to Florida together, and in the predawn hours we settled into the viewing area to watch history being made.

As the countdown was happening I could feel my heart pounding. But at about nine minutes to go something went wrong. We all held our breath, waiting for the launch, but after a while an announcement was made that the mission was being scrubbed. There was a timing discrepancy between the computers at Kennedy and in Houston, and even though it was a very tiny one, the computer engineers needed a day to correct it. So the launch was postponed two days, to April 12.

No biggie, I thought. We'll just stick around in Florida for a couple of days and watch the launch on the twelfth. Even better—April 12 was my birthday! What an amazing birthday gift this would be.

Except . . . *Oh, no!* I had completely forgotten that Gigi was planning a big party for me on that day. It was a Sunday, and she had pulled out all the stops, inviting a huge crowd of people to celebrate my forty-first birthday. Quincy Jones was coming, and Kareem Abdul-Jabbar, and Billy Dee Williams, and all my family and tons of musicians I'd played with over the years. Gigi had been organizing this event for months, and before Bryan and I left, she'd said, "Have fun, Herbie, but you'd better be back by Sunday."

I couldn't believe it. There was nothing I wanted to do more than watch the first space shuttle launch that day. I didn't care about celebrating my birthday! But I did care about Gigi, and I knew she'd be hurt if I didn't come home. More important, I knew she'd be angry, and she might take my head off. So reluctantly I flew back to L.A. on Saturday, so I'd be there for the party.

On Sunday the twelfth I turned on the TV and watched the launch, and I just felt sick to my stomach. But I also chanted that morning, and I looked for a way to find peace with the fact that I'd missed seeing it in person. This almost worked until I was actually at the party and I made the mistake of telling a few people I'd flown home rather than staying to watch the launch. "What the hell are you doing here?" my friends asked me. "Are you insane?" I felt about two inches tall. As grateful as I was to Gigi for loving me enough to have thrown me a wonderful party, I just couldn't get over missing that launch.

The shuttle was scheduled to be in orbit for two days, then land at Edwards Air Force Base in central California. Of course, nobody knew for sure what would actually happen when it reentered the atmosphere and landed, because this was the first time it had ever been tried. The day after the launch Bryan and I were in the recording studio, busy pretending we didn't mind the fact that we'd missed it, when all of a sudden I said, "Do you think those passes might work to get us in for the landing?" All of a sudden we were like a couple of kids again, hurrying to make plans to get to Edwards on April 14.

Keith Lofstrom was there for the landing, too, and he invited us to sit in the seats where members of his space club, L5, were sitting. But I walked up to a guard and said, "I'm Herbie Hancock, with Columbia"— Columbia Records, not Columbia TV and radio, but he didn't know that! Presumably thinking I was a reporter, the guard escorted us right down to the front row. After feeling so disappointed at missing the launch, I was really happy to see the landing, which happened as smooth as silk, right in front of me.

||||||||||

In late 1981, I noticed something strange going on with my left hand. My pinky finger was swelling up at the joint between my finger and palm, and it hurt whenever I'd hit the keys on the piano. For a while I tried to ignore it, but soon the swelling and pain were bad enough that I had to get it checked out because it was affecting my playing.

I went to an orthopedic hand specialist named Dr. Charles Lane, who I'd been told was the best in the business. As he poked and prodded my hand, he said, "It looks like you have a tumor in your finger." Well, that certainly got my attention. I was forty-one at the time, and cancer had been just about the furthest thing from my mind. "It doesn't act like a malignancy," Dr. Lane continued. "But we'll need to remove it surgically anyway, and then I'll have it examined."

Of all the places on a piano player's body where a tumor might appear, the finger is pretty much the worst option. While it might not be a big deal if you lose a little bit of nerve sensitivity in another part of the body, if you lose it in your fingers it can seriously hinder your playing ability.

I knew Dr. Lane was a very skilled surgeon, but it would be no easy feat to cut a tumor out of my little finger without damaging the nerves. As he explained to me, nerves also have tiny hairlike extensions that are numerous and difficult to see, and it was inevitable that he'd end up damaging or removing some of them during the process. The worry was that the damage would be extensive enough that the feeling in my finger would be impaired.

We scheduled the surgery to take place a couple of days later, and I began spending hours chanting in preparation. With the help of two friends, Susie Sempers and Kathy Lucien, I even chanted for ten hours straight in one stretch, with just a five-minute break every hour. Having Susie and Kathy chant with me helped give me strength, and when it came time for the procedure, I felt ready.

Dr. Lane had explained that this was an outpatient surgery, which meant I'd have just a local anesthesia and be awake the whole time. "Can I watch?" I asked him, half joking. I thought it would be interesting to see the process, but he just smiled and said, "No, Herbie. Because if you flinch at anything, you could lose the finger." The nurse put up a partition so I couldn't see what he was doing, and she gave me a sedative, which settled me. The ten hours of chanting made me feel confident and even, oddly, lighthearted, and before I knew it the procedure was over.

Normally, Dr. Lane would slice the skin down the finger in a straight line right across the middle of the joints—but because he was concerned that the healing process at the joints might make it difficult and painful to bend my finger to play the piano, he decided that day to do it a different way. He cut a zigzag W-like pattern from the top of my palm up through my little finger, the scalpel tracing a path through the edge rather than the center of each joint.

When the surgery was finished, he told me, "Herbie, I think this is the best of this type of procedure I've ever done." He said he'd taken out the tumor without too much nerve damage and would send it right away for a biopsy. In the meantime, he told me, "Sometime during the week, you should regain feeling in the finger." The nurse dressed my hand and I went home.

As he predicted, the tumor turned out to be benign, which was, of course, a huge relief. But a week after the surgery I still had no feeling in my little finger. I decided to give it more time, but at the end of the second week I still couldn't feel anything. Now I was getting really concerned. I called Dr. Lane and asked him, "When will the feeling come back?" He explained that while normally the feeling would have come back already, we still had every reason to believe it would— though he couldn't say when that might happen. "It's not within the realm of science for me to make that prediction," he said.

My finger still had the dressing on to protect it, so I really couldn't do anything but wait and chant. By the end of the third week, when it still had no feeling, I couldn't stand the waiting anymore. I carefully peeled off the dressing and sat down at the piano. I knew my little finger wasn't working—it wasn't even moving. I thought, *What if it never wakes up? What will it feel like to play with only nine fingers?*

Very gently, I started to play. And then something really strange happened. My ring finger started sliding over to play the notes my little finger would normally play! I wasn't doing this consciously—my ring finger just naturally compensated by playing the lower notes. It was an amazing thing to witness, but it didn't change the upsetting fact that my finger still wouldn't work.

At that moment I knew I needed to prepare myself for the possibility that I would never play with all ten fingers again. This was a sobering thought, but now I had my Actual Proof that I could do it. I had a gig coming up about a week later, the first since my surgery, so I decided to practice gently and play, even if I only had nine working fingers. I might as well get used to it.

The gig was an unusual one, a concert organized by the well-known jazz writer Conrad Silvert. Conrad was in his early thirties, but he'd been diagnosed with testicular cancer and knew he had only a short time to live. One of his dreams was to organize a concert featuring some of the greatest jazz players in the world, and because so many players loved and respected Conrad, he was able to book an incredible group. The concert was scheduled for February 22, 1982, at the War Memorial Opera House in San Francisco, and the featured musicians included Jaco Pastorius, Tony Williams, Bobby Hutcherson, Wayne Shorter, Wynton Marsalis, Pat Metheny, Sonny Rollins, and Carlos Santana.

The night before Conrad's concert, I sat down at the piano for the rehearsal . . . and just then I felt a tiny tingling at the base of my finger. I actually gasped. I wondered whether I was just imagining the feeling, but as I started to play the tingling became stronger. I could finally use my little finger, and by the end of the song the complete feeling was back. I could hardly believe the irony—that my own cancer scare would find its ultimate resolution in playing for a friend who was fighting cancer.

The concert the next night was amazing, with so many great musicians playing and the hall filled with emotion for Conrad. We played for three and a half hours, and by the end everybody was emotionally and physically spent. Conrad had given us all a rare and special night. He'd fulfilled his dream, and just a few weeks later he died at age thirty-four.

CHAPTER
EIGHTEEN

I n February of 1982 David Rubinson had a heart attack.
He was just thirty-nine at the time, and he'd always been healthy,
so this came as a real shock. David had been working long days and
nights, but he'd always done that without any problems. But now, after
bypass surgery, it was clear that he needed to slow down. There was no
way he could keep working in the studio the way he'd been doing, so
for the first time since 1970 I took on another producer for my next
record, *Lite Me Up*.

Yet David's health wasn't the only reason our producing partnership needed to end. David had done amazing work with me over the
years, staying with me every step of the way as my music morphed
from spaced-out Mwandishi to funky Headhunters to the throwback
sounds of V.S.O.P. Our collaboration had been incredibly fruitful. But
as I began to contemplate new directions in the '80s, our working relationship no longer felt productive.

One problem was that David lived in San Francisco, while I was
in L.A. This was pre–e-mail, pre-Skype, pre-everything except phones
and faxes. And even though we had always worked at this distance, it

was starting to wear on us. Too often, when we talked, we weren't communicating as we'd been able to in the past. And this was doubly frustrating now, because although David had always been supportive of changes in my musical direction, now he was questioning where I was going. I was pushing even further into electronic music, writing songs with more of a disco and R&B feel to them, and David had reservations about some of it.

In some ways, I did, too. I was forty-two now, and I knew better than to think that I had my finger on the pulse of new music. No matter how hip or connected a musician in his forties may feel, the truth is that cool new stuff usually comes from kids—teenagers and twenty-somethings. I didn't have a lot of people of that age in my circle of friends, so I wanted to find a way to tap into the younger generation's creativity.

That's when I met a guy named Tony Meilandt. Tony was the student concert producer at UC Berkeley, and he ran the Berkeley Jazz Festival. He was in his mid-twenties, very smart, and totally into music—especially jazz. When he moved down to L.A. after college, I knew I wanted to hook up with him. He was the kind of guy who could sniff out new music and new sounds, the people who were off the radar. He was young and hungry, and that was what I needed.

I hired Tony to co-produce *Lite Me Up,* and from the get-go he and David Rubinson did not get along. Tony felt that David didn't want him to get any credit, and David felt that Tony was a bad influence on my music and, to a certain extent, on me personally. This was the early '80s, and cocaine was rampant in the music scene, but for some reason David thought that Tony was supplying me with coke, or that I had started doing more of it once he'd come around. Neither of those things was true, but David's perception of the situation only added to the hostility between them.

For *Lite Me Up* I collaborated with Heatwave's Rod Temperton, who wrote most of the songs. I was excited to work with Rod, not only because he's a great guy but because he was a great songwriter and had written some monster hits for other artists, including "Off the Wall," "Thriller," and "Rock with You" for Michael Jackson. We also got the amazing recording engineer George Massenburg to work with us, so I had really high hopes for the album. Somehow, though, it didn't quite come together. I sang a couple of songs with vocoder, and even one without, but the record just didn't turn out the way I'd hoped. Rod wrote great material, but I didn't deliver it very well.

For my next record I wanted to find a bold and unexpected sound. But what was next on the horizon? I asked Tony to keep his ear to the ground, and I also started poking around myself, talking to younger musicians. One afternoon Tony said to me, "You know, there's a couple of guys in New York, Bill Laswell and Michael Beinhorn, who are doing some cutting-edge stuff." I hadn't heard of them, but Tony told me they worked as a team, under the name Material. Material had started in 1978 as a band, with Laswell on bass, Beinhorn on synthesizer, Martin Bisi as the engineer, and the fourteen-year-old whiz kid Fred Maher on drums. Now, in the early '80s, Material was also collaborating with other artists, creating electronic backdrops and funky beats.

New York had become the epicenter of a new genre of black music. In the city's streets and playgrounds, especially in the Bronx, people were exploring spoken-word poetry and sharp, percussive beats, combining them in a new musical form called rap. In 1979 the Sugarhill Gang released "Rapper's Delight," introducing this new style to a wider audience. But as a musical genre, rap was still in its infancy.

"If you let those guys do something for your next record, even if it's just on spec, I bet they'll come up with something cool," Tony told me. I thought that was a great idea, so Tony called them up and they said they'd prepare two song ideas for me, things they thought would be hip and new for my record. We agreed that they'd come out to L.A. the following week and show me what they'd been working on.

In the meantime, I decided to ask my godson, Krishna Booker, what he was listening to. Krishna's dad, Walter, was a jazz bassist with Cannonball Adderley's band, and Wayne Shorter was his uncle, so Krishna had grown up around jazz, but I knew he was into other genres of music, too. "Can you make a tape for me?" I asked him. "Just give me some stuff that you think I should be aware of, that younger people are listening to right now."

Two days later Krishna brought me a cassette. I couldn't wait to hear it, so I popped it right into a tape deck in my studio and sat back to listen. I don't remember everything that was on the tape, but one thing really struck me: a song called "Buffalo Gals" by the English artist Malcolm McLaren, the former manager of the New York Dolls and the Sex Pistols. McLaren had collaborated with a pair of DJs who called themselves the World's Famous Supreme Team, and on the record they created a rhythm by moving a vinyl record back and forth on a turntable, making a scratching sound with the needle.

Normally you'd never want to have a needle scratching across a vinyl record, because it just messes your record up. But this was fresh, the idea of creating a rhythm with that sound. Scratching sounded avant-garde, like the kinds of sound we were always seeking out during the Mwandishi days. Just as I had initially heard Buster's sister chanting as a mesmerizing potential song rhythm, now, ten years later, the scratching on "Buffalo Gals" affected me the same way.

Right then I knew I wanted to use scratching on my next record. Now I just had to wait and see what Bill Laswell and Michael Beinhorn were bringing me from New York, and hope that it sounded as innovative as what Malcolm McLaren was doing.

When Laswell and Beinhorn arrived, we settled into my home studio and I said, "All right, let's hear it." Laswell played the tape—and, wouldn't you know it, the sound of scratching started coming out of my speakers. I clapped my hands and said, "Yes! This is exactly what I want to do!" The guys had recorded an idea for a direction with scratching, drums, and a cool bass line. They'd already laid down the perfect foundation of a new song.

Laswell played the second idea they'd brought, and although it didn't have scratching, it was every bit as fresh as the first one. I had a big smile on my face as I listened, and when the tape ended, I looked at Laswell and Beinhorn and said, "Let's make a record together."

||||||||||

We used that first idea as a base for a new song, which we called "Rockit." I started building other instrumentation around it, and then we brought in the hot young New York turntablist who'd been on Laswell and Beinhorn's tape, DST, to add more of his scratching. What I didn't realize was that guys like DST (who later changed his name to DXT, in honor of Malcolm X) had already honed skills far beyond mere scratching. A lot of the sounds on the album that resulted from that collaboration, which we called *Future Shock,* came from DST and his turntable—not synthesizers, which was what most people thought.

This was a music revolution! Before Laswell, Beinhorn, and DST, I had been only dimly aware of what was happening in the Bronx. Now I was thrilled beyond words to be in the middle of it, working with guys who had skills I hadn't even imagined before. This music was exciting and unpredictable, because scratching lets you change direction suddenly, cutting to another sound or groove. It was totally avant-garde but within the popular-music context. Exploring all these new possibilities made me feel more energized than I had in years.

When we finished the first cut of "Rockit," Tony and I took it to David Rubinson. We played it for him, and he made a face like he'd eaten a lemon.

"Oh, man," he said. "Do you really want to do *this*? Come on—you're Herbie Hancock!" My mouth fell open. Here I thought this new direction was the hottest thing going in music, and I was lucky to be on board in its infancy. And David thought it was somehow . . . beneath me? I couldn't even get my head around that. I was disappointed that David and I were so far apart now on our musical vision, primarily because even though he wasn't producing my records anymore, he was still my manager—so I was really going to need him to support the new record.

But David wasn't the only one who had doubts. One day in the studio I played a couple of tracks for Bryan Bell. Bryan and I were coming to the end of our partnership, too, but he was still working with me as we were recording *Future Shock*.

When Bryan listened to the tracks, he said, "You know, Herbie, your fans might not like this."

I just shook my head, suddenly feeling very tired. "Bryan," I said, "I am so over this, I can't even tell you."

"What do you mean?" he asked.

"Listen, my mother is still mad that I left the symphony!" I said, throwing my hands in the air. "When I stopped playing classical music and went to jazz, I got crap for it. When I left jazz to do space music, I got crap for it. When I left space music to do funk, I got crap for it. And when I left funk to do what I'm doing now, I'm *still* getting crap for it.

"Everybody else is so concerned about what I'm doing, but I'm not doing it for them," I told him. "I'm doing this because I *have* to do this. If the fans come, great! If they don't come, it doesn't matter, because I *have* to do this—because I *want* to do this."

Twenty years had passed since I joined Miles Davis's quintet, and if I had spent my time paying attention to what other people wanted me to do, I would never have explored any other styles of music. Why was it so difficult for people to believe that a musician might want to venture into new music from an artistic standpoint rather than a financial one? I'm not saying I didn't want my records to sell—of course I did! I wanted my music to reach as many people as possible. But the difference is, I never chose what kind of music to make strictly for the goal of maximizing sales. I made the music my heart led me to make—and some records sold millions of copies, while some sold very few.

When we finished *Future Shock,* David Rubinson took it to the Columbia marketing executives. By now David was on board with the record, which was fortunate, because he knew he was going into the lion's den again. He had done this so many times, with so many of my records, and the response had often been the same: confusion and consternation. But was there a chance that this time the New York–based execs might see that this was an exciting new direction for music?

Here's how David describes the meeting:

Whenever we delivered a new record, I'd go to New York, assemble twenty people, have coffee and sandwiches, and play it loud. But this time the music was too revolutionary, so I played it for six people—the people who ran the marketing for Columbia.

It was on a cassette tape, and the first tune was "Rockit." It starts with that *whicka whicka whiiiiicka* of scratching—and as soon as that came on, one guy actually reached over and turned off the tape! "This is going to alienate all of Herbie's fans," the guy said. "This is going to kill his career."

I literally went to his side of the desk, opened the door, and threw him out of the room. I couldn't take it anymore. Tony Meilandt was sitting there, and the room just erupted—it was bedlam! I said, "Anybody else want to leave?" And then I played them the rest of the tape.

According to David, Columbia came very close to refusing to release *Future Shock.* They never said that to me, but they definitely didn't put it high on their priority list for marketing—and in fact, they declined to provide a budget for making a music video, which was becoming a cornerstone of how songs got promoted. MTV had launched in the summer of 1981, and millions of people were tuning in to watch videos of the latest songs. But Columbia told us that if we wanted to make a video, we were on our own.

||||||||||||

I had never done a music video before, but Tony Meilandt told me, "We need to make a great one." He absolutely loved "Rockit," and he believed it was going to be a big hit.

"Okay," I said. "So where do we start?" Tony told me about two guys who were making some of the most popular music videos on MTV, Kevin Godley and Lol Creme. Godley and Creme were English musicians who'd gotten their start in the rock band 10cc. In 1979, even before MTV, they'd started making music videos, first for their own songs and then for other artists.

"Which ones are theirs?" I asked Tony.

"They made two for the Police," he told me. " 'Wrapped Around Your Finger' and 'Every Breath You Take.' "

"Those are my two favorite videos!" I said. And it was true. I'd only recently started watching MTV after Jessica, who was now thirteen, turned me on to it. I mostly watched it to keep up with what was happening in rock and roll, which was a genre I didn't follow much otherwise. Music videos were in their infancy, so a lot of them were pretty rudimentary, but I had noticed that the Police were putting out visually sophisticated, really engaging videos.

If Godley and Creme were the guys behind those videos, then they were the guys I wanted. I asked Tony to send them a copy of "Rockit," and if they were into it, I would pay their fee myself. Fortunately they loved the song—but there was one more conversation we needed to have before I could set them loose to work their magic.

MTV had been on the air for nearly two years by that time, and people had noticed one glaring fact: The channel almost never showed any videos by nonwhite acts. In the year or so I had been watching the channel, the only video I'd seen by a black artist was Eddy Grant's "Electric Avenue." Years later some of MTV's early executives would say that the reason they didn't air videos by black artists was that the channel was based on Top 40 radio, which was almost all white acts back then. But whatever the reason, it was clear that, for a black artist, getting on MTV wouldn't be easy.

So I called Kevin Godley. "Listen," I said, "you have free rein to do whatever you want on this video. But I have just one request. I don't want it to look like a 'black guy' video. I want it to look like something that could have been made by Duran Duran or the Police." I knew that if we could get "Rockit" onto MTV, the song would find a whole new audience. And while I was never willing to tailor my music in a certain way just to enhance sales, I honestly didn't care what the video looked like, as long as it was brilliant. I wanted Godley and Creme to do whatever they needed to do to get it on MTV.

The guys said they understood, and they got to work. A couple of weeks later Godley called me.

"Lol and I just went to this exhibition of kinetic art," he told me. "And we saw these really cool robotic figures. We thought something like that might be interesting for your video."

"Great!" I said. "Whatever you think works, you have my approval." I think they thought I'd want to be more involved, but I didn't know the first thing about making a music video, so I was happy to leave it entirely up to them. "I'm a musician, so I make the music. You're the video artist, so you make the video," I told them. "I trust you guys."

So they forged ahead, shot a little footage of me, and about a month later Tony Meilandt and I flew to London to see the finished product. We all went into a screening room, the lights dimmed, and up on screen I saw a two-story housing block, then a close-up of bottles of milk on a front step . . . and then the madness started. Crazy dancing robot legs!

A giant robot bird! Headless mannequins, interspersed with clips of my hands playing the synthesizer, and camera work that shook back and forth with every *whicka whicka whicka* of the scratching.

And honestly, as I sat there watching, I had no idea what to think. I'd never seen anything quite like this video, and I wasn't sure what to make of it.

Meanwhile, Tony, who was sitting beside me, was flipping out. "This is brilliant! This is so fucking brilliant!" he kept saying. I laughed and said, "It is? Are you sure?" I mean, I *hoped* it was, but I really didn't know. Something about the video just kind of eluded me.

"Let's take it to Columbia and show them!" Tony said. So after the screening, we took the video to Columbia Records' London office. And when we showed it to them, *they* flipped out, too—there were a lot of young people in the room, and they were going nuts, congratulating us, slapping me on the back. "This is gonna be huge!" one guy said. I just smiled.

I wish I could say that I knew immediately how great that video was. I didn't dislike it, but I wasn't really enamored of it. I didn't know where to put it in my mind—which is, I later realized, probably how some people felt about my more avant-garde music. Everybody was so excited that I felt a little stupid, like I wasn't getting something. I could only hope that if the video did get picked up by MTV, the response from viewers would be just as rapturous.

I had steeled myself for the possibility that MTV wouldn't accept it, but when we sent the video over, they aired it right away. I'm not sure if they made that decision because the video was of robots rather than me, or because MTV was now adding videos by Michael Jackson and other black artists into their rotation. Ultimately it doesn't really matter, because the result was the same. "Rockit" went from light rotation immediately into heavy rotation, and it ultimately became one of the highest-rated music videos of all time.

People still congratulate me on that video, giving me credit for a piece of visual art whose creation I had little to do with. All I did was say yes to Godley and Creme, and to Jim Whiting, the artist who created the robots. This was a trait I'd learned from playing jazz and honed through Buddhism. When I played with Miles Davis, he always trusted us to do what he'd hired us to do, allowing us to tap into our own creative skills. In letting Godley and Creme do the same thing, we all benefited.

||||||||||

When it came time for the tour, I knew I'd have to put together a very different kind of band. We had to figure out how to reproduce the sounds of *Future Shock* on the road, so Tony and I started fiddling with different onstage configurations.

Like all turntablists then, DST used vinyl LPs for scratching and for playing samples. He needed a lot of different records to make those sounds, and when we recorded in a studio, he could take his time finding what he needed. But playing live was a completely different beast— he didn't have enough time to find and switch the records on and off the turntables. I was thinking about how to make the process more efficient, and it suddenly occurred to me that instead of having a dozen records with all the different songs DST needed, we could put all those songs and snippets on a single vinyl record.

Tony thought that would work, so we compiled a dozen or so songs onto one tape and then used that to press about twenty-five vinyl copies. We needed those extras so that when copies broke, as vinyl records inevitably do, we'd have enough to get us through the entire tour. Nobody presses just twenty-five copies of a record, of course—so if any of those still survive from that tour, they would be collectors' items today. I don't have one, and I have no idea whether any of them still exist.

We had a few other firsts on that tour, too. DST saw that I had various pedals attached to my equipment—a wah-wah pedal, an

Echoplex, and an expression pedal for my Clavinet—and he decided it would be cool to attach those to his turntable, too. He used them during the shows to create effects that no other turntablist had. He also got wireless headphones with a little antenna, which was then new technology, so he could hear his turntables wirelessly while in the middle of the band onstage.

We designed the show specifically so we could play the record live, right up to the solos. We had two drummers, one on a regular drum set and one on electronic drums. We also brought in a second keyboard player, Jeff Bova, who was a sound designer for the album. Somehow, without Bryan Bell, who'd just left to work with Carlos Santana, we managed to get this raft of new gear and new players ready, and we took the whole circus on the road to venues across the United States. I hadn't felt like such a rock star onstage since *Head Hunters* came out ten years earlier. But the excitement was really only beginning.

In February of 1984 I was invited to play at the Grammy Awards. "Rockit" was nominated for Best R&B Instrumental Performance, and the song had become a smash hit since its release the summer before. Over eight months "Rockit" had become more than just a single; people were calling it the herald of a new musical style, hip-hop. And because of heavy airplay on MTV, it had been able to cross the color barrier, attracting both black and white audiences.

For the Grammys performance we decided to use Jim Whiting's robots onstage. We had the whole band, with DST at his double turntable and me out front with my clavitar—a combination synthesizer, keyboard, and guitar—and we were surrounded by robots! We had three dancing-legs robots suspended above the stage and a few others in various poses—sitting in an armchair, lying on a bed—all of them doing repetitive mechanical moves, just like in the video. I was rocking out with my clavitar, just jamming, when about halfway through the song . . . four of the robots really came to life.

The four robots, who were actually dancers, got up and moved to center stage—and everybody in the audience jumped to their feet, screaming. The robots started popping and moonwalking, and when two of them began break dancing, it was absolute mayhem. I looked out into the audience and saw Michael Jackson grooving along, in his military jacket with epaulets, and Brooke Shields beside him in a white dress, and their friend Emmanuel Lewis, who was just thirteen then and starring in the sitcom *Webster*. Everywhere I looked there were musicians and artists and actors dancing and clapping their hands.

I loved every minute of it. Those robots turning human was some seriously hip shit, and when we finished, the crowd gave us a standing ovation for what felt like forever. I won my first Grammy that night, but if I had to choose between the two moments, I'd take that exhilarating performance. It was one of the greatest nights of my life.

Later that year MTV held its first MTV Video Music Awards. "Rockit" was nominated for eight awards and won five, the most by any song that night. (Michael Jackson's "Thriller" was next, with three.) It was another huge night for "Rockit," whose impact was surpassing anything I could have imagined. Around that same time I heard about a break-dance contest in New York City, where twenty-five groups were competing, using any song they wanted. Well, twenty-four of them chose "Rockit." So people had to sit through the song twenty-four times! I really love the song, but that's a show I'm glad to have missed.

Future Shock would go on to become the fourth-best-selling jazz record in history, and the success of "Rockit" marked the beginnings of hip-hop as a mainstream musical style. And the ironic thing is, to this day I still really don't know much about hip-hop music. I'm happy to have helped open that door, but so much of the credit has to go to Tony Meilandt, Bill Laswell, Michael Beinhorn, Kevin Godley, Lol Creme, Jim Whiting, and DST (now DXT). I just happened to be at the right place at the right time with the right people, and I opened myself up to what emerged.

But as fantastic as everything was going, I also had a scare during the "Rockit" period—a warning that maybe I was pushing myself too hard.

||||||||||

One afternoon, as I was walking down a flight of steps at my house, I started to feel strange. My heart was beating like crazy, and I felt dizzy and sick in a way I'd never felt before. I started freaking out, and I called to Gigi, telling her I needed help. I thought maybe I was having a heart attack.

We called a doctor out to the house, and he checked my vital signs. He asked whether there was any reason I might be feeling this way, and I told him the truth. "I might have done too much cocaine," I said. He told me to lie in bed and try to relax, which of course was impossible in the state I was in. I had overdone it, and now I was really scared, because this had never happened to me before.

In the music scene in L.A. and New York, snorting coke was just about as common as drinking. You could find it set out on people's coffee tables like an appetizer, and it was freely available in bars and clubs. Most musicians didn't see cocaine as a big deal—certainly nothing like heroin, which was far more addictive and had destroyed some great musicians' lives, some of whom died from an overdose or had an early death from its toll on the body.

I never did a lot of coke, but I did do it occasionally in moderate amounts, mostly for fun but sometimes when I had to stay awake to write music. This particular time I'd done more than usual over the last couple of days because I had a big deadline coming up. For the first time since *Death Wish* I had gotten a job writing music for a film: Norman Jewison's *A Soldier's Story*.

Just as with *The Spook Who Sat by the Door* and *Death Wish*, I didn't have much time to write the music for *A Soldier's Story*. I had procrastinated, and now I was really feeling the pressure to create something great. Quincy Jones had recommended me for this job, and Norman Jewison was one of the most accomplished directors in Hollywood, having directed films like *Fiddler on the Roof*, . . . *And Justice for All*, and *The Thomas Crown Affair*. So I really didn't want to screw this up.

I spent hours upon hours in my home studio, but the music just wasn't coming out. It felt like the well had run dry, and I was unbelievably frustrated. As the deadline crept closer I snorted some coke in the wee hours to keep me awake. I didn't have time to sleep! I had to keep going, keep going . . . but now, walking down that flight of steps, my body was rebelling.

I was supposed to go to the studio to record that day, but there was no way I could do it. After seeing the doctor, I had to call and let the producers know—and of course that's the last thing movie people want to hear. Time is money, and every day that production activities get postponed is a day that adds to the budget. I couldn't believe I had gotten myself into this state, but somehow, later that day, I managed to pull myself together enough to get some work done. But I was a mess, and other people on the movie knew it.

When I'd meet with Norman Jewison or the music editor, Else Blangsted, I'm sure they could tell I was wired. I was leaning on coke to keep me awake, but the problem was, simply staying awake wasn't actually helping me get the work done. When I was doing coke, I wasn't really myself—I wasn't whole, so I couldn't write music. In trying to fix my problem, I was actually perpetuating it.

David Rubinson saw what was happening, and he was really upset. Here's how he describes that period:

> There would be times when I'd go to Herbie's house in L.A. and he'd been up for two or three days, in his bathrobe. It was

hard for me to handle. He was doing *A Soldier's Story*, and he couldn't—he wasn't really functioning. So I was going down, meeting the producers, and we hired a guy to help with the music, under Herbie's direction. And we set the scoring dates, when you actually record. And I went down to L.A., and I got to the studio, and there were forty or fifty musicians sitting there, and Herbie didn't show up. We ultimately had to pay for the session ourselves.

About a week later I sat down with him in San Francisco and said, "Herbie, this can't continue. It's really hurting you." And he said, "Look, David, you're not my father. You're my manager. I don't need you to look after me." And that was the coke talking.

Two years earlier I'd had a heart attack that ultimately saved my life, because it made me slow down. And now I felt like Herbie was destroying himself. It was very difficult to watch, and I didn't handle it well. We argued a lot.

I don't remember that conversation with David, but that's not surprising for me. I've always had a tendency to suppress things I want to get away from. It's almost as if I want to bury them, to help me move past them—it's a protective device. Maybe for that same reason I also don't remember this period of time as having been indicative of some kind of larger problem. I know I overdid it on that one occasion, because I had to call the doctor. But after that I was able to cut back without any trouble.

This was a turning point for me, in terms of doing cocaine. I realized that I could have ruined my reputation completely, and while it's easy to ruin your reputation, it's almost impossible to get it back. I needed to get my act together, so that's what I did.

I apologized profusely to Norman Jewison and Else Blangsted, and ultimately the soundtrack turned out fine. But while Else was really cool about everything, I'm not sure Norman felt as forgiving. I saw him at the Oscars a couple of years later, and I definitely felt a little distance from him. I hoped that, over time, I could restore his faith in me and repair any damage that might have been done. And I also hoped that I'd get more opportunities to do soundtracks, which I really loved doing.

Fortunately, not long after *A Soldier's Story* came out, I would get that chance. And the movie was about jazz.

CHAPTER
NINETEEN

One afternoon in early 1985 I got a call from Bruce Lundvall. Bruce had brought me to Columbia Records back in the Mwandishi days, but he'd recently taken on the job of reviving Blue Note Records, which had fallen on hard times. Bruce was, and still is, one of the most connected, knowledgeable, and respected people in the jazz world, so a call from him usually meant something interesting was about to happen.

Bruce told me that a French filmmaker named Bertrand Tavernier was making a movie about jazz for Warner Bros., and that Dexter Gordon had been chosen to star in it. This was surprising, because Dexter wasn't an actor; he was a saxophonist. In fact, Dexter had played saxophone on my very first record, *Takin' Off,* back in 1962.

"I recommended you to do the score," Bruce said. "Would you be interested?" Oh, man! I'm sure Bruce knew the answer before he even asked, but I said, "Absolutely!" So we set up a lunch for me to meet with the director.

About a week later I flew to New York and had lunch with Bertrand. He told me that the movie, *Round Midnight,* would be loosely based on a book called *The Dance of the Infidels,* by the French writer

Francis Paudras. In the late 1950s Paudras had met the great jazz pianist Bud Powell, who was living in Paris at the time. Like many black American artists, Bud had moved to Europe to escape the racism and oppression of postwar American society. He was a brilliant musician but in a state of decline, as he suffered from alcoholism and had also contracted tuberculosis, which Paudras nursed him through.

Dexter Gordon was perfect for the role, because much of his life mirrored Bud Powell's. He had moved to Europe in the early 1960s, for the same reasons Bud had. Dexter actually knew Bud during his time in Paris, and he'd even invited Bud to play on his 1963 record *Our Man in Paris*. So for *Round Midnight*, Dexter didn't just understand his character's life; in many ways, he had lived it himself.

Over lunch Bertrand explained to me why he wanted to hire musicians instead of actors for *Round Midnight*. He was a huge jazz fan, and the purpose of the movie was to bring attention to the art form. He intended the music in the film to be completely authentic—to be played and recorded live, rather than dubbed in later. For that reason he had to have real jazz musicians, rather than actors playing musicians. This was an audacious idea because of the technological difficulties involved, but Bertrand was determined to do it this way.

At the end of the lunch Bertrand said, "Herbie, I would like for you to do the score." I was thrilled—what a fantastic opportunity! I thanked him and said I'd love to. And then, almost as an aside, he said, "Also, there's a part for a piano player in the film. Would you be interested in playing the role?"

"There *is*?" I said. I mean, my eyes lit up like a kid's at Christmas. Bertrand had been looking at me pretty intently over lunch, but I just figured he was an intense guy. Now it turned out he'd been trying to decide if I was right for an on-camera part. I told him I'd love to do it, even though I had acted only once before in my life, in 1981, on a TV show called *Concrete Cowboys*.

When the *Head Hunters* record became such a big success and I started getting interviewed on television, I was always really nervous. I'd start sweating, and my mind would go blank. I just couldn't get comfortable. The first couple of appearances were agonizing, and when it didn't seem to be getting better, I made a decision: The only way I could cure myself of being frightened on TV was to seek out more opportunities to be on TV. So I accepted every interview request I got and tried to get more relaxed in front of the camera.

Then, in 1981, I was asked to audition for a role in a TV show starring Jerry Reed. It would be a onetime appearance, and I'd be playing a musician who was leaving the music business to develop engines for hot-air balloons. I thought that sounded pretty cool, so I agreed to come in and audition.

I rehearsed my lines with my next-door neighbor, a saxophonist named Joe Miller. Joe was an aspiring actor in addition to being a musician, so I asked him for advice. "You have to really believe what you're saying, so it doesn't come across like you're acting," he told me. "Deliver your lines like you're really talking to the person." I wasn't very good at first, and when Joe would run lines with me, he'd say, "I don't believe you." So I kept working on it, right up to the day of the audition.

I read for George Schlatter, a big-time producer who'd done shows like *Rowan & Martin's Laugh-In* and *The Judy Garland Show.* I was nervous, but George just asked me to read the lines in a few different ways, and then he said, "You know, I think I'd like to take a chance on you, Herbie. Who's your agent?"

My agent? For acting? I just started laughing. "I don't have one," I told him.

"Are you in SAG?" he asked. I told him I wasn't in the Screen Actors Guild, and he said, "We'll take care of that." And they did. I acted in only one episode of *Concrete Cowboys,* but they got me my SAG card, which I still have. It was a lot of fun, especially one scene where I play in a jam session with Jerry Reed, who was not just an actor but a country music star, too—and a really good guitar player.

So that was all the acting experience I'd had before Bertrand Tavernier offered me the role of piano player Eddie Wayne in *Round Midnight*. But Bertrand didn't mind. He hired a lot of other musicians for appearances, too, including Wayne Shorter, John McLaughlin, Ron Carter, Tony Williams, and Freddie Hubbard. I headed to Paris in the late spring of 1985 for filming, and although I had a lot on my plate between writing the score, arranging the musicians' parts, and preparing for my role, I was really looking forward to spending a few months there.

|||||||||||

Warner Bros. sent a car to pick me up at Charles de Gaulle Airport, and we rode to an apartment building on rue Vaneau, on the Left Bank. When I walked into the apartment the studio had rented for me, my eyes just about popped out of my head. It had three floors, and the living room ceiling was two stories high, with a balcony off the bedroom overlooking the living room. The place was lovely.

After the Warner Bros. people showed me around, we talked about what I would need while I was there. "We know you're going to be very busy," said one, "so we have arranged for you to have a housekeeper, to keep the place clean. He can also make breakfast for you in the mornings, if you prefer."

I thought about that for a minute and said, "Well, you know, I don't have a lot of time to write this score, so if I'm in the middle of writing, I don't want to have to stop and go to a restaurant to eat. Can he make my dinners, too?" They conferred for a moment, and they said yes, that could be arranged. I just smiled. I was going to have it made here.

Warners hired an African student who lived nearby, a guy named Edouard Kouassi, to be the housekeeper, and we soon became friends. Edouard was young and from the Ivory Coast, but he knew Paris, and he knew the hot places to go. Now, for movies shot in the States, you often have to be on set at 6 a.m., which would put a damper on any late-night activities. But for *Round Midnight* we didn't have to be on set until the afternoon—this was a film about jazz, after all, so a lot of it took place at night. The earliest Warners ever sent a car for me was 11 a.m., which meant Edouard and I could go out and explore the Paris nightlife, including the hottest club there in the mid-'80s, Les Bains Douches.

Because "Rockit" had been a big hit in Europe just the year before, I got the royal treatment in the clubs: We were swept into private areas and presented bottles of Cristal while gorgeous French models were ushered to seats beside us. I had never experienced this kind of celebrity treatment before. I might have been procrastinating a bit in writing the film's score, but I was having the time of my life doing it.

Tony Meilandt came to Paris, too. He always had his ear to the ground for cool happenings that nobody else knew about, and one day he told me the Rolling Stones were in town. We went to the studio where they were recording, and I played around with them during one of their sessions, though they didn't end up using the track. Another time I went to Studio Grande Armée, where Simon Le Bon, Nick Rhodes, and Roger Taylor of Duran Duran were recording as a new band called Arcadia. I played on one of their tunes, and that did make it onto the record, which was called *So Red the Rose*. I got big points for that with Jessica, who was a big Duran Duran fan in the '80s.

Sting was in Paris at that time, too, rehearsing a new jazz-oriented band for his first solo album, *The Dream of the Blue Turtles*. Sting is an artist who's always reinventing himself, exploring new musical styles. Like Madonna, he's never been afraid to change direction completely, doing 180-degree turns even after very successful albums. In 1985 Sting had just left the Police, which was one of the most popular rock bands in the world. This was an audacious move, but not as audacious as what he did next, which was to put together a jazz fusion band, with Branford Marsalis on saxophone, Kenny Kirkland on keyboards, and Omar Hakim on drums.

Sting played at a theater in Paris for about a week. The place was always packed with young people digging him and his new hot band, and I was drawn to that energy. He was gracious enough to invite me to sit in, and from the stage I'd look out into the crowd and see all these beautiful young women dancing and screaming for Sting, who was not only a rock star but a movie star, too, having just appeared in the movie *Dune*. I loved sitting in and ended up doing it for two or three nights.

Soon it was time to settle down and write music. At my request, Warners had flown the arranger David Blumberg to Paris to work with me, and he assisted me throughout the process, giving me ideas and encouragement and making sure I had everything I needed on a day-to-day basis. Dave had a lot of experience writing scores, orchestrating, and composing, so he was an invaluable help to me during the composition of *Round Midnight*.

Early on I realized that even though the movie was about jazz, the music had to be palatable to the average American moviegoer. This was similar to how I felt when I started writing for *Head Hunters:* I wanted to broaden the audience, to make the music accessible even to non–jazz fans. But the songs still had to be authentic; they would have to be pieces that jazz bands might have played in the 1950s.

I didn't want to copy the music from the '50s, because anything that's a copy is by definition not real. So the question I asked myself was, how can I, in 1985, write music that sounds as if it could be from the '50s but is advanced enough that contemporary musicians— Wayne, Ron, Tony, Freddie—can freely play it without the restrictions of the period? In other words, could I write songs that were fresh enough that we would simply be musicians playing music, rather than musicians *playing musicians* who are playing music?

My mind went right to the harmonies of the great French composer Maurice Ravel. Over the years I had often used Ravel's harmonies in my music, and they were also used in popular music of the early twentieth century. Musical styles were very different from decade to decade, of course, so I decided to construct the music for the film so it walked the tightrope between what harmonies were *possible* in the '50s and what harmonies were *probable*. The songs incorporated harmonies that existed in the '50s even though people didn't really play them back then the way we'd be playing them now.

I took some existing songs—standards like "'Round Midnight," "Body and Soul," and "How Long Has This Been Going On?"—and reharmonized them, so the musicians would have something fresh to play. So even though many people knew these songs, they sounded new because of those harmonies. That's how we walked the tightrope.

I also wanted to feature vocals, because I felt that non–jazz fans would respond to songs with lyrics. The very first song in the movie, which runs over the opening credits, is a vocal performance—though you might not realize it on first listening. The song is "'Round Midnight," and the singer is Bobby McFerrin, who sang the melody an octave higher than he normally would while making his voice sound like a muted trumpet. Bobby is the master of disguising his voice, and throughout the piece it's hard to tell it was a human singing.

One of the most important songs in the movie, and one I wanted to make especially sure we got perfect lyrics for, was called "Chan's Song." In a key scene in the film Dexter Gordon's character, near the end of his life, regrets not having been a real father to his daughter, Chan. He writes a song dedicated to her—a song that after his death continues to influence other musicians. Bertrand wanted me to write a piece that would plausibly be played for generations to come, which is not something you can just pluck out of a hat.

I started thinking about how to compose a song like that—something written by a musician in the '50s, dedicated to his daughter, that would live on for decades afterward. I wanted a song that could be played instrumentally but that also had lyrics and a vocal. A song that would be timeless but that young people could relate to. I spent a few late nights trying to come up with the right melody and harmonies, and finally I hit on something I liked.

Stevie Wonder and I were good friends, and I decided to ask him if he'd write lyrics for "Chan's Song." When I had most of the music written, I called him up—and he said he'd love to do it. I was so happy! I made a tape and sent it to him and gave him the deadline we were working under. Stevie said he'd get something back to me as soon as he could.

Days went by, and then a couple of weeks . . . and nothing from Stevie. I didn't want to push him, but we finally got to the point where we couldn't wait any longer. I called him on the phone, and he said, "Oh, yeah! I have them right here." And he started singing me the lyrics he'd written:

Never said, never heard / though within every word
Lives a heart / filled with love for you

They were perfect. Nobody writes better lyrics than Stevie Wonder, and he nailed this, capturing the regret a father feels at never having told his daughter he loves her. But unfortunately, it turned out to be too late to incorporate the lyrics into the movie. We used the song twice in the film, as an instrumental played at Birdland in New York, and also a version Bobby McFerrin recorded without lyrics, which played over the end credits, with Bobby's muted-trumpet vocal.

I wish we could have gotten Stevie's lyrics into the film, but in the years since, other artists have recorded the song, including Dianne Reeves. So it lives on, just as Bertrand wanted.

Bertrand's insistence that the music be recorded live, as the cameras rolled and we were in character, required some creativity. The makeup and costume people would dress us like 1950s musicians, and we'd get up onstage at the "club" that had been built on a soundstage. We had to use microphones of the period, for the sake of authenticity, but those older mics weren't as good for recording—so the sound engineers took them apart and hid modern equipment inside, so we'd have the look we wanted without sacrificing sound quality.

Many people had told Bertrand it would be impossible to record the music live, because of camera noise and other acoustic factors. But he used any methods he could to deaden extraneous sound around the set, and whatever noise did manage to creep in would just have to be there.

One afternoon we had played for about nine hours straight and the guys were all exhausted. But just as we were about to quit for the night, somebody pulled me aside and said, "Chet Baker is here."

A few weeks earlier I had invited Chet, who was living in Europe at the time, to sing and play trumpet in the movie. Chet was a brilliant musician, and I knew he'd come across as authentic to the era. But he also had a well-known problem with heroin, as well as a reputation for not always showing up, so even when I asked him, I knew there was a chance it wouldn't work out.

Instead of giving Chet a specific time and date, we told him to come at any time in the next two weeks, and we would accommodate him. Unfortunately Chet happened to show up right at the end of a long workday. I thought, *How am I gonna get everybody pumped back up for this?* We couldn't just tell him to come back at another time, but the guys were already packing up their stuff. So I hurried over to them and said, "Hey, guess what! Chet Baker just showed up! Let's record him while we can!" I tried to turn it into the most amazing opportunity ever, and somehow it worked.

We all gathered back on the stage, and I put sheet music on everybody's stand. I sat down at the piano, and just as I was about to count off I remembered that Chet couldn't read music. *Oh, shit!* I didn't want to embarrass him, but how was I going to fix this? Everybody was waiting for me to begin, so we could get the song done and get out of there.

Just then Chet said, "Why don't you guys play it first, so I can listen to it?"

"Okay!" I said, and so we did. The song we chose, "Fair Weather," is a complicated ballad, with unexpected chord changes—not the kind of piece you can just hear once and then jump in and play. But Chet did exactly that, and on the next take he sang it and played a beautiful trumpet solo, finding notes, common tones, and phrases that connected the chords. He was in his fifties at the time, and not in the best of health—just three years later he would be dead. Yet that day he showed all of us the great talent that made him so special.

IIIIIIIIIII

Around that time I got a call about possibly doing another movie score for Warner Bros. I didn't really have space in my schedule to do it, but I couldn't bear to pass it up, either. *Clan of the Cave Bear* was an adaptation of the popular novel about an orphaned Cro-Magnon girl raised by a Neanderthal family, and I was really intrigued by the notion of writing music for a movie about prehistoric man.

I had a brief window of free time toward the end of shooting *Round Midnight,* so I turned my attention away from 1940s jazz and started thinking, *What kind of music and sounds would be appropriate for the Neanderthal period?* I wasn't sure, but I figured that getting in touch with some really ancient part of the earth might help me figure it out. As it happened, I was scheduled to play a gig in Iceland, and I wondered if there was a particular place there where I might be able to get close to something ancient. I did a little research and discovered a glacier called Snæfellsjökull, which was also said to be a vortex, a kind of focal point of spiritual energy.

I decided to visit the glacier, or to get as close to it as I could, anyway. I wasn't sure how to do that, but once I was in Reykjavik, I asked around and ended up meeting this redheaded Icelandic guy who knew it well. "You can only fly over the glacier," he told me. "There's no place to land, and no other way to get there." Incredibly, this guy actually had his own plane, a little four-seater, and he offered to take me to the glacier the very next day.

We picked up two other people, and the four of us took off. I was sitting right next to the window, and I practically had my nose pressed to the glass, hoping to get a good feel for it. Suddenly the glacier came into view, a sprawling mass of ancient ice. And as we flew directly over it, I suddenly started sobbing for no apparent reason. I was completely overcome with emotion.

I kept staring out the window, trying to hide the fact that I was crying, because the whole thing felt so weird. Tears were streaming down my face, and my shoulders were shaking—but then, as soon as we passed over to the other side of the glacier, it stopped. I instantly went back to feeling normal, and I had no idea what had happened. I wiped the tears off my face and tried to pull myself together, but finally I couldn't help myself—I turned to the others and said, "I just cried like a baby when we passed over it, and I don't know why!"

And the redheaded Icelandic guy said, "Yes, you felt it. That's the power, that's why they call it a vortex." He wasn't surprised at all, which surprised me even more. Even now I really can't explain what happened to me over that glacier—it was one of the weirdest experiences I've ever had.

Clan of the Cave Bear was about indigenous people, so after the glacier visit I decided to make one more trip, to the Gambia, on the west coast of Africa, to spend some time with an African tribe. I had recorded a song for the 1984 Winter Olympics in Sarajevo with a Gambian musician named Foday Musa Suso, so I got in touch with him and asked if he could help me set things up.

Around the time I left for Iceland, Jim Henson's company asked if I'd be willing to make an appearance on *The Muppet Show*. They were planning an episode about Muppets and technology, and since I had developed a reputation as a musician interested in science and had actually made an appearance on *Sesame Street* a couple of years earlier with the Fairlight synthesizer, they wanted me to demonstrate new musical uses of technology.

I needed to do more research for *Clan of the Cave Bear,* so I thought, *Why not kill two birds with one stone?* I asked the Henson people to fly me to the Gambia, and I told them that if they could send some Muppets there, I could demonstrate a new kind of portable sampling keyboard in a remote African environment—maybe even on a boat, floating down a river.

I had no idea if they'd go for it, but they said yes. They flew one of their puppeteers to the Gambia with the Muppet characters Miss Piggy and Kermit, and in the meantime I called the Ensoniq Corporation, a musical equipment maker based in Pennsylvania, and asked to borrow their newest product, a battery-powered portable sampling keyboard called Mirage. The Mirage wasn't on the market yet, so I needed to get one directly from Ensoniq—but it would be amazing exposure for them, of course, to have Kermit and Miss Piggy showing off their brand-new keyboard while floating down a river in West Africa.

And that's when Ensoniq told me they had only one prototype, and it wasn't available. *Oh, no!* We had made all these arrangements, and the Muppets were on their way to Africa, and now I had no keyboard to show off. I panicked and said, "Listen, you've got to send me one, because Miss Piggy and Kermit are on their way here!" But they needed the prototype for a meeting with potential investors that week, to show them the technology. They promised to ship it as soon as the meeting was finished, to wherever I needed it, and with any luck it would arrive in time. So I gave them Sosu's address.

That's how I ended up on a boat in the Gambia with Miss Piggy and Kermit, playing a portable keyboard as we floated on a river, looking for sounds to sample while I improvised a casual conversation with the Muppets, explaining the technology of sampling sounds to use for music. I couldn't believe how well it worked out, and that I was able to shoot scenes for *The Muppet Show* while I did my *Clan of the Cave Bear* research.

After all that, the Muppets clip never actually aired—and I didn't get hired to write the score for *Clan of the Cave Bear,* either. But the Gambia trip was an amazing convergence, of the kind I seemed to experience more and more often since I'd started practicing Buddhism.

In my Buddhist belief, whenever we're faced with challenges, we can transform them into opportunities, which strengthens our resolve and builds confidence in our ability to overcome obstacles that will surely arise in the future. Joy and suffering are a part of life, but we can transform suffering into joy through the power in our own life that awakens through our Buddhist practice. Every obstacle contains within it a jewel, and my life felt so filled with jewels right now, I could hardly believe my good fortune.

I went back to Paris to finish up final details for *Round Midnight,* and then, at long last, it was time for a vacation. V.S.O.P. had a gig coming up in Athens, so Gigi and Jessica flew from L.A. to meet me for a week on the Greek island of Corfu. I couldn't wait to see them, couldn't wait to share all the wonderful things that were happening. We scheduled a celebratory dinner for August 2, 1985.

But before that dinner was finished, all our lives would be turned upside down.

CHAPTER TWENTY

Gigi and Jessica were already in Corfu when I arrived, and I was excited to see them. It had been months since we'd had time for a vacation, and I was really looking forward to some downtime with my family. Our friend Maria Lucien had come along, too, and the four of us went to the hotel's restaurant for the dinner we had planned.

About halfway through the meal, the maître d' came to the table and said, "Mr. Hancock, you have a phone call." I got up and followed him out of the dining room, and he took me to a phone nearby. This was pre–cell phone days, so it wasn't unusual for me to get calls at hotels where I was staying. It was surprising that the hotel staff had tracked me down in the middle of dinner, though, so I wondered what was up.

"Herbie, it's David," said the voice on the line—it was my manager, David Rubinson. "I'm sorry to have to ask you this, but have you heard about the plane crash?"

"No, what crash?"

"There was a plane crash in Dallas," he said. "And it appears that your sister might have been on board."

"Might have been . . . but maybe she wasn't?" I asked. He told me that he'd gotten a call from Delta officials who were trying to reach me, and that Jean's name was on the passenger list, so it seemed pretty certain that she was on the flight. But that wasn't even the worst of it.

"Herbie," David said, "they believe Jean was killed in the crash. I'm sorry."

Delta flight 191 had taken off from Fort Lauderdale–Hollywood International Airport in Florida, with a stop scheduled in Dallas–Fort Worth before heading on to Los Angeles. But the flight ran into a thunderstorm on the way to Dallas, and on approach to the airport a sudden wind shear pushed the plane violently into the ground, where it crashed and caught fire, killing 137 people. There were 28 survivors, most of whom were in the rear of the plane. My sister had been sitting up in the front, in first class.

My brain started racing, trying to process what David was telling me. I was horrified at the thought that Jean was dead, but just as quickly I thought, *Somebody has to hold it together here. And it's going to have to be me.* I knew that I would have to go back into the restaurant and tell Gigi and fifteen-year-old Jessica that Jean had died, and I would have to be strong for them, because they were going to be devastated.

I told David I would catch a flight back to Los Angeles first thing in the morning, and after sorting out a few more details, we hung up. I took a deep breath, trying to collect myself, and started to head back into the dining room. But I ran into Gigi, who'd gotten worried and come to look for me.

Gigi took one look at my face and asked, "Herbie, what happened?"

"Let's go back to the table," I said. "I'll tell you there."

We walked back to where Jessica and Maria were still sitting, their faces pale with worry. "I'm sorry to say that I have some really terrible news," I told them. "Jean has died in a plane crash."

Gigi burst into tears, clasping her hands over her mouth. She is an emotional, compassionate, empathetic woman, and this news was almost too much for her. She was nearly wailing with grief as Jessica, Maria, and I hugged her. None of us could believe that Jean, who was so vibrant, so alive, and so young—only forty-one years old—was actually gone.

As I later learned, Jean wasn't even supposed to be on that flight. She had been booked to fly home to San Francisco the day before, but she'd run into her friend Phyllis in Miami, and they were having such a good time that she decided to stay an extra day. Then, instead of taking the same Miami–San Francisco flight she'd skipped the day before, she decided to fly from Fort Lauderdale to L.A. instead—through Dallas.

My mother was still living in L.A., but without my family there, and with my father and brother living in Chicago, she was alone. And because Delta didn't immediately release the names of dead and injured passengers, my mother had no idea Jean was even on that flight.

My father and Wayman flew immediately to L.A., and we decided that I would call around the time they arrived so we could tell her together what had happened. My mom had been doing really well in Los Angeles, practicing Buddhism and making progress in dealing with her bipolar illness, but this would be the most horrible news she could ever hear. The moment we told her that Jean had died, she just started sobbing. I knew I needed to come home to help her, but I told Gigi and Jessica to stay in Corfu, as I'd be coming back in a few days anyway. I wanted them with me while I was in Athens for the V.S.O.P. gig, and it didn't make sense to have them make that long trip twice.

The next morning I flew home to L.A. I had called our friends, several of whom were Buddhists, and asked them to meet my mother at my house, where we would have a gathering that evening to celebrate my sister's life. After twenty or so hours in transit I finally made it to LAX, and in the car on the way to my house I wondered what kind of state my mother would be in. How can any parent face the grief of suddenly losing a child? I was really worried about whether she'd be able to deal with this.

When the car arrived at my house, my mother was sitting on the front steps, waiting for me. I got out of the car and walked up to her, and she looked at me and said something funny, some little affectionate joke about Jean. And at that moment I knew she was going to be okay. I hugged my mom, feeling relieved, and then the two of us went inside, where the celebration of Jean's life had already started.

IIIIIIIIII

As person after person got up and talked about how incredible Jean was, I realized that I had never fully appreciated that fact. We often don't realize how amazing people are, especially those who are close to us, until they're gone, and that was certainly true for me where Jean was concerned.

It wasn't until she died in that plane crash that I started to really think about and appreciate the remarkable things she had accomplished in her life. Jean was gifted at everything she attempted, including sports like waterskiing and snow skiing and tennis. And from becoming one of the first black flight attendants to helping develop the ATM, to writing lyrics and music for songs, to teaching herself to play guitar, she truly was an extraordinary person.

Less than a year before her death Jean wrote a short autobiography for a class she was taking. When I read it, I was floored: In addition to everything else, she was a beautiful writer. She described her life, her work, and her dreams so eloquently that the essay was almost painful to read. And it was especially difficult to read her musings on air travel, turbulence, and plane crashes—all subjects she'd been obsessed with since her years as a flight attendant.

In the late 1960s, during the Vietnam War, Jean had worked on charter flights carrying soldiers to and from Southeast Asia. She saw excited young men going to war and the devastated veterans who returned. Here's how she described it in the autobiography:

> World Airways carried those young men to their one-year tour of duty, and brought them home—sometimes as changed men, sometimes even quieter, encased in coffins in the belly of the plane. . . .
>
> Although they were only one year older chronologically, we now had a group of changed men. I expected happy, celebrating soldiers, glad to be on their way home, but found quiet, subdued, almost haunted passengers. We were all accustomed to being flirted with, barraged for details on what was happening back home, summoned for inane questions just to detain us for a time on an armrest . . . these soldiers sat stolidly and stared out of the window or down at their hands. Food was refused more often than not, and even the cartons of fresh milk from the States were accepted without comment.

She wrote about trying to comfort these soldiers when the returning planes hit bad weather:

> The only times that I dreaded were when we would hit turbulence in the winter skies. Sometimes it would be quite severe, and I would see the men go stiff, gripping their chairs, staring straight ahead. I knew the shaking would pass without event, but to them it seemed a possible, horrible irony—that they had endured Vietnam but would die at the hands of a Pacific storm. The crew always wished for a smooth sky, to save the soldiers from that final fright.

Jean had been through turbulence hundreds of times as a flight attendant, and she always knew that the plane would make it through.

I wondered if she'd felt any differently on that Dallas flight, or whether she'd faced the final moments of her life with the same stoicism she'd shown in front of those returning soldiers.

Later in the autobiography she described her feelings about air travel. She was fascinated with crashes, but that never put a damper on the thrill she felt at being in the sky:

> Because of my experience as a flight attendant, I'm committed to air travel and maintain very close relationships with friends in cities around the world. I read every book that I can about commercial aircraft, with particular interest in reports of air crashes or unexplained phenomena (such as the Eastern Airlines Flight 401, which went down in the Florida Everglades but resurrected through ghostly apparitions of dead crew members on other flights).
>
> I shunned the DC10 long before the Chicago disaster [a May 1979 crash in which all passengers and crew died] because of my knowledge of cargo door problems encountered on a Canada run. I've experienced engine fires on takeoff, severe turbulence in the center of a thunderstorm, and being hit by lightning.
>
> At World, we flew Boeing 707s exclusively, and in my opinion, it is the best airplane made. I came to believe unconditionally in the structural integrity of that aircraft. The rumble of those massive Pratt [&] Whitney engines became a favorite, comforting sound. I never tired of staring out of the window at the swept-back wing, the ailerons and flaps rising and retreating in aerodynamic combinations, guiding the steel ship through the thin, cold air.

As I reflected on Jean's too-short life I thought back to our conversation six years earlier about whether she could ever become a professional singer. It pained me to recall the disappointment on her face in that moment, and I found myself wishing once again that I'd been able to encourage her in any endeavor she chose.

But as I read more of her autobiography I took comfort in the resilience she'd shown in turning her attention to writing songs, and the joy it brought her:

> My brother has recorded two of his melodies with my words (he rarely does vocals on his albums) and one of his jazz standards entitled "Maiden Voyage" has been recorded by four artists with lyrics by Jean Hancock printed right there on the album jacket for all to see.
>
> Flora Purim, a Brazilian singer, fell in love with and recorded a composition of mine (words and music) on one of her albums. In fact, one of the greatest thrills I've ever felt was in 1984 while I was vacationing in Puerto Vallarta. Another guest at the villa was telling a friend about a favorite song of his by Flora that he had heard on the radio and went to great lengths to locate because he liked it so much. He started reciting the song, and in a hot flush of disbelief and joy, I heard him repeating <u>my work</u> . . .
>
> My world has been full of friends, challenging work, good books, much-loved music, citizenship and appreciation for a flawed but wonderful country, and an awesome realization of how rewarding and pleasant my life has become.

I didn't cry when Jean died, but not because I wasn't sad. From the moment I got that phone call from David Rubinson, I'd felt very focused on taking care of others—Gigi, Jessica, my mother. I was used to holding things back, shutting off emotions so I could take care of other people, but it disturbed me that I still hadn't cried about my sister's death.

Ever since I was a boy I had been trying to control my emotions. I never wanted to feel victimized, so I would just shut down rather than feel them. It's not that I was incapable of having feelings, or even crying, but more often than not those feelings came from experiencing music or beauty—listening to the record *Miles Ahead* or flying over the vortex at the Icelandic glacier. When it came to family and relationships, I kept my emotions in check for fear of being hurt. My family meant a lot to me, but I just couldn't, or wouldn't, allow myself to get emotional about them.

But over the years my practice of Buddhism broke through that fear, slowly knocking down the walls I so dutifully put up around myself. Where I had a naturally selfish streak, my Buddhist practice taught me to take others into account. And though I'd never been a particularly compassionate or empathetic person, over time Buddhism began breaking down those walls, too. A few weeks after Jean's death the emotions I'd been holding so tightly inside finally came out.

We had gone to Hawaii to scatter my sister's ashes when the tears finally came. As we sailed out into the ocean I knew Jean's soul was no longer in her body, but there was a finality to seeing her ashes float away on the wind, then settle on the sparkling water, that finally overcame me. I celebrated my sister's life and wept that it had ended too soon. Jessica was with me, and she had never seen me cry before. "Dad, are you okay?" she asked.

"Yes," I told her. "Now I'm really okay."

||||||||||

When the film *Round Midnight* was released, in 1986, everybody raved about Dexter Gordon's performance. He was so natural in the role, he really seemed to become the character, and people were impressed. As awards season rolled around, critics started naming him as a possible Oscar nominee, which was exciting for all of us who had worked on the movie.

Tony Meilandt and I were in New York on February 11, 1987, the day the nominations were announced, in an apartment we had rented for business trips to the city. The announcement comes early in the morning, so I was still asleep when the TV news broadcast was about to start. Tony banged on my door and yelled, "Herbie, wake up!" I dragged myself into the living room and sat down on the couch, but pretty soon my blood started pumping—what if Dexter really did get a Best Actor nomination? How cool would that be? Dexter was in his mid-sixties, and not always in the best of health. This would be an amazing honor for him, and I was praying we'd hear his name that morning.

When Dexter's name was announced, Tony and I started whooping and clapping, just so thrilled for him. Not long afterward the nominees for Best Original Score were presented—and that's when I heard *my* name called.

What? I was so stunned, it practically pinned me against the couch. As Tony began screaming and jumping up and down, I just sat there, my mouth hanging open—I couldn't believe what I'd just heard. It was really early in Los Angeles, but I had to call Gigi. "You are not going to believe this!" I said. "I got nominated for an Oscar!" And she started shrieking with joy. This was so amazing, it was almost too much.

The Academy Awards ceremony was scheduled for six weeks later, on March 30. Tony immediately went all out, like Sherlock Holmes, making calls to try to figure out what my chances were. He went under the radar, poking around and doing research, and about a week before the ceremony he said, "Not looking good, Herbie." Most people expected the great composer Ennio Morricone to win for *The Mission*. Morricone had been composing music for films since the early 1960s, and the quality and quantity of his work were legendary. By the time he did *The Mission*, Morricone's scores included *The Good, the Bad and the Ugly; La Cage aux Folles; Once Upon a Time in America;* and *Days of Heaven,* which had garnered him his first Oscar nomination.

Besides Morricone, the other Best Soundtrack nominees that year were James Horner for *Aliens,* Jerry Goldsmith for *Hoosiers,* and Leonard Rosenman for *Star Trek IV: The Voyage Home*—all films that had sold a lot more tickets than *Round Midnight.* I wasn't sure whether that made a big difference to voters or not, but in the weeks leading up to the ceremony I had to assume my chances weren't very good. At the same time I knew how much that Oscar would mean to jazz players, who often feel like the redheaded stepchildren of American music, so I did dare to let a little bit of hope creep in that I might actually win.

The Academy hosts informational meetings for nominees, so they'll know what to expect on Oscars night. The day I attended they told everybody, "Please write out a speech whether you think you'll win or not, because there will be a billion people watching you up onstage." I went home after that and sat down on our porch with a pen and paper, but I didn't know how to start. It felt strange to be composing an acceptance speech that I probably would never give, but I had to write something. Then I hit on an idea. I scribbled down a few thoughts, and they became the basis of a short speech.

Finally the big night arrived. I dressed in a tuxedo and folded up my speech, slipping it into my jacket pocket. When we got to the Dorothy Chandler Pavilion in Hollywood, Gigi and I made our way to our seats to find we were sitting right next to one of my heroes, my favorite film composer, Jerry Goldsmith, who had been nominated for his magnificent score for *Hoosiers.*

It's incredible being in the audience at the Oscars, surrounded by some of the greatest actors and musicians in the world. There were three hosts that night—Chevy Chase, Goldie Hawn, and the Australian actor Paul Hogan—and I was laughing so much I didn't even feel nervous as the first few awards were presented. But when Bette Midler took the stage to award the Oscar for Best Original Score, my heart started pounding.

Bette started making all kinds of jokes, but the one I remember most is when she said, "I'm honored to present this award because, as you may have heard, I love this category: scoring!" Everybody cracked up, and when she started reading off the five names, I thought, *Well, here we go!* And then . . . she opened the envelope and announced, "The Oscar goes to" . . . and incredibly, she said my name. It was as if I heard it and didn't hear it at the same time, but everybody around me started going crazy, so I immediately gave Gigi a kiss. I had to walk past Jerry Goldsmith to get to the aisle, and I felt bad for him. But I had to get up to the stage!

Bette handed me the Oscar . . . and it was so heavy I just about dropped it. I had won a few Grammys by then, but they were much lighter. I held the statue in one hand and pulled out my speech with the other, and although my hands were shaking I felt good about what I was going to say, because when I'd been sitting on my porch, pen in hand, I had finally hit on the idea of turning the thank-you speech upside down:

> In accepting this award, I salute the same unsung heroes that you so boldly have chosen to applaud. Some are with us today and some are not. Many have suffered and even died for this music, this greatest of all expressions of the creative spirit of humankind—jazz.
>
> From their suffering and pain we can learn that life is the subject, the story that music so eloquently speaks of, and it is not the other way around. We as individuals must develop our lives to the fullest, to strengthen and deepen the story that others can be inspired by life's song.
>
> I thank Bertrand Tavernier, Irwin Winkler, Francis Paudras, Dexter Gordon, Bruce Lundvall, William Flageollet, and the cast and crew for their sincere efforts through love and respect for this American-born art form called jazz. Praise has been long overdue for Bud Powell, Lester Young, Thelonious Monk, Charlie Parker, Billie Holiday, and many, many others.

Along with you, I thank them.
Along with them, I thank you.

I didn't thank Gigi in my speech, but I thought she would understand, since I wanted to accept the award on behalf of jazz and jazz musicians. But even more important, I wanted to express gratitude going both ways, because we owe gratitude to those who would honor jazz, but we also owe a great debt to all the musicians who have continued to develop and expand it, keeping it going strong for all these years. Even though that Oscar sits on a shelf in my home, it truly belongs to the many, many men and women who have poured their hearts and souls and very lives into this original and greatest American art form.

CHAPTER
TWENTY-ONE

I n the years after my sister's death I went through some changes in my life. David Rubinson and I ended our working relationship for good, and Tony Meilandt took over as my manager. After living in L.A. for seven years, my mother finally moved back to Chicago. And although I'd made dozens of records over the past twenty-five years, that pace slowed way down as new opportunities in TV and movies began to open up for me.

Not long after I wrapped *Round Midnight,* PBS asked me to host a show called *Rockschool,* which had started out as a BBC program. PBS wanted to make an Americanized version, with each episode covering a different element of rock music—things like tuning, equipment, and music styles that influenced or grew out of rock. I loved doing *Rockschool,* because it was educational not only for the public TV audience but for me, too. I learned from musicians who appeared on the show, like funk bassist Bootsy Collins and Jamaican reggae artists Black Uhuru.

Rockschool ran for two seasons, and then I got a call from the producer Ken Ehrlich offering me a job hosting *Coast to Coast,* a new program that would take viewers behind the scenes of musicians on tour.

We'd travel with cameras to wherever an artist was playing, and I'd interview and perform with him or her, showing viewers life on the road. Just as I had on *Rockschool,* I got to showcase a lot of amazing artists on *Coast to Coast:* Sting, Van Morrison, Pat Metheny, Rick James, Stevie Nicks, David Sanborn, Joni Mitchell—and the list went on.

At the same time I was getting requests to do more movie scores. Between 1986 and 1989 I composed four scores in addition to *Round Midnight: Jo Jo Dancer, Your Life Is Calling,* starring Richard Pryor; *Action Jackson,* starring Carl Weathers and Sharon Stone; *Colors,* starring Sean Penn and Robert Duvall; and *Harlem Nights,* starring Eddie Murphy and Richard Pryor. I enjoy doing scores, but after a while the combination of touring and scoring led to a feeling of burnout. This was especially true when I was doing *Colors*—I just couldn't tap into the well, so I ended up getting help from Bill Laswell and Bob Moses, who really deserve the credit for that one.

All these projects took me in different directions—an experience unlike those years with Miles and Mwandishi, when my focus was on touring and recording with one band. By the end of 1988 my deal with Columbia had come to an end, and given the broadening scope of my projects, I wondered whether it was time to enter a different kind of arrangement, one that would encompass the full range of what I was working on.

I decided to ask Quincy Jones if he was interested in forming some kind of partnership with me. Quincy had been a friend for years, ever since I'd met him playing at Birdland in New York in the early 1960s. He had been an up-and-coming trumpeter as a teenager, and by the time I met him he had played and recorded with Lionel Hampton and Dizzy Gillespie. He became the first black senior executive with a major recording label, and he also moved into writing and arranging music and doing film and TV scores, including that for the groundbreaking miniseries *Roots.* And then his career really exploded.

In the '80s Quincy Jones was the man who could do anything. He produced Michael Jackson's *Thriller*, which became the best-selling record of all time. He produced and wrote the score for *The Color Purple* and created the philanthropic pop sensation "We Are the World." Quincy knew absolutely everybody in music, television, and the movies, and he'd just signed a ten-year deal with Warner Communications to create his own entertainment company, Quincy Jones Entertainment.

Quincy and I have always had a great relationship. He's a few years older than me, and he'd always been a source of encouragement, talking about me to directors and recommending me for film scores. Yet even though he was so accomplished, I felt that, between music, film, and TV projects of my own, I brought a lot to the table, too. I also brought something that he didn't have: technology. Quincy had always been interested in what computers and new electronic gadgets could do in the world of music, but he wasn't an early adopter, as I was—in fact, he was usually the one asking *me* for advice. If we combined our strengths, I was convinced the two of us could create a powerful force in the entertainment world.

I approached Quincy about forming a partnership when I left Columbia Records, but he kind of skirted around the issue for a while. In fairness, he'd only just signed his own deal with Warners, so he was naturally focused on that. Instead he told me, "Let's start with you making your next record under my label," Qwest Records. I said, "Okay, Q. Let's do that"—but I hoped that during the period I was recording that album he would see how I worked and reconsider the partnership proposal.

For the moment, it wasn't happening, so I felt a bit at loose ends. I'd been playing professionally for thirty years now, through many different musical styles, instruments, and historical eras, running at a full sprint ever since I first set foot in New York City. There was no blueprint or guidebook for what I was doing; my life and career had just unfolded at their own pace, with their own twists. Now, at the beginning of the 1990s, I wasn't exactly sure where I was heading next.

Judging by a conversation I had with Miles Davis around that same time, I wasn't the only one feeling that way.

||||||||||

After I left the quintet, I saw Miles off and on through the years. He had a lot of serious health problems, including arthritis, diabetes, bursitis, and ulcers, and for a four-year period between 1975 and 1980 he was so sick and out of sorts, he didn't play the trumpet at all. Miles started doing too much cocaine during that time, and he rarely left his house. I'd go by and see him occasionally, but he wasn't well and didn't seem to be getting better.

In 1976, after years of suffering terrible hip pain, he finally had hip-replacement surgery. I went to the hospital to visit him, and he was in worse pain than I'd ever seen him in before. He was in such a state, I just wanted to do anything I could to help him.

"Miles," I said, "I know you'll do anything to help ease that pain, right?"

"Yeah," he said, grimacing. He still never said one word more than was necessary.

"Well, the only thing I know that will help is to chant," I said. He just looked at me cockeyed, as if that were the silliest thing I'd ever said. But I really wanted to get him to say *Nam Myoho Renge Kyo,* even if he only ever said it just this once. Suddenly an idea popped into my head.

"Yeah, that would have helped you," I said, "but I know you can't say it anyway."

"Shit," Miles said, and looked away. "I can, too."

"No, don't worry about it," I said.

"I can say it!" he snapped. And then, his voice quiet, he said, *"Nam . . . Myoho . . . ,"* and I helped him with *Renge* and *Kyo.* I was really happy to hear those words come out of his mouth.

"You were right, Miles!" I said. "You did it." I would have hugged him, but he was in too much pain, and, besides, Miles wasn't what you'd call a hugger. "If you do that a bunch of times, I promise you, it will help," I assured him. I'm not sure if Miles ever chanted again, but eventually his health did improve enough that he got back to touring and making records.

In the late 1980s I was scheduled to play a gig in Madrid, and I heard that Miles was in town, too. I got to Madrid the night before our gig started, so I decided to go hear him play—I hadn't heard him live in a long time, and I wondered how he'd sound after having so many health issues.

One tune he'd taken up in the '80s was the Cyndi Lauper hit "Time After Time." Miles brought a new sensibility to the song, slowing it down and giving it a softer, more R&B-like beat than the original. In the Palacio de Deportes that night I sat in the audience and watched as Miles led his band through the song. It was just unbelievable, what he did—the spaces that he picked, and just how he constructed the whole thing. It was superb, so gorgeous and so perfect, it brought me to tears.

Then, at the end, the band played a tag, which is a chord sequence that repeats over and over again, like a loop. Miles played on top of it, a different phrase each time—and every one connected with the previous one in a gorgeous way. You'd think that he would run out of ideas, but he just kept going, each idea more beautiful than the last. No matter what he'd been through, Miles was still a genius onstage. I watched that concert in a state of amazement at the level of musicianship and emotion he brought to every song.

But Miles wasn't feeling well that night, and after the concert he collapsed and was rushed to a hospital. Afraid he was going to die, he told the Spanish doctors, "I don't want to die here!" The next day he insisted on flying back to New York so he could be at home in his final hours. He didn't end up dying then, of course, but I've sometimes wondered if he felt a hint of his own mortality onstage that night, leading him to play with the depth of emotional intensity he brought to those songs.

Not long after that Miles was too ill to play at a scheduled gig in Rome, so he called me up. "Can you take my place?" he asked.

I was shocked, because I had never known Miles to ask anyone to take his place with his band. Most guys would just cancel the gig, but Miles trusted me to step in. As I was considering what synthesizer to bring, I realized I had one Kurzweil synthesizer that could be programmed to sound like Miles's muted horn, so I decided to bring that one. I didn't want to piss Miles off, so I asked the band when I got to Rome whether he'd mind, and they all said, "Cool, go for it!" Someone gave me a rough live concert tape, so I'd know what songs and arrangements the band had been playing, and I stayed up all night writing out sketches of those arrangements, trying to figure out how best to approach the music. The next evening I played with the band, and even though I'd gotten very little sleep, it was exhilarating. Everything just clicked.

In the end, I think that Miles knew exactly what he was doing. Any stand-in trumpet player is a letdown when you're hoping to see Miles Davis. But getting a keyboard player—at least that brought something fresh to the gig. Miles's band was hot, with Kenny Garrett playing saxophone and flute, Ricky Weldman on drums, Marilyn Mazur on percussion, and Benny Rietveld on bass. I had a blast being up onstage with them, using that Miles Davis–like sound with my keyboard. No matter how many years had gone by, Miles's music was still capable of giving me a new and exciting experience.

Miles was always looking forward, never back. When a Spanish journalist asked him in 1984 whether he'd ever want to reunite the quintet, putting together a tour with Ron, Tony, Wayne, and myself, he said, "No. That would be like making love to the first woman over again." In other words, what's the point? Once you've already done something, it's time to try something new.

That's why I was so surprised when, in 1990, Miles suggested reuniting to Wayne, Tony, and me. We'd just played a gig together in Paris, and as we were shooting the shit with some other musicians afterward at La Villette, Miles said, "Okay, everybody else out of the room except Wayne, Tony, and Herbie." People began shuffling out, and Miles got up and closed the door behind them.

"What would it be like if we got back together?" he asked us. And I could tell that he meant it.

My first thought was *That would be cool!* because we all had so much more to bring to the table now. All of us had been bandleaders: Wayne with Weather Report, Tony with Tony Williams Lifetime, and me with Mwandishi and the Headhunters. We all had new compositions, new experiences, new ideas. Yes, Miles was in poor health, and he probably wouldn't be able to execute like he had in the past—but that wouldn't matter, would it? Because whatever Miles does is always hip.

I didn't take Miles's suggestion lightly, but at the same time it didn't make me suddenly want to drop my plans for the future. It would be tricky pulling together the quintet again, in large part because none of us were sidemen anymore. We'd have to make a serious adjustment, and even then I wasn't sure the arrangement would work.

In the end, we were all intrigued by the possibility of getting back together, but it never rose above that level. We had played together and had loved it, but then we had all moved on. And we had all learned— from Miles himself—that the secret is to keep moving forward, never to look back. There are always new avenues to explore and new mountains to climb, and for that reason it made me a little torn when Miles suggested getting back together, because it seemed the opposite of what he'd always taught us.

Not long after that I played at a Miles Davis and Friends show at the Zénith outdoor arena in Paris. Before the show Miles told me he wanted to do "Watermelon Man," and asked me to play my portable keyboard. That gave me an idea, and while we were up onstage I played a little joke on him.

The band had run through the melody, and when it was time for my solo, I switched programs so my keyboard would sound like Miles's muted trumpet. I had done that with Miles's band at the Rome gig, of course, but I'd never done it with him onstage. I played a solo riff with that trumpet sound, phrasing it as much like Miles as I could, and Miles looked so surprised that everybody on the stage cracked up.

The joke was over, so I started to switch the sound back to electric piano, but Miles winked and then pointed to me, indicating that he wanted me to play that same muted trumpet sound for the rest of my solo. Now I had to laugh—he actually liked it! So I did as he said, reveling in Miles's enjoyment of it. I never got tired of playing with Miles, of watching him behave with such generosity toward everybody in his band, and of seeing him acknowledge a shared moment with a wink and a smile.

That night was the last time I ever played with Miles. He died on September 28, 1991, and the following year, ironically, the rest of us did have that reunion when Tony, Ron, Wayne, and I went out on a "Tribute to Miles" tour. We hadn't toured together in many years, but I felt the need to honor my musical mentor, and who better to do that with than the rest of the quintet? It was amazing to be back on the road with some of my best and oldest friends in the world. Gigi came, too, and Wayne's wife, Ana Maria. We traveled by tour bus with the young trumpeter Wallace Roney, laughing and joking our way across Europe, going out to restaurants with our wives, catching up, and just generally having a really cool time.

All of us except Wallace were experienced bandleaders by now, but you wouldn't have thought that, watching Tony in his free time. Because entering into the fourth decade of his career, even with all the amazing success and accolades he'd received, he still sat on the tour bus every day, studying music. He was taking lessons in orchestration, so he had books and notepads out and was constantly scribbling. If anything exemplified the spirit of Miles, it was Tony's ongoing effort to improve himself as a player and learn something new every day.

People still ask me if I miss Miles. The honest answer is, I don't. But that's only because I don't think of him as being gone.

For me, Miles never went away. He may not be here physically, but he's still here, because he's in me, he's in Ron, he's in Wayne—he's in all the people who played with him over the years. Miles's artistic expression is reflected somehow, in some way, in everything we do, in our music and in our lives. As long as there are people playing music, stretching themselves and exploring new ideas, Miles Davis lives on.

||||||||||

In 1990, while I was talking to Quincy Jones about pairing up, I'd already started working on a new record. We had agreed that Q's label, Qwest, would put out my next album, and I had thought this would be the one. But before it was finished, Qwest released *A Tribute to Miles,* a combination of studio and live recordings from our tribute tour, and the partnership I'd hoped for didn't seem to be happening. So I decided to take my new record to a label that had a connection with technology, because I wanted it to have a technological component that no other record had ever had.

I wanted to make the songs interactive, enabling listeners to make their own choice of bass line, background, drum beats, and so forth. There was a lot of new technology out there—MIDI, CD-ROMs, erasable CDs—since the days when Bryan Bell was jury-rigging computer systems for me. The electronic world had expanded, and I wanted to be on the cutting edge of the new technologies. I thought if we made a CD-ROM of a record, with listener options for each song, people would flip for it. I also wanted to make it in quadraphonic sound, or "surround sound."

The two labels I thought might be capable of doing this were Sony and PolyGram—but I'd just left Columbia, which was now owned by Sony. I didn't want to go back there, so I set up a meeting with Polygram, and I went down to their offices one afternoon to talk about my ideas. PolyGram was owned by Philips, an electronics company, so I figured they'd be receptive to the idea, or at least not throw me out of the room for being crazy.

At the meeting I asked whether they had anybody at the label working on new technologies. When they told me they did, I said, "Great! Because I want to do something nobody's tried before." I explained my concept of letting people construct the songs they wanted to hear, and the executives seemed intrigued, so we set up another meeting with their technology guy to find out what was really feasible.

This tech guy was amazing, just full of creative ideas. One I remember was that he wanted to put all of PolyGram's music on a server, so customers could download songs directly. This was long before iTunes, so it was a radical concept. And he had a lot of other ideas, too—none of which PolyGram ever instituted. In fact, PolyGram was so closed off to this guy's ideas that he ended up quitting before my record, which we titled *Dis Is Da Drum*, was even released.

To be fair, it took a lot longer to finish *Dis Is Da Drum* than I ever imagined. When I first started working on it, with a group of musicians that included Bill Summers, we started putting together a song that we named "Call It '91." With each year that went by, we had to keep changing the title—"Call It '92," "Call It '93" . . . and by the time the record finally came out, the song was titled "Call It '95."

One reason it took so long was that I kept trying to figure out how to record all the different bass and drum lines we wanted to include. At the time I had a Neve mixing console, which was a top-of-the-line analog device. But it had only thirty-two tracks, and for some of the songs that wasn't enough.

So in the middle of making the record I sold my Neve and bought a Euphonix console, which had more tracks because it was digital. One of my songs actually had seventy-two tracks—and there was no medium at that time for recording seventy-two tracks! The closest was a Mitsubishi forty-eight-channel recorder, and that thing was so big, you needed a forklift to pick it up. I had to figure out a way to piece together different storage mechanisms in order to play back all the tracks simultaneously.

Ultimately we weren't able to create the interactive CD-ROM version of *Dis Is Da Drum,* but I was proud of the record and had one other idea for how to make it special. I knew a producer at Industrial Light & Magic who was a fan of my music, so I decided to ask him if ILM would be willing to make a video for me.

ILM was founded by George Lucas, the visionary behind the Star Wars films, and his team created some of the most amazing special effects in the movies. Along with John Lasseter and Pixar, ILM was a pioneer in putting computer-generated (CG) characters on screen, using CG special effects, and integrating live action with CG characters. For a tech geek like me, the people at ILM were like superheroes. All I could think was how cool it would be if they'd do a video for me.

Because ILM was used to working with huge budgets, the first thing I said to my friend there was "This is the record business, not the film business. You can forget about the kind of budgets you're used to." If they were going to do this video, they'd have to do it because they wanted to. He told me, "I think I can get a team together—but you won't be able to call it 'Industrial Light & Magic.'" I didn't mind that at all, of course—I was doing this for the magic behind the name, not the name itself.

I went back to PolyGram and told the executives, "I have people from Industrial Light & Magic who are doing the video. And they're doing it within our budget." They thought I was out of my mind! They didn't believe me, so I said, "Okay, call them yourselves. Here's the guy I'm dealing with." I gave them his information, but when one of the PolyGram people called him, he asked the wrong question: "What does Industrial Light & Magic charge to do a music video?"

The answer to that particular question was, of course, *way too much,* so the PolyGram exec just decided I'd made the whole thing up. I was eager to do the video, but I hadn't heard anything back from the label, so I finally had to call them and ask what was happening. It took a while for me to straighten everything out, but I finally got the ball rolling. The "unofficial" ILM team created the video for "Dis Is Da Drum," and it was a visual feast, with morphing totems, plants, snakes, and dancing African figures. The ILM guys even used software modifications that weren't on the market yet, creating strange morphing bubble forms. It's fantastic to watch, a psychedelic jungle come to life.

||||||||||

By the mid-1990s I came to a conclusion: I wanted to make every new record absolutely different from any I'd done before. And different from any record *anybody* had done before.

I was fifty-five now, and I had been playing music seriously since the age of seven. It's rare for a person to find the thing he wants to do for life at such an early age, but ever since my parents bought me that first piano, I considered myself a musician. When I graduated from elementary school and we had to write little captions for our yearbook photos of what we wanted to be when we grew up, I wrote "concert pianist."

Twenty-five years after becoming a Buddhist, I thought of myself as a human being first and a musician, father, and husband next. Ever since making that change, I'd been thinking less about just writing tunes and more about my purpose in creating a musical project. What could I create as a musician that would have deeper purpose and meaning? How could I serve humanity in some way? One way I knew was to translate that idea into musical expression.

My perspective had been changing over time, and I finally came to the inevitable conclusion that I should never do the same thing twice. If music, and Buddhism, had taught me anything, it was that the world is full of infinite possibilities, and there are infinite numbers of ways to look at things. This is what jazz improvisation is all about, and it's what Miles Davis demonstrated to all of us every time he played. Miles looked at every note, every sound, as an opportunity rather than an obstacle.

I tried to do the same thing, incorporating new sounds and rolling with the punches whenever anything surprising popped up. Once, when I was playing at a jazz festival in New York, I sat down at the piano to discover that one of the keys didn't work: Instead of emitting the correct note, all you could hear was a dull thud, because the string was broken. I could have raised a fuss, but I decided I liked the sound of that broken string. It gave me an unexpected slap of percussion at the touch of a finger! So I incorporated that sound into the songs we were playing, just to see how it came out, opening up a whole new avenue of possibilities that I didn't usually have on an acoustic piano.

When you never stop exploring, you stay active and vital, no matter what you may be doing. People stop exploring in their lives for various reasons—fear of criticism, of failure, of disappointment. But even if you decide you don't love the direction in which you're moving, you can always change directions. Making every record of mine completely different from any other record would be the ultimate expression of exploring every facet of myself. With each record I wanted to jump off the cliff in a different spot.

Unfortunately, around this same time, I ended up jumping off another, different kind of cliff. And before I was even halfway to the ground, I realized that I had made a huge, terrible mistake.

CHAPTER
TWENTY-TWO

One night I drove to a friend's place in Beverly Hills for a birthday party, and as I was parking I saw two women I knew getting into their cars. "Are you leaving?" I asked.

"Yeah," one of them said. "You might not want to go up there." Before I could ask what she meant, the car started up and they were gone.

I decided to head in and see what was happening. When I walked into the apartment, I didn't see my friend and didn't know most of the people there. They were mostly standing around, talking and drinking, but there was also cocaine on the coffee table. I got myself a drink, and after a while I noticed that people were coming in and out of one of the bedrooms. It seemed like they were trying to hide whatever was going on back there, but when they came out of that room, I could see that they were high.

Somebody finally asked me, "Have you ever smoked cocaine?"

"Nooo," I said. "I'm afraid to do anything like that." For me, there was a clear line between snorting cocaine and smoking it. Crack cocaine was a relatively new drug, but to my mind it fell on the same side of the line as heroin, which I would never touch. I knew what heroin had done to musicians like Charlie Parker, Chet Baker, and John Coltrane in his early years. It wasn't a drug you could take recreationally; it was a drug that took over your life, and that was my impression of crack, too.

As the party went on, though, I found myself getting more and more curious. What is this thing that people are talking about that's so bad? Crack was a cocaine derivative, and I didn't have a problem with cocaine. What was so different about this drug? After a while I couldn't contain my curiosity. "Hey, I changed my mind," I said. "I want to try it."

My friend asked, "Herbie, are you sure you want to do this? It may not be a good idea." Then someone else standing nearby said, "It's all right! Let him try it."

I said, "I want to see." So I was led down the hallway into the bedroom, where somebody put a pipe in my mouth and lit it. "Draw it in and hold it," the person told me. I did. And when the high hit me, it was like nothing I'd ever felt. Crack overloads the pleasure center of your brain, hitting you with a wave of every pleasurable sensation you can imagine, physical and emotional, all at once. I closed my eyes and thought, *Oh, shit. I should never have done this.* This stuff was obviously way too dangerous to mess with.

I decided that night that this would be the last time I ever smoked crack. Unfortunately that resolution lasted only about a month before I picked up the pipe again.

For a while I managed to smoke only once every couple of months or so, and every time I did, I swore it would be the last. I made rules for myself: I'd never do it on tour, or when my family was around. And I never told Gigi—never told anybody, in fact, except the very few people I actually smoked with. I was super paranoid about being found out and having my career, and maybe my life, ruined.

But I just could not stop doing it, even though months would go by between sessions. I was sure I'd be able to quit at some point, but I had no idea how far in the future that might be. In the meantime, I guarded my secret and tried to keep things under control. As time went on, that would become more difficult to do.

||||||||||

In 1995 I made a record called *The New Standard,* the first since I decided to make every one of my records different. I had just signed a new contract with Verve, and one of their A&R guys thought he had a good idea for my next album. "Why don't you make a record of pop tunes by today's artists?" he suggested.

My first instinct was not to do it, because I knew it would smell of trying to make a commercial record for the sake of money, not quality. Over the years I'd heard many people accuse me of doing exactly that, and I never minded because I knew it wasn't true. But recording an album of pop hits *did* feel like pandering to the label's desire for greater sales, so I said no.

Yet whenever I answer a question with no, it always gives me pause—I have to stop and think about why I'm rejecting something. Part of my training with Miles Davis, and also in my Buddhist practice, was learning the art of turning the impossible into the possible—of turning poison into medicine or transforming lemons into lemonade. Often it's a matter of perspective, because there's always more than one way to look at things. As a jazz musician, if you're playing in a band, you can't stop and think about whether you like what the guitarist just did, because as soon as you start judging the other musicians, it stops the flow. Whatever happens, you've got to accept it as fact, as reality, and then figure out a way to make it work. That's the nature of improvising.

So I began to examine whether Verve's suggestion could have musical merit if seen from another perspective, and wondering whether there was a way to say yes to it while holding on to my musical integrity. I started taking apart the situation like a clock: Verve wanted me to do pop songs, and "pop" is short for "popular." Popular songs had been part of the jazz repertoire for years—not *current* popular songs, but ones from the '20s and '30s, which are what we call "standards" now. Even though those songs had started out as "pop" songs in their time, nobody today was considered a sellout for playing and recording standards.

I started wondering, what songs will be the standards of a hundred years from now? Will it still be those same tunes from the '20s and '30s? Or will there be new standards—songs from current eras that would have stood the test of time? That's how I hit on the idea for a record called *The New Standard*.

I decided to take songs written by current artists and treat them as though they were originally written as jazz standards. The trouble was, most current pop songs were somewhat simpler than the old standards—they didn't have as much meat, in terms of the structural elements of harmony and rhythm. Some did, such as Stevie Wonder's "You've Got It Bad, Girl," which I decided to put on the record. But for the ones that didn't, I thought, why not restructure these new songs to give them some meat?

There were many great composers to choose from, but I finally narrowed the list down to Don Henley, Peter Gabriel, the Beatles, Babyface Edmonds, Stevie Wonder, Sade, Simon & Garfunkel, Prince, Donald Fagen, and Kurt Cobain. I spent a lot of time collaborating with the producer, Bob Belden, to rework and reharmonize the material. Some of them, such as Don Henley's "New York Minute," don't sound anything like the originals. Others, like Nirvana's "All Apologies," I decided to play pretty straight, with just a bit of my own flavor.

I put together a band with drummer Jack DeJohnette, percussionist Don Alias, bassist Dave Holland, guitarist John Scofield, and saxophonist Michael Brecker, and we recorded the album over a couple of days at Manhattan Center Studios. After the last take was done, when all the guys had left, I decided to record one more thing—a song that had been composed a quarter-century earlier but that had never been recorded before.

The song was called "Manhattan," and my sister and I had co-written it back in the late 1960s. Jean had written great lyrics for "Maiden Voyage" and some of my other songs, but for this piece she and I had collaborated on the melody, too. Both Jean and I loved Tony Bennett's recording of "I Left My Heart in San Francisco," so we decided to present this song about Manhattan to him in hopes he'd want to record it. At some point we did present it to Tony, but for various reasons he never used it. So I put it aside, and over the next twenty-five years I rarely thought about the song again.

In 1995 I found myself thinking about Jean a lot, maybe because we were coming up to the ten-year mark since her death. As we started recording *The New Standard*, I suddenly recalled "Manhattan." It had been years since I'd played the song, but I decided that if we had room, I wanted to put it on the record. When we finished the last session, it still wasn't clear whether we'd have enough space for it or not, but I said to the producer, Guy Eckstine, "I want to do this."

The band was gone by now, so I was alone in the studio. I sat down at the piano, and the song just flowed out of me; it was as if I could feel the connection with Jean. I did the song in one take, and we put it at the end of the record as a sort of finale, a place of honor. It was the only solo piano piece on *The New Standard*. I was happy to have had a chance to record it, as a kind of tribute to Jean. But I never could have imagined what would happen next.

Jean and I were nominated for the Grammy for Best Instrumental Composition, in a field that included my friends Arturo Sandoval, Billy Childs, and Wayne Shorter. I thought of how proud Jean would have been to see her name listed as a Grammy nominee, especially in the company of those great composers. Our nomination for "Manhattan" was the only one *The New Standard* received.

And then . . . we won. Twelve years after her death, my sister, who'd so badly wanted a career in music, won a Grammy Award. My parents came to the ceremony, even though my mother wasn't in the best of health at the time. They were thrilled to be there, primarily because of Jean. We all knew that this would have been a dream come true for her, and I'm sure her presence was there with us that night.

|||||||||||

Wayne Shorter and I had been playing together since the early '60s, and not only was he one of my favorite people to play with, he had become my closest friend. Both he and his wife, Ana Maria, had grown close to Gigi, too, and the four of us had been through a lot together, good times and bad, over the decades.

Wayne had been there for us when my sister died in the Dallas plane crash. Tragically, in the summer of 1996 we were called to do the same for him when his dear, beautiful Ana Maria and teenaged niece Dalila Lucien died in the crash of TWA flight 800, which went down in the Atlantic Ocean shortly after taking off from JFK airport. Ana Maria and Dalila were flying to Rome to see Wayne, who was on tour, and unbelievably, just like Jean, they weren't even supposed to be on the plane that went down. Their original flight to Rome had been canceled, so the airline bumped them up to first class and switched them to TWA 800, which was routed to fly through Paris.

Ana Maria and Wayne had been married for more than twenty-five years. Her sudden death was a profound shock, but both Wayne and Ana Maria had been practicing Buddhism since the early 1970s, which enabled him to face it head-on with courage and strength. He had also stopped drinking in the late 1980s, after decades of doing it heavily. Consequently he was able to face his grief with a greater degree of physical and mental health. Many of their friends, having difficulty coming to terms with her death, would come to console Wayne—but more often than not he ended up consoling them.

Less than a year after Ana Maria's death, Wayne and I decided to do an album of duets. We had played together on dozens of records over the years, but never anything like this, an all-acoustic album with only the two of us. We wanted it to have an intimate, spontaneous feel, so we asked Tomo Suzuki, who was brilliant as both a studio recording engineer and a live concert sound engineer, to come from Japan to my home studio and record us while we played in the living room.

Instead of trying to write ten brand-new songs, we decided to look at scraps of musical ideas we'd saved over the years. Wayne had some pieces that he'd composed earlier but never recorded, and I had various fragments of ideas that I had never turned into songs. Most of our ideas were written on manuscript paper, though I wrote mine in pencil, while Wayne—who was not only fearless but seemed to have most things figured out in his head—wrote in ink.

We dug out pieces of music paper from our files, spread them out on a table, and began trying to figure out how to turn these scraps into songs. Just by cutting and pasting, moving things around, changing a key or shifting a chord structure, we were able to create new pieces. If we decided to put one of Wayne's melodies on top of a structure I'd written, we'd literally take his sheet of paper and tape it onto mine.

We must have looked like a couple of overgrown kids doing an elementary school project, but when we were done, we had eight songs—including two that were different versions of the same melodic content. The tune was so flexible, we ended up with takes that sounded like two different songs, so we named them "Visitor from Somewhere" and "Visitor from Nowhere" and put them both on the record. To round out the album, we decided to record revised versions of two older compositions: Wayne's song "Diana" and my own "Joanna's Theme," from *Death Wish*.

Tomo Suzuki came over and set up a camera facing the Hamburg Steinway piano in my living room. Then he ran audio and video tie lines to the studio, in another part of the house, so he could record there while seeing and hearing Wayne and me playing in the living room. We made the record in a week, playing up to six hours a day. It was so comfortable recording like that, in my living room, as if Wayne had just dropped by to shoot the breeze. We called the album *1+1*.

Wayne and I toured all over the world in support of *1+1*, and as soon as we were back Verve had another suggestion for my next record. They wanted me to do a tribute album to one of the Great American Songbook composers, like Rodgers & Hart, George Gershwin, or Cole Porter. Gershwin is one of my favorites, but once again, as with Verve's earlier suggestion, I wasn't totally keen on the idea.

These were all great American composers, but why should I make a record celebrating a great white American musician? Especially when that musician had gained fame by creating music in a style that was actually founded by black musicians—who never got the credit, the fans, or the money they so richly deserved. Gershwin's music was obviously infused with the influence of the African American cultural tradition, which became the American cultural tradition in the '20s and '30s "jazz age," through tap dancing, shimmying, the Charleston, and other popular artistic movements. I knew I'd get flak for it from the black community, and understandably so. What message would it send for me, a black musician who'd managed to achieve a certain degree of stature, to use whatever capital I had to celebrate white composers?

And yet . . . was there a way I could approach it from another perspective, a way that would allow me to make such a record in good conscience? Once again I started taking apart the problem. Let's say I chose George Gershwin for my tribute: I understood why Verve suggested him, because he had a broad scope of music, was incredibly talented as a composer and pianist, and was very popular. But I also knew that a lot of that popularity came because he was white.

Gershwin's creative output included classical music, Tin Pan Alley, ragtime, jazz—but I didn't want to buy into the distorted view that made it look like George Gershwin was an inventor of jazz. In Gershwin's world, in the '20s and '30s, jazz music was synonymous with American music, which meant that jazz had a big influence on the majority of Gershwin's music—and *then* Gershwin, in turn, made a big contribution to jazz.

So . . . instead of making an album about Gershwin, why not make it about Gershwin's *world*? That way I could include pieces by Duke Ellington and James P. Johnson—pieces that weren't written by Gershwin but that clearly influenced him. This approach would give credit where it was due, which made me comfortable enough that I could do the record.

In addition to the Ellington and Johnson pieces, I wanted to include Concerto for Piano and Orchestra in G, by the French composer Maurice Ravel. Ravel had been a big influence on not only Gershwin's composing but my own. I had Ravel in mind when I was reharmonizing songs for *Round Midnight,* and I really wanted to record this concerto as a kind of tribute to him as well. But I ran into some trouble trying to do that.

With nonclassical music, which I was most familiar with, once a song has been recorded, you don't need permission to make subsequent recordings of it. With classical music, anything written prior to the establishment of copyright laws is in the public domain, so you don't need permission to record that, either, which is why works by Beethoven, Mozart, and Bach can be recorded without permission, fees, or royalties. However, newer classical music, such as this piece by Ravel, fell within copyright guidelines. This meant that I'd have to get permission from whoever owned the copyright if I played it in any way other than the exact original version. And of course I never play the "exact" version of anything—I was revising and improvising on a lot of the piece.

Unfortunately I had no idea I needed permission until after we'd already recorded the piece with a chamber orchestra. When Verve asked whether I'd gotten permission for the Ravel, I just about fell through the floor. "How hard will that be?" I asked. They weren't sure, but they advised me to get in touch with the French music publisher, Durand, which would contact the Ravel family. I soon discovered that the family was known to be very strict about rights, and they almost always said no to these types of requests.

I was incredibly disappointed, because I had to have that Ravel piece on the record. But I knew what I had to do next, and that was to chant. A representative from Durand was contacting the family to see if anything could be done, so I just sat tight, chanting for hours, hoping we could secure that permission.

A few weeks later the rep from Durand called me. "So, what's the verdict?" I asked.

"It's very interesting," he said. He told me he'd given the family a call and discussed with them my plans for the piece. He'd explained to them that I was a respected artist and that having a Ravel concerto on an album by a well-known jazz musician would expose his music to a wider audience. And then the family did something really unusual: They asked him what he thought.

"That never happens," he said. "I told them they should do it, and they said okay." Just like that, my Ravel problem was solved, and *Gershwin's World* was saved.

An amazing group of artists collaborated on that record, including Joni Mitchell, Stevie Wonder, Chick Corea, and Kathleen Battle. This was the first time since I was a teenager that I was doing anything with an orchestra, and we got a great one in New York's Orpheus Chamber Orchestra. When it was time to tour, I took a quartet with me and we played with the local orchestras in each city. It was a throwback to my classical music days, but the wonderful twist of Gershwin and jazz fit nicely with my desire to do things I'd never done before.

But as enjoyable as it was to do *Gershwin's World,* another project I undertook in 1998 didn't turn out so well.

Twenty-four years after the release of *Head Hunters,* we reunited the Headhunters band one more time. Bennie Maupin, Mike Clark, Bill Summers, Paul Jackson, and I got together and made a new record, *Return of the Headhunters!* The guys were thrilled to be back, and I think they hoped to recapture the rush and excitement of those earlier days. When Dave Matthews graciously invited us to open for his band on their upcoming tour, I said yes immediately—Dave has a unique talent, is a true gentleman, and was one of the hottest young artists around in the late '90s. Opening for him might bring us a whole different audience. I couldn't wait to get on the road with him and his smoking band.

Unfortunately fans of the Dave Matthews Band didn't pay much attention to us. We'd usually do a short forty-minute set before Dave's band came on, and it felt as if I were back in Central Park, opening for Iron Butterfly, wondering how to get the audience interested. I actually didn't mind it too much, because I thought it would make us focus more and become stronger as a result. But the guys in the band hated it. I'm not quite sure why—maybe they thought we'd be recapturing the magic of our '70s funk heyday, but I was never that big on trying to recapture things anyway.

So the Headhunters reunion tour wasn't all that pleasant a time for me—but it wasn't nearly as difficult as what was coming.

||||||||||

Ever since I'd first smoked crack cocaine at that birthday party, I had been trying without success to stop. I managed to keep it under control for several years, sometimes going months without smoking it. But then Gigi would go out of town and I'd think, *I have a few days, I'll just do it one more time.* There were only a couple of people who knew that I did it, because they were doing it, too. Even my best friend, Wayne Shorter, and his new wife, Carolina, never knew.

I didn't feel good about hiding it from Gigi, but I was more embarrassed about the fact that I was doing it at all—and not only because she had quit doing coke in the '70s and quit drinking not long after that. The truth is, smoking rock cocaine wasn't like smoking weed or snorting coke—there was a stigma attached to it. Even the musicians I knew who did coke would have looked askance at smoking crack. It's just a different kind of drug.

I couldn't seem to quit, so I tried a way of lessening the effect. Instead of smoking a rock of pure crack in a pipe, I would take a cigarette, empty out some of the tobacco, and then mix the tobacco with coke or rock cocaine, and put it back into the cigarette. Smoking it that way gives you a rush, but not like smoking it in a pipe. I tried that a few times, but I always ended up going back to that pipe.

In 1999 I started smoking more often. I had kept my cravings for it under control for a long time, but now, instead of doing it every other month, I was doing it every other week, and then every week. On crack your heart beats fast, your breathing speeds up, and because it affects your nerves, your breathing sometimes comes in gasps. Depending on how much you smoke, you might be in an altered state for hours, and when you finally come down, you feel numb—no emotion. You're just drained. I didn't want to see Gigi until the whole cycle played out, so I would often go out at night and not come home until the next day, because it's not a short high.

This wasn't so unusual for me, as I've always been a night owl, and Gigi was used to my staying awake until all hours, often with friends or in a studio somewhere. For a while she didn't think anything of my nighttime absences. But eventually she noticed how tired I looked, and that my face was drawn. I didn't look healthy, even though I didn't notice that myself.

Crack also makes you paranoid. I mean, I was scared already, because I really didn't want to get caught doing it. I knew that a night of indulging in crack meant being somewhere for a long period of time, because I definitely didn't want to be in public in case someone saw me and figured out I was high. Beyond these normal fears, though, I'd think the FBI was outside, and peek through the blinds, imagining things. Once I had to check out of a hotel where I'd been smoking in my room, and I was paralyzed at the idea of having to go down to the lobby, where people would be milling around. I was sure they'd be able to tell, just by looking at me, what I'd been doing.

Toward the end of 1999 things were getting out of control. I was smoking a lot now, and acting in ways I'd never acted before. One day in November Gigi had an asthma attack, but instead of taking care of her or taking her to the doctor, I left the house. I couldn't handle it.

On November 11 Jessica turned thirty. I had gone out the night before and hadn't made it home yet, so Gigi called me on my cell phone. "Herbie, it's Jessica's birthday today. Remember, we're going out to dinner tonight." Gigi had arranged a small birthday dinner for her, just me, Gigi, Jessica, and Jessica's best friend, Rebecca.

"Yeah, I'm good," I told her. "I'll be there." I had been smoking the night before, and although I was fine when I talked to Gigi—I wouldn't have picked up the phone otherwise—I smoked again that afternoon. I completely forgot about Jessica's birthday dinner, and the three of them sat at the restaurant, waiting for me, until they finally gave up and ordered, realizing I wasn't coming.

I was going down the rabbit hole now, frequently in search of my next high and sometimes oblivious of the consequences to others. I knew I needed to quit, but I still didn't realize quite how bad it had gotten. By now Gigi was aware that something was very wrong, but she didn't know what. Then, a few weeks after Jessica's birthday, the last straw came.

I had been out of town and was flying into Burbank airport. When the plane landed, I called Gigi and let her know I was coming home— but as I got into the car that was waiting for me, I asked the driver to take me to a particular house. I wanted to get high.

The driver took me to the address I gave him, and I asked him to wait. I went into the house and smoked, as I'd done so many times before, and the hours ticked by. When I was high on crack, I had no real concept of time and didn't really care.

By around 7 a.m., the driver, who was still sitting in his car outside the house, was tired of waiting. We were in a nice neighborhood, so he wouldn't have had any real reason to worry about my safety, but hours had gone by with no sign of me, so he decided to call the house. Gigi answered and he said, "Herbie asked me to drop him off somewhere, and he never came back out."

"Oh, my god," she said. "Give me the address. I'm coming there now." She told the driver to go to our house and drop off my luggage, and that he could go home after that.

Gigi got in her car and drove to the address the driver had given her, but it was an apartment building, so she still didn't know exactly where I was. She'd been calling my cell phone, but I was so high, and so paranoid, that of course I didn't answer. I didn't want to speak to her until I could come down enough to talk normally.

Gigi was so scared and frustrated that she started crying. She called our friend Susie Sempers. "I don't know where he is, Susie," Gigi cried. "I don't know if he's dead or alive." She'd been sitting in her car in front of the building for an hour, and had no idea how to find me, so finally, at Susie's urging, she decided to drive home. But before she did, she tried my number one more time.

This time, I picked up. I don't remember much about the conversation, but I know that Gigi told me that she'd called the police and that they were on their way to the apartment building—so if I didn't want to be arrested, I'd better get out now and find myself a taxi home. She hadn't called the police, but I didn't know that. It was her way of making sure I actually left the apartment, which I did.

I called a taxi and hurried out of the building, scared but finally coming down from my high. When I got home, I tiptoed up the stairs in case Gigi had gone back to bed. I was so tired, I just wanted to sleep and deal with any fallout in the morning. Despite the fact that my Buddhist practice had made me more empathetic and more compassionate, doing crack brought out the exact opposite in me. I just wanted to be able to get high and not think about the consequences, not answer to anyone about it.

But as I was tiptoeing up the stairs, I heard Gigi call to me from the chanting room, across the hall from the bedroom. "Herbie, can you come in here for a second?"

I opened the door and saw Gigi, Jessica, and our dear friends Susie Sempers and Matilda Buck sitting there. These were the people I cared about most in the world, the people I felt most embarrassed to see in the state I was in. They *knew*. And I felt so sorry, so terribly sorry, for having disappointed these people whom I loved and who loved me. It all just came crashing down on me in that moment, and I burst into tears.

Gigi's eyes were red from crying. "Herbie, I'm not going to watch you die," she said. "If you continue this way, you are going to have to move out." I just looked at her, my heart aching. "I made some calls, and here are the numbers for some rehab places. But I'm not going to force you. You have to do it for yourself."

"I'm so sorry," I said, to Gigi and everybody else in the room. I didn't know what else to say. This was an intervention, and I was so embarrassed, but there was another feeling creeping in, too: relief. I had been struggling with this habit, and this secret, for so long. I looked at my daughter and sobbed, wondering how I had gotten to this place but thankful that it was finally going to end.

I called Hoag Memorial Hospital rehab services that night and booked myself a stay. But before I could go, there was one gig in Las Vegas that I was afraid to miss. I never canceled gigs, and I was scared that people would find out I had missed this one because I was going to rehab. I had finally revealed my secret to Gigi, Jessica, Matilda, and Susie, but I never wanted anyone else to find out. And in fact, I never told another soul for years, until I decided to reveal my addiction and rehab in this book.

I used a false name in rehab, and I don't want to say too much about the program, to protect the other people who were there at the same time I was. But I do want to give credit to the doctors, nurses, and staff at Hoag, because they took care of me with grace and discretion. I'm sure some of them realized who I was, but nobody ever revealed it.

From the moment I walked into Hoag, I wanted to do everything I possibly could to make the rehab work—no excuses. I didn't want to be the kind of person I had become over the last few months, a person who was trapped in addiction. At that point, separated from my family, my friends, and my music, I was stripped bare. The only thing I had to hold on to was Buddhism, and because the facility allowed me to bring in my Gohonzon, I was able to chant while I went through the program. My Buddhist faith helped me, giving me hope and the conviction that I could stop.

Gigi and I decided to tell our friends that I was going away for a month to write music and start working on a new project. Nobody seemed to suspect anything, so when my three weeks of rehab were finished, I came back home as if nothing had happened. By this time it was nearly Christmas, and Gigi, Jessica, and I had been planning a trip to Bali with our friends Tom and Cheri Carter. We were going to spend New Year's Eve there together, the big celebration of 1999 turning to 2000.

I had always loved drinking champagne, and the Carters had brought Cristal to Bali. But I was attending AA meetings now as part of my continuing treatment, so I knew it wouldn't be a good idea to drink. As always, Gigi was looking out for me—she had brought bottles of Martinelli's Sparkling Cider for us to celebrate. And as the clock ticked down to midnight I realized I felt good about not drinking. In fact, I decided right then that I would never drink again, and that's how I entered the new millennium. I haven't had any drugs or alcohol since.

For years I buried the secret of my addiction and rehab. I wanted to suppress the memory of it, because I was ashamed of it. I suppose I thought that if I never revealed it, I could pretend it never happened.

But it did happen, and I finally understood that trying to keep it hidden is the same as lying about it. If one of our goals in life is to overcome obstacles and turn them into opportunities for victory, then how can I try to ignore the biggest obstacle I ever faced? The fact that I was able to overcome my addiction, thanks in large part to my family and my faith, was a victory, not something to hide from, and that's why I'm sharing it now. The truth can set you free, and maybe sharing my experience will encourage someone else who is fighting this battle, too.

CHAPTER
TWENTY-THREE

Earlier in my career I was making new records left and right—
sometimes two or even three in a single year. But once I
decided that every new record had to be completely different
from anything I'd done before, my focus changed.

Now I asked myself, *How can I contribute to solutions for the problems humanity is facing?* I wanted to use culture as a canvas to illuminate and encourage positive action and critical thinking. I no longer saw myself as a musician; now I was a human being who happened to make music. When you look at yourself that way, the purpose behind the music becomes more important than the music itself.

That's why, in the first decade of the new millennium, I made just four records. I could have made more, and at this point in my career maybe people expected me to. But I only wanted to make records that I felt broke new ground. I also decided to create my own label, Hancock Music, because the birth of Napster and file sharing meant that it was possible for artists to get their music directly out into the world. There were still benefits to signing with a big label, because they do have marketing and production engines, but that was no longer the only solution. When you sign with a label, they own the pie and just give you a few slices. I wanted to own my own pie.

In 2001 I made *Future 2 Future,* which was based on a concept from Bill Laswell. Bill and I had collaborated on three albums—*Future Shock, Sound-System,* and *Perfect Machine*—and my first two Grammy Awards were for music we had made together. Almost twenty years had passed since Bill and Michael Beinhorn had introduced me to scratching, but Bill was still right on the cutting edge of music. He seemed to have his hands in every musical genre, and he loved putting together unusual pairings of artists and styles.

Bill wanted me to collaborate with the top electronic musicians, guys like the hip-hop turntablist Rob Swift and techno pioneer Carl Craig. Both had been influenced by my early forays into hip-hop on *Future Shock.* They were just kids when "Rockit" came out, and they came of age on that first wave of hip-hop music in the mid-1980s. Fifteen years later, they were pushing the envelope in that genre even further—so now I was coming around full circle to learn something new from *them.*

Future 2 Future was a cross between electronica and jazz, and we brought in Wayne Shorter and Jack DeJohnette to play on some of the tracks. Bill provided the basic structure of the songs, using rhythmic elements he brought me on tape, and we stretched even further than on the records we'd done together in the past. Our palette was larger than before; now we had elements that hadn't even been in our sights the previous times we had worked together. Many records are like a carpet that's been woven together, but this one was more like a networking, a webbing, with space in between. *Future 2 Future* was right on the edge, and like a Michelangelo Antonioni movie, it left a lot of room for interpretation by the listener.

Chaka Khan sang on the record, too, but the one artist I really wanted to showcase was Tony Williams. Tony had died a few years earlier, suffering a heart attack after he had gallbladder surgery. It was reported that either he was misdiagnosed or the medical staff had missed signs of his heart attack, and that he actually might have survived it. He was just fifty-one when he died, and it's devastating to think of how much more music he could have given us, how much of his creativity we will never get to see realized.

As a tribute to Tony, the brilliant spoken-word artist Dana Bryant recited a poem over a sample of his drum work, with electronic music laid over it. The resulting six-minute song, called "Tony Williams," is a haunting tribute to an amazing man, with Dana, a former jazz singer, repeating these words:

Only once every millennium
comes a son as prophetic as this one

Tony Williams burned through life like the brightest flame. When I met him, he was just sixteen, but he was already one of the greatest drummers on the planet. He had tremendous, otherworldly skills, but that's not what made him so remarkable. No matter how good he was, he never stopped studying, never stopped trying to improve himself as a player and composer.

While we were with Miles's band, I would watch Tony try to play the piano. He'd plunk on it with his two index fingers, trying to pick out melodies for the compositions on his first album, *Life Time.* Back then he needed me to help him play and transcribe his compositions, but that didn't last long. He not only began studying music transcription but learned how to play piano, too—with both hands. Later he studied orchestration, and by the time of his last album, *Wilderness,* he was able to write out full orchestrations.

Tony was always pushing boundaries, not just for himself but for entire musical genres. Miles Davis usually gets credit for being the pioneer of jazz-rock fusion, thanks to his brilliant 1970 album *Bitches*

Brew. But what few people realize is that Miles was actually influenced by Tony's band, Tony Williams Lifetime, which was already forging that new territory with the double-album jazz-rock classic *Emergency!* in 1969. When Miles heard what Tony was doing, he said, "This is the shit," and he followed in Tony's footsteps with *Bitches Brew*.

Lifetime was the true cornerstone band of jazz-rock fusion—and it's also the reason I wear a hearing aid now. Tony's highly amplified band played extremely loud, and I went to see them on quite a few nights. I was fortunate enough to spend a lot of time watching Tony Williams do his thing, and even luckier to have had him as a dear friend. Starting with our time together in the Miles Davis Quintet, we became like brothers.

||||||||||||

The next record I did after *Future 2 Future* was called *Possibilities*, and it started with a very simple idea. Most musicians get easily pigeonholed: Whatever the sound was on the record that made them famous, that's the sound their fans want to hear over and over again. And very often the artists do stay in that particular box, because that's where they're comfortable.

I started thinking, *Wouldn't it be cool to invite a few really good artists to explore a genre that's completely different from whatever made them famous?* I thought it would be really exciting to hear Christina Aguilera work her magic on a Leon Russell song, or see what would happen when the Irish singer-songwriter duo Damien Rice and Lisa Hannigan took on a Billie Holiday song. You never know what will happen when people dare to step outside their comfort zones, and that's what I wanted to get them to do on this record.

I figured that some of the artists might surprise themselves, but what I didn't count on was how much they'd surprise *me*. John Mayer came in and almost knocked me flat with his guitar playing. I'd never met him before and didn't realize that he'd not only studied at the

Berklee College of Music, which has its foundation in jazz, but he'd also been exposed to a lot of jazz players. Many rock and roll instrumentalists don't read music, and they don't know much about formal structure, but John did. He was very gifted, and also generous—he brought in an idea he'd been playing around with, and when we developed it in the studio, he gave me half the credit for the song.

I didn't know Damien Rice or Lisa Hannigan either, but I'd heard some things they'd done and loved both their voices. You don't hear a lot of modern harmonies on a Damien Rice record, so I wanted to see what he could do when we threw different harmonies his way. During our sessions I played piano the way I always do, changing things up with every take, and both Damien and Lisa ate it up.

Lisa in particular surprised me, because she could go off the deep end, mixing up the harmonies to a degree that I wouldn't have expected. She improvised like a jazz musician, singing ninths and elevenths with such artistry that it reminded me of choices Miles Davis would make. And she sang with incredible emotion, in an ethereal voice that just cut through everything, right to the heart. We did a few takes, and somewhere around the fourth one, everybody in the studio could feel it come together. That was the take we used.

One of the most challenging songs for me was Paul Simon's "I Do It for Your Love," a gentle, rolling tune off his 1975 record *Still Crazy After All These Years*. Paul suggested the song because it had a lot of chord changes and different keys, a kind of built-in complexity that lent itself to a jazz treatment. In fact, it had already been covered by Bill Evans and David Sanborn. So Paul said, why don't we do it as a jazz number on *Possibilities*?

My feeling was, if two other artists had already done jazz interpretations of the song, why would we want to do that again? I proposed a new spin, something nobody had tried yet: giving the song a different rhythmic feel by replacing the trap set with percussionists, which was something cool that I'd heard Don Was do on a solo album. Paul agreed, so we set up a date and time for recording the instrumental. He was supposed to show up later to record the vocal, but instead he showed up early, and by the time I got to the studio, he had already worked with the percussionists to lay down an amazing rhythmic feel.

Paul said, "You know, this song has a tender message, but these rhythms have a dark, exotic flavor. What if we did the entire piece with just one minor chord, laying the melody over the top of it?"

I loved Paul's adventurousness, but the original song had so many chords and key changes that it seemed impossible to do what he was suggesting. But "impossible" was not in my vocabulary for this—or any—project, so I started thinking about whether there was another perspective that could make it work. I sat at the piano and started playing around with the idea, and eventually I hit on a solution. I put a single bass note, or pedal note, onto the bottom of new harmonies that fit the melody, which gave the illusion of one pivotal minor chord. It wasn't exactly what Paul had asked for, but it got the effect. And Paul loved it.

For Annie Lennox we decided to record a piece by the singer-songwriter Paula Cole. The song was called "Hush Hush Hush," and Annie did a gorgeous interpretation, her pure soprano soaring over the piano. Paula's lyrics are simple but powerful:

Hush, hush, hush, says your daddy's touch
Sleep, sleep, sleep, says the hundredth sheep
Peace, peace, peace, may you go in peace . . .

All of us in the studio were congratulating each other on having recorded "the take," but we soon realized we weren't actually sure what the song was about. Everybody had a different idea. Was it a historical allegory? Or the tale of a daughter's disappointing her father? We went around and around until finally Annie said, "Herbie, you've got to call Paula!" So I did.

I told Paula that we had seven or eight different interpretations of what "Hush Hush Hush" was about and that we were desperate to know, to make sure our rendering was appropriate to the song's meaning. She told me it was about a young man dying of AIDS, who finally comes out to his father on his deathbed. The song was actually based on a true story of someone Paula had known, making it all the more poignant and giving Annie's rendition that much more emotional weight.

Then Annie got on the phone. As it turned out, Paula had been a huge fan of hers for years, and she'd seen Annie on every one of her tours since "Sweet Dreams" back in 1983. In fact, Paula was almost in tears, speaking with the woman who had been her musical idol for so long. It was such a lovely moment, bringing together these two fantastic artists—who are now linked forever through the recording of "Hush Hush Hush" we did that day.

My intention for *Possibilities* was to showcase artists performing in unusual musical settings. But I liked having the opportunity to put songs in different settings, too. With one minor chord we had turned Paul Simon's "I Do It for Your Love" from a pop song into something darker and more exotic. I wanted to figure out a way to re-create the last song on the album, too: Stevie Wonder's "I Just Called to Say I Love You."

The song was such a huge hit in the 1980s that just about everybody on the planet knew its straight-up Euro-pop beat and Stevie's vocal interpretation. We asked the guitarist and vocalist Raul Midón to record it, and we decided to use an arrangement I'd prepared for Diane Schuur and Take 6 to perform at the 1999 Kennedy Center Honors, when Stevie was an honoree.

In that arrangement the song's opening was so radically different from the original, it was almost unrecognizable. Stevie had written the original with a kind of turn-of-the-century harmonic flavor, but I reharmonized it, which reshaped it into a different presence. On *Possibilities* the song opens with slow, lush piano and orchestral sounds, and when Raul starts singing, his voice is so pure and high that he was actually able do it in the same key I wrote for Diane Schuur! Raul's range was just phenomenal, and toward the end he soared to a note that reminded me of Jiminy Cricket singing "When You Wish Upon a Star." It was a fantastic performance from an amazing artist, perfect for ending the album.

||||||||||||

Nearly all the records I'd done over my career were completely instrumental, and even the few that did have songs with vocals were mostly instrumental. *Possibilities* was the first one I did in which all the songs had lyrics, though that wasn't the purpose behind making it. So . . . what if, for my next record, I specifically chose to explore lyrics? That was something I'd definitely never done before—which of course meant that as soon as the idea popped into my head, I knew I wanted to do it.

At the time I was under contract with Verve, so I had a conversation with one of their A&R people, Dahlia Ambach Caplin. Dahlia's very hip, a huge jazz fan who knows all kinds of other music, too. As she and I talked she mentioned Joni Mitchell, who's a lyricist of the highest caliber. "You could do a whole record of Joni's songs," Dahlia suggested, which I thought was a brilliant idea.

Joni is a real poet, a genius at creating portraiture through lyrics. Her songs are incredibly evocative, painting pictures in your mind. She also had a vast repertoire I could choose from, much of which had the basic elements of jazz already in place. And she had been a good friend of mine ever since we'd first worked together almost three decades earlier.

In the spring of 1979 I got a call one night from the bassist Jaco Pastorius. "Hey, Herbie," he said, "I'm over here rehearsing for a record with Joni Mitchell, and we have all the pieces of the puzzle together except one: you." He told me Joni wanted me to play on her new record and asked me if I'd be willing to come over.

I hesitated. As far as I knew, Joni Mitchell was a folk-rock singer, and that wasn't a style I was particularly interested in. "Joni Mitchell, huh?" I said. "Who else is on it?"

Jaco said, "Well, there's Wayne Shorter—"

"Okay!" I said. "I'm coming down." That was all I needed to hear.

I drove down to A&M Studios in Hollywood, and when I walked in, I didn't see Joni. Jaco was leading the session, with Wayne on saxophone and Peter Erskine on drums, and I thought, *Great, we can stretch out!* I knew that, with those guys, we could open up all kinds of avenues, but was that going to throw Joni off?

I asked Jaco about it, and he said, "Oh, no, you just go ahead and play your thing. That's what Joni wants." *Really?* I thought. I still didn't quite believe it.

Joni finally came in, and she counted off one of the songs. I started doing my thing, throwing in little moments here and there, and she was all over everything I did. I had never seriously listened to her sing before, and I realized she had an artistry I hadn't been fully aware of; she was so smart in her choices, with such an amazing musical sense. Here I'd been worrying that she wouldn't be able to keep up, and she was keeping *me* on *my* toes. She means every word she sings, and I'd put her up against anybody in jazz. She's one of the best I've ever heard.

Later on, when I got to know Joni better, she told me she'd been raised on jazz. She remembered her parents playing Billie Holiday records and told me that those songs triggered her interest in singing. The only reason she'd gotten into folk music was because she was a poet, and she thought that was the easiest way to get her lyrics exposed. Joni taught herself to play guitar, but right from the start she experimented with alternate tunings. If you've ever been to a Joni Mitchell concert, you've seen the result of that, with multiple guitars lined up onstage, each one with a different tuning.

Throughout the '70s Joni had been branching out from folk-rock into different styles of music, and she began hiring jazz musicians in her band. She was a far more accomplished musician than I knew, and after we played together on that first album, *Mingus,* we collaborated many times over the years.

Yet even having known Joni for so long and being such a fan of hers, I was a novice when it came to working with her lyrics. I really wanted to do this record, but I needed help, so I turned to Larry Klein, a wonderful producer and bass player who also happened to be Joni's former husband. I knew Larry would be able to give me perspective on the meanings and stories behind Joni's lyrics, and he also had a lot of experience working with all kinds of singers. With Larry's help I believed we could create a record we'd be proud of.

We had to figure out which songs to choose, who the guest vocalists would be, and who would be the best personnel for the band. We brought in bassist Dave Holland, drummer Vinnie Colaiuta, and guitarist Lionel Loueke. And I knew I wanted Wayne, not only because he's the best at what he does but because he and Joni have a special bond.

In public Joni tends to let her music do the talking for her, but the truth is, she loves to talk! She has very strong opinions, and she can be argumentative, but she backs up everything she says and is incredibly articulate about it. I love listening to her, because she talks the way she writes—beautifully, poetically, and with great imagery. But what I *really* love is to listen when she and Wayne are having a conversation.

Hearing Wayne and Joni talk is like having an out-of-body experience. They speak the same language, and it's a language I'm not sure anybody else in the world speaks. They both use a lot of metaphors, and they can just make leaps from one thing to another and still understand each other perfectly, even when everybody else in the room has lost the thread. I never really heard them talking directly about music, but they would often talk about life, and emotions, and experiences. Whenever I find myself in a room with the two of them, I try to do the smart thing: just shut up and listen.

They have the same kind of relationship musically. Joni will count off a song, and Wayne just goes with the flow, playing off her lyrics, applying his amazing intuition. Somehow he always nails it, right on the first take—and then Joni will say, "That's perfect." And then they're on to the next thing.

I was excited about this record, but I didn't want it to be necessarily a Joni Mitchell project. I wanted it to be Joni's songs as heard through my prism, and through the prisms of the people who would be performing on the record. Joni did sing one of the songs, but she wasn't directly involved in the rest, and that's how we both preferred it. Her lyrics were the driving force, but the music was the stylistic creation of the band and the guest vocalists, which included Tina Tuner, Norah Jones, Corinne Bailey Rae, Luciana Souza, and Leonard Cohen.

Because Joni's words were the centerpiece for the record, I decided to write out a copy of each song's lyrics for every musician who was playing. We all would read through them and then talk about what feelings and images they evoked. I'd talk about any backstory I'd learned from Larry, and we would explore what we thought the meaning was behind each song. In all the years I'd been playing I had never done that with musicians before, and it was such a cool feeling to try to dig deeper, to gain some greater understanding of what was going on beyond a song's melody, rhythm, and structure.

I wanted us to play not just the music but the words—the *meaning* of the song. And the truth is, if we hadn't done that, the record wouldn't have sounded at all like it ultimately did. Paying attention to the lyrics took us in directions we hadn't imagined before, and the result was a deeper, more satisfying connection to the music.

||||||||||||

In late 2007 my assistant Melinda Murphy came down to my home studio from her office upstairs. Melinda had been with me for years, and she was, and still is, like my right arm—she's one of the most loyal, hardworking people I've ever known. She started out as my assistant, but over time, on her own initiative, she taught herself everything there is to know about touring and the recording business, and now she's my co-manager. Together with my daughter, Jessica, who also works with me, they cover all the bases.

Melinda told me that I'd been getting calls from the Recording Academy, which produces the Grammy Awards. "They want you to be one of the people who announce the nominees," she said, and I grimaced. Melinda knows that I don't like getting up early in the morning, and those announcements take place before dawn. "It seems really important to them," she told me. "They've called a couple of times." I sighed and said, "Okay, tell them I'll do it."

On December 6, the day of the announcements, I got up at five thirty in the morning to chant before heading out. At that hour I'm much more likely to be going to bed than getting out of it, but I tried to wake myself up enough to look presentable.

The announcements took place at the Henry Fonda Music Box Theatre in Hollywood, and I was one of about eight artists who were called into service that morning. Dave Grohl was there, and Taylor Swift, and Fergie, and the rapper Akon. The producers gave us all envelopes to open and read for different categories, and we stood on a stage in front of a small army of reporters and photographers.

Each of us took a turn announcing nominees, and I honestly don't remember which category I had—I just opened up my envelope and read off the names. Then, for the last announcement, the hip-hop pioneer Jimmy Jam, who was also the producer and chairman of the National Academy of Recording Arts and Sciences, stepped up to the microphone. He announced the nominees for Album of the Year, and I heard him say Amy Winehouse, the Foo Fighters, Herbie Hancock . . . *What?*

Jimmy Jam turned around and smiled at me, and I just stood there dumbfounded. Taylor Swift grabbed me in a hug, but I still couldn't process that my name was one of those he'd read out. Jazz albums almost never got nominated for Album of the Year. In my wildest imaginings it never would have occurred to me that *River: The Joni Letters* would be selected.

This was the fiftieth anniversary of the Grammys, and as it turned out, the five records nominated for Album of the Year were all from different genres: The Foo Fighters were rock, Amy Winehouse was R&B, Vince Gill was country, Kanye West was hip-hop, and I was jazz. These artists made for some rarefied company, so I was happy just to have been nominated. By this time I had already won ten Grammys, but I knew my chances of winning this one were almost nil. Only one instrumental jazz record had ever won Album of the Year: Stan Getz and João Gilberto's *Getz/Gilberto*, which introduced bossa nova to the American audience, way back at the 1965 awards.

For a few weeks I couldn't wrap my head around the fact that I'd been nominated. I kept thinking about it, trying to take the situation apart. If I had learned anything in practicing Buddhism, it was that everything is connected somehow, so I found myself focusing on why this might have happened to me. The only thing I could come up with was the fact that, at this point in my career and my life, I was striving to give people a sense of empowerment, as that was a message I felt was worth sending. We're all capable of succumbing to our demons, and some of my fellow nominees were publicly battling theirs. I had battled my own demons, too, but had managed to come out on the other side, and I really wanted to take this opportunity to send out a positive message to people.

Everybody knew the chances that I would win were very slim, so what would it mean if I actually did? For one thing, it would be fantastic for America's greatest gift to the world, which is what I really believe jazz is. The award would be a tremendous encouragement for the whole jazz community and might inspire young people to listen to and create jazz.

It would also be an incredible demonstration of the power of Buddhist practice—Actual Proof that the practice of chanting and the strategy of the Lotus Sutra can overcome anything. Once I started seeing the award as a personal campaign to make the impossible possible, I got excited. I spent many, many hours chanting in front of my Gohonzon in the six weeks before the show. And although I might have been the only one who thought so, I came to believe I would actually win.

Part of the strategy of the Lotus Sutra is removing doubt from the equation, so that's part of what I chanted for—to break down the barrier of doubt. At first it was scary trying to do this, but I felt that I had no choice. This was where the practice of Buddhism had led me, and now that I was here it was time to put up or shut up. So I did.

When I wasn't chanting, I was spending hours practicing an arrangement of "Rhapsody in Blue." Even before the nominations had been announced, the Grammys' producer, Ken Erlich, had called to ask me if I'd be willing to perform a duet with the classical pianist Lang Lang during the show. Now, I hadn't played classical music seriously since I was a twenty-year-old college student, and Lang Lang was one of the greatest classical pianists in the world. So when Ken proposed the idea, I said, "Come on, man! Don't do this to me!"

It isn't so easy to just switch back to classical music after a lifetime of jazz, funk, hip-hop, and every other kind of improvisation, so my first thought was *It would take me a year to prepare for this*—and that was speaking conservatively. I told Ken I'd think about it, but in the end, of course, I couldn't refuse. So in the weeks leading up to the show I was not only spending hours chanting; I was also spending hours at the piano, trying somehow to get back the classical chops I'd last had nearly fifty years earlier.

On the night of the Grammy Awards, Lang Lang and I played our duet, and everything just felt relaxed. I was completely confident and played the piece better than I'd ever done it in rehearsals. It was a blast to be up there with Lang Lang, who has a playfulness to his style that's really energizing. Then, once our duet was finished, I went back to my seat in the front row for the rest of the show.

Album of the Year is announced at the very end of the show, and my friend Quincy Jones walked up to the microphone with the rapper Usher to present the award. And then a really strange thing happened. Although I had been chanting for so long, trying to knock down the barrier of doubt and believe that I would actually win, at that moment everything just fell away, and my mind went blank. So when Quincy opened the envelope and said, "*River: The Joni Letters*. Herbie Hancock!" I just about went into shock.

I really couldn't believe what was happening. Larry Klein was sitting right behind me, and we looked at each other and then hugged. I couldn't speak, but Larry said, "I guess we won!"

I said to him, "Come on, let's go take this thing!"

We walked to the stage, and once I got up there I just stood silently for a moment and looked around with a big grin on my face. Finally I was able to blurt, "What a beautiful day this is in Los Angeles!" And then I proceeded to drop my speech as I was trying to pull it out of my jacket pocket. Quincy bent over behind me to pick it up as I kept rummaging around in my jacket, completely unaware that it had fallen to the floor.

I started my speech by thanking the person who'd made the record possible:

Joni Mitchell. Joni Mitchell. Joni Mitchell, thank you *so much*. You know, it's been forty-three years since the first and only time that a jazz artist got the Album of the Year award. And I'd like to thank the Academy for courageously breaking the mold this time. And in doing so, honoring the giants upon whose shoulders I stand—some of whom, like Miles Davis, John Coltrane, unquestionably deserved this award in the past.

But this is a new day that proves that the impossible can be made possible. *Yes, we can!*—to coin a phrase.

The audience laughed, recognizing the allusion to then-candidate Barack Obama's presidential campaign slogan. I went on:

My thanks, of course, to Joni Mitchell—her music and her words. And without the vision of Larry Klein, the producer, this could never have happened. I want to thank my mother and father. I want to thank my wife, Gigi, Jessica, my daughter, Melinda Murphy, all the musicians, Wayne Shorter, Dave Holland, Vinnie Colaiuta, Lionel Loueke, Tina Turner, Corinne Bailey Rae, Norah Jones, Luciana Souza, Leonard Cohen, Sonya Kitchell, Helik Hadar, Dahlia Ambach Caplin, everyone at Verve . . . Thank you *so much*. Thank you! Thank you!

It's still hard to believe that the impossible became possible, but it did.

CHAPTER
TWENTY-FOUR

One night Larry Klein and I decided to watch a PBS documentary called *Journey of Man*. It's a fascinating two-hour examination of the culture and genetics of human beings all over the globe, but there was one part that stunned me: New research suggested that every human on the planet was descended from one African man who lived sixty thousand years ago.

Hearing that, I got very emotional. Life is about connection, and the idea of all humans sharing a common ancestor is one of the most meaningful connections imaginable. However different we might be from each other in terms of languages, skin color, religion, or customs, we are all one family. Watching the documentary gave me hope—and it also gave me an idea.

It was late 2008 when Larry and I watched *Journey of Man,* and the big news at the time was the economic crisis that had begun a few months earlier. Giant financial institutions were failing, causing an economic meltdown not only in the United States but around the world. That year "globalization" was on people's minds, but not in a good way. It called to mind the collapse of many interdependent economies.

I wanted to reclaim the word "globalization," to recapture the positive elements of being interconnected with other human beings all over the world. If humanity is to survive, we have to reap the benefits of being interconnected. We have to work together, to help each other find answers to the tremendous problems affecting the planet today, from economic inequity to global warming.

In jazz every member of the band works with every other member to create something beautiful. There's no judgment and no competition, just a collaborative effort that ideally lifts everybody's performance. I found myself wondering, *What if the planet were run like a jazz collective?* What if we could find a way to harness globalization for the common good, rather than just suffering from its ill effects?

The most visible platform I have right now as a human being is music. So I decided to make a record speaking to this issue—a record that would be truly global in scope and encourage people all over the world to come together. When you take people from different cultures, who speak different languages, and unite them to make music, you get something that no one group could have achieved by itself. That's the true essence of globalization, and that's what I wanted to convey with this record.

Not long after watching *Journey of Man,* I was talking to my friend Ken Hertz, who's also my attorney, about that idea. "Why don't you use John Lennon's song 'Imagine' as the centerpiece?" Ken asked. As soon as he said it, I knew it was the perfect choice. Lennon was very proactive on peace issues, and the lyrics in "Imagine" really captured perfectly what I was trying to accomplish. I titled the album *The Imagine Project.* Larry Klein seemed as excited about it as I was, and he agreed to come on board as the producer.

Now that I had the basic concept, I started taking apart the clock once again. At this point in the twenty-first century the music that has been most "global" is American music, which is played and performed everywhere. However, I noticed that American artists tend to make records for America—meaning the songs are almost always in English, and the cultural sensibilities are American—and then the rest of world either jumps on board or not. To me, this was classic twentieth-century thinking, rooted in the past. How could we make a twenty-first-century record with truly global sensibilities?

For one thing, I wanted to acknowledge that America is the largest immigrant country, with roots in every other country on the planet. We're always hearing about immigrants supposedly overrunning our borders and taking our jobs, but almost everybody in America is an immigrant. Our ancestors are from everywhere, and almost all of us came to this land later, so I wanted to explore those global roots, to bring back an awareness and a reconnection to them.

I started with the basics: The songs would be in multiple languages, not just English, and those languages wouldn't just be European, either, but from all over the world. I also wanted to record artists in their home environments, on their own turf, so the music would truly have the flavor and feeling of the places where it originated. Finally, I didn't want the record to be a "world beat" record, because those tend to get marginalized. I wanted talented stars on the record, people whose commitment to the project would create awareness of it, and I wanted it to be something they could feel proud of.

As the record started taking shape I realized this was going to be the most ambitious, far-reaching album I had ever done. We ultimately ended up with songs in seven different languages, with artists from eleven different countries, and no two tracks sounding remotely alike. Pulling all that together sometimes felt impossible . . . which is exactly why I was driven to do it.

||||||||||

In February of 2009 I traveled to India for the anniversary of Martin Luther King, Jr.'s trip there in 1959. King had gone to India to study the nonviolence teachings of Mahatma Gandhi, and now, fifty years later, his son Martin Luther King III was leading a U.S. State Department-sponsored delegation to celebrate his father's legacy.

Officially I was joining the delegation in my capacity as the chairman of the Thelonious Monk Institute of Jazz, a nonprofit founded in 1986 to promote jazz music education. The institute has done incredible work, providing education programs and scholarships for music students, and putting on the annual International Jazz Competition since 1987. I'd been working with the institute for years, teaching classes, judging competitions, and working on programming. The Thelonious Monk Institute does more than any other organization to promote and support jazz both in America and internationally, so I was happy to expand my work there when I was named chairman in 2003.

Our musical delegation to India included Chaka Khan, singer-songwriter Dee Dee Bridgewater, pianist George Duke, and a number of young people who were studying jazz through the institute. We were scheduled to perform concerts in four cities in India, including Mumbai and New Delhi, and to work with Indian music students at the Ravi Shankar Institute. But I was also looking forward to our one day off in Mumbai, which meant I'd be able to go into a studio with Chaka to record a song for *The Imagine Project*.

Larry Klein had written a piece called "The Song Goes On," based on a Rainer Maria Rilke poem. He had the poem translated into Hindi, and we brought those lyrics to the studio. I had asked an Indian vocalist named K. S. Chithra if she'd be willing to sing on the piece, and she joined Chaka, sitarist Anoushka Shankar (daughter of Ravi Shankar), and me in the studio. We recorded Chaka singing the song in English and Chithra singing it in Hindi, with the two of them trading vocals back and forth. It was the perfect start for our global project, and later we would overdub Wayne Shorter playing soprano saxophone to round out the international flavor.

Larry and I had talked a lot about the kinds of songs and artists we wanted, and he did amazing work pulling them together. This was a huge, complicated task, as we had musicians from places like Mali, Ireland, Australia, India, and the Congo. We even had a nomadic Tuareg troupe from the Saharan desert, a group called Tinariwen, which we teamed with the Latino rock band Los Lobos and the Somali-born rapper K'naan to do Bob Marley's "Exodus." And because I had loved Lisa Hannigan's rendition of "Don't Explain" on *Possibilities* so much, I asked her to sing in English and Irish on *The Imagine Project;* we teamed her with Malian kora player Toumani Diabate, the Irish band the Chieftains, and Lionel Loueke to record "The Times They Are A-Changin'." These were radical groupings of musicians and styles, and Larry deserves much of the credit for making them happen.

Not surprisingly, with all these moving parts and so many miles separating the participants, we started running into problems. Sometimes artists would commit to recording and then back out, having said yes to too many things. Others sent us their recordings late or mistakenly recorded the wrong thing. K'naan was in Japan but promised to send us his overdub for "Exodus." Larry and I told him we needed it within twenty-four hours, and he actually got it to us in time—but then it turned out he'd done an overdub for the wrong place in the song! I called him in Japan to ask if he could stop whatever he was doing and record another overdub for us. He hadn't planned to go back into the studio, but I was so frantic that he agreed to do it, and he sent us a perfect recording just in the nick of time.

It seemed as if every time I turned around another obstacle was thrown in our way—but that's how I knew I was doing the right thing. In my Buddhist practice I had learned that whenever you're undertaking an action for the greater good, opposing forces will surely arise. Meeting resistance when you're moving forward is similar to how a car moving forward meets resistance from the wind. The fact that you can feel that resistance tells you that you're moving, so even though these obstacles were frustrating, I never stopped believing that we would overcome them.

Larry and I were working like crazy, but it became obvious that we were going to miss our deadline for getting the record to the mastering engineer. This date had been set long ago, and I knew it would cost a hell of a lot more money if we missed it—and because we were releasing this on my own label, Hancock Records, I'd be the one paying those extra fees. Whenever I wasn't working on the record, I was chanting, focusing all my energy on somehow getting this thing finished without either going broke or giving myself a heart attack. But as it turned out, I had completely miscalculated what the extra cost would be, and it ended up being much less than I had feared.

Then, just as we were pulling together all the recordings and overdubs, Dave Matthews called me to say he really didn't like the song he'd done for the album. We had recorded him up in the Bay Area when he had a concert there, and he'd created a really cool tune, with a nice rhythm that morphed throughout, finally coming back to the original groove after my piano solo. I really liked the song, and we had already edited and mixed it, so it was ready to go. But now, at the eleventh hour, Dave said, "I want to do a different one."

What!? "Dave," I said, "your song is great! Don't worry about it, this one is perfect for the record." But he insisted, and he ended up doing a gorgeous version of a psychedelic Beatles song called "Tomorrow Never Knows," and incredibly enough, he happened to be in L.A. at the time, so I was able to come record with him, too.

I went down to the studio, and the song felt so amorphous that I had a hard time figuring out how to play. I tried the acoustic piano, but it didn't fit. Then I tried the Fender Rhodes, but that didn't sound right either. Then I happened to notice an old beat-up piano that wasn't even on legs anymore but just lying right on the floor. Now, *that* looked interesting. I walked over and started playing around on it, hitting the strings with a spoon and doing some things on the mixing console to modify the sound. I worked out a kind of melody on it, but it didn't sound at all like what I would have played on a regular piano—which was perfect, of course. There was nothing else on the record that sounded like what we did that day, so the song added a whole new dimension.

Even though we turned the record in late, the mastering engineer loved it, and he spent a lot of time after hours pitching in to make the finished product great. So, in the end, every problem we had encountered was solved by finding an even better solution. Actual Proof!

I put a lot into that record, and I think the message of connection is something that people need to hear. But the really cool thing is, the message came through not only in the songs themselves but in the way the record was actually made. *The Imagine Project* is a testament to facing the impossible and making it possible, which is the message not only of my music but of my life.

|||||||||||

More than forty years after I started practicing Buddhism, I still chant every day. Yet, when I think back to those early days, as I listened to fellow Buddhists talk about what they were chanting for—cars, a spouse, a house—I see those desires differently than I did back then. These things aren't the root of happiness, because even if you have a spouse you may eventually want to divorce, and even if you have money you may want more. People tend to look outside themselves for things to complete them. But what Buddhism has taught me is that we must look inside ourselves for that happiness. The transformation that Buddhism offers is an internal transformation, one that will awaken you to things you never dreamed of before.

What Buddhism awakened in me was the desire to apply my humanism and humanistic vision toward the goal of world peace—not just through my music but through every means at my disposal. It's true that as we get older we get wiser, so I can't say exactly what I would have been like at this point in my life without Buddhism, but I do believe that Buddhism has led me in directions I probably wouldn't have followed. I probably would have continued to focus obsessively on music, as I did when I was younger, rather than shifting that focus to the larger issues facing the world.

In 2011 I was named a UNESCO Goodwill Ambassador, something that probably wouldn't have happened if it weren't for my Buddhist practice. UNESCO, the United Nations Educational, Scientific and Cultural Organization, has a mission of developing peace in the world, promoting dialogue among all people to achieve human rights, respect for the sanctity of human life, and the alleviation of poverty. These are all issues that I've become especially attuned to through my practice, so I was excited to have the chance to work on them through this organization.

One of the first things I proposed to UNESCO was International Jazz Day, a day of collaborative concerts staged throughout the world, with musicians and artists from various cultures working together; the first celebration was held in 2012. But my UNESCO activities involve more than music: I hope to host symposiums with thinkers, scholars, and artists—creative people with ideas. I just want to play a part, whatever part I can, in helping to rid ourselves of the kind of ignorance that separates people, causes misunderstandings, and creates conflict.

The transformation I've experienced—and continue to experience— through my Buddhist beliefs is the reason I'm not sitting down in a studio every day focused only on making music. I never would have considered myself an educator, but now I am, even teaching classes at Harvard University in early 2014 as the Charles Eliot Norton Professor of Poetry. I have a new relationship with young people, who are the future, a relationship that has been enhanced by my practice. It's a continual process, a continual battle within myself for self-improvement and self-realization.

And that includes going back to classical music, which—apart from that one Grammys performance with Lang Lang—I hadn't played since I was twenty years old. My musical output had gone through a chameleonlike evolution, from classical to jazz to funk to hip-hop and beyond, but now, in my seventies, I was coming back around full circle.

In February of 2012 I agreed to play a classical piece for the New York Philharmonic's Chinese New Year celebration at Lincoln Center. "Er Huang" was written by a Chinese composer named Qigang Chen, and it was the hardest piece of music I have ever tried to learn in my life. It was written on four staves, or musical staffs—which is normally done for four hands—and about three-quarters through, it starts going really fast and jumping around.

I mean, this piece kicked my ass. For months before the performance I practiced between three and four hours a day—and I've never practiced that much for any music I've performed, with the possible exception of playing "Rhapsody in Blue" with Lang Lang at the Grammys. For "Er Huang" I was practicing beyond what I'd done when I was eleven years old, preparing for my debut at the Chicago Symphony. My friends were wondering what had happened to me, and even my brother, Wayman, called to ask if everything was okay.

When I was rehearsing for the Grammys performance with Lang Lang, I hired a tutor named Joanne Pearce Martin, who's the keyboardist for the Los Angeles Philharmonic. I hired her again for this, and three or four times a week she'd come over to my house to try to help me get back my classical chops. She started me off doing scales, and as she watched me play she said, "Herbie, you don't pay any attention to your left hand. You pay attention to your right hand, and then your left hand follows."

I hadn't thought about it, but once she pointed it out, I noticed she was right. I thought back to years before, when Miles Davis pointed out that my left hand was holding back my right. I obviously still needed improvement, just as I did when I was a younger player. "Do the scales with just your left hand sometimes, and leave the right hand out," she told me. "That way you'll get used to paying attention to it." I had been playing piano for sixty-five years by this point, but you never stop learning, never stop improving, if you keep your mind open.

Even with Joanne's help this piece was still terrorizing me. I would practice for hours and then hit a plateau where my playing never seemed to improve. I very rarely get stressed out, but I was getting nervous, worrying that I wasn't going to be able to perform the piece up to the standards I wanted.

It was on my mind so much that I decided to go to a Buddhist meeting to regain my perspective on the problem. And the amazing thing was, the simple act of deciding to go to that meeting helped me realize that playing this piece wasn't about me at all but about others. It was about having the opportunity to do something for others.

Once I'd shifted my focus and gained this new intention, I was able to stop worrying. And that cleared my mind enough to realize how I could solve my problem: Instead of playing the most difficult parts exactly as they were written, I could use improvisation to get through them. I didn't have to be so rigid in my playing—in fact, the composer himself had said he welcomed my improvising and that the more important thing was to perform the true spirit of the piece. Finally I was able to relax and look at how I might play the piece *well,* even if that meant not sticking completely to the notes on the page.

That broke everything open. At the concert I walked out onstage feeling confident, and from the first chord I was smiling. I even played the most difficult parts as written, which I never expected to do. Backstage after the show, people came and told me that the piece sounded beautiful, and several said I had been smiling the entire time I was onstage, which I hadn't even realized. They could see that I was enjoying myself, and I really was—because I'd finally figured out how to turn my obstacle into an opportunity, which opened up a whole new world of possibility.

Thinking about that performance reminds me of another one—a

night fifty years ago, on a stage in Stockholm, when I played what I thought was a "wrong note." I had felt so embarrassed, having made such an obvious mistake in front of an audience while playing with the great Miles Davis. But when Miles turned that obstacle into a new opportunity, he taught me a lesson I never forgot.

Miles taught me many great lessons in music, but everything I learned from him, I learned for the sake of playing well. I never really saw past that, because at that time playing music was the most important thing in my life. Once I started practicing Buddhism, I learned even greater lessons—about not just how to play but how to live. Buddhism illuminates everything I've learned in new and profound ways, and it keeps teaching me new things every single day. I can hardly wait to see what tomorrow will bring.

ACKNOWLEDGMENTS

In life, as in jazz, there is great beauty in collaboration. I've been very fortunate throughout the years to have wonderful family members, friends, and colleagues who've made my life's journey all the richer. And there are many—far too many to list in the pages of a book.

In particular, I would like to thank:

The managers, agents, and others who have helped me throughout my life and career: Melinda Murphy, Bruce Eskowitz, Marc Allan, Red Light Management, David Rubinson, Tony Meilandt, David Passick, Barry Marshall and Marshall Arts, Ken Hertz, David Jackel, and Adriane Hibbert.

The talented engineers who've helped bring my music to life: Bryan Bell, Fundi Bonner, Fred Catero, Helik Hadar, Brian McCullough, Rudy Van Gelder. And those who have helped me put words to paper: Bob Barnett, Rick Kot and Clare Ferraro, Lisa Dickey, and Shelby Fischer.

The producers, directors, studios, and festival creators who've provided stages both literal and virtual for jazz: Michael Beinhorn, Dahlia Ambach Caplan, Laura Connelly, Ken Erlich, Quincy Jones, Larry Klein, Bill Laswell, Bruce Lundvall, Claude Nobs, Bertrand Tavernier,

George Wein, Richard Saul Wurman, Blue Note, Sony, Verve, and Warner Bros.

The makers of the instruments and technology that have enhanced music and its creation over the years: Paolo Fazioli, Steve Jobs and Steve Wozniak, Apple Inc., Korg, Harold Rhodes.

The people and organizations who are working tirelessly to better our world: President Daisaku Ikeda, Danny Nagashima, Kay Yoshikawa, and Soka-Gakkai International; Tom and Cheri Carter, Bill Powers, Stuart Subotnick, Carolyn Powers, and Thelonious Monk III of the Thelonious Monk Institute of Jazz; Mika Shino; UNESCO; former secretary of state Madeleine Albright.

The many musicians who have both inspired me and given me the honor of playing with them: Chris Anderson, Krishna Booker, Jeff Bova, Donald Byrd, Ron Carter, Mike Clark, Vinnie Colaiuta, Chick Corea, Miles Davis, GrandMixer DXT, James Genus, Pat Gleeson, Godley & Creme, Don (Goldberg) James, Billy Hart, Eddie Henderson, Freddie Hubbard, Paul Jackson, Lang Lang, Lionel Loueke, Wynton Marsalis, Harvey Mason, Bennie Maupin, Joni Mitchell, Julian Priester, Carlos Santana, Sly Stone, Bill Summers, Wah Wah Watson, Buster Williams, Tony Williams, and Stevie Wonder.

My dearest friends: Wayne and Carolina Shorter, Lou and Kelly Gonda, Kathy and Maria Lucien, Valerie Bishop, Susie Sempers, and Matilda Buck.

And finally, my family: My brother and sister, Wayman and Jean; my parents, Wayman and Winnie Hancock, who taught us as children to believe in ourselves; my daughter, Jessica, who lights up my world; and my wife, Gigi, the love of my life.

For more information:

SOKA GAKKAI INTERNATIONAL—USA (SGI)
606 Wilshire Blvd.
Santa Monica, CA 90401
(310) 260-8900
www.sgi-usa.org

UNITED NATIONS EDUCATIONAL, SCIENTIFIC
AND CULTURAL ORGANIZATION—UNESCO
7 place Fontenoy
75352 Paris 07 SP, France
+33 (0)1 45 68 10 00

2 United Nations Plaza, Room 900
New York, NY 10017
(212) 963-5995
www.unesco.org

THELONIOUS MONK INSTITUTE OF JAZZ
1801 Avenue of the Stars, Suite 302
Los Angeles, CA 90067
(310) 284-8200
www.monkinstitute.org

INDEX